GLADIATOR

NO EASY WAY HOME

(to Norm Hewitt)

Autumn: the time of booty,
the lazy, exact plunder
of the bumble bee;
now winging home, heavy
with nectar into the teeth
of a northerly — a hero
who did not please the gods.

This muscled, banded bee is No Man.
Not for him the leviathan myth of a Jonah;
he is mortal, weary
with the struggle home — an Odysseus:
No Man, Norman, Everyman

beating into the wind, the heart
of a hurricane, for fourteen years
with deliberate power, a broken leg
bearing still an orb
of pollen. A cannonball
with wings that they said could never fly
but did despite the gods who decreed
a winter wilderness,
no easy way home.

— James McNaughton
from *The Stepmother Tree*

GLADIATOR

THE NORM HEWITT STORY

Michael Laws

DARIUS

By the same author

The Demon Profession
Dancing with Beelzebub

Published by Darius Press
PO Box 3368
Wellington
New Zealand

First published 2001

© Michael Laws 2001

The author asserts his moral rights in the work.

ISBN 0 473 07825 2

Designed by Mary Egan
Typeset by Egan-Reid Ltd
Cover photograph by 'The Evening Post', Wellington
Printed in New Zealand by Publishing Press

CONTENTS

ACKNOWLEDGEMENTS:

Thanks to Susan Brierley, Karen Laws, Graeme and Wendy Taylor, Mary Egan (and the good people at Egan-Reid), Jason Weller of Publishing Press and to all those who consented to be interviewed for this book, especially John Hart and Graeme Mourie.

For the photos contained herein, credits to Photosport, Fotopress, Getty Images, *'Daily Telegraph'* Napier, Associated Sports Photography (UK), Norm's personal collection and to the *'Evening Post'* Wellington for the front cover photograph.

Preface

It had been a long day. There had been a trail of constituents through the office — each with a harder luck story to tell than the last. It had started with a delegation of grumpy orchardists and ended with a solo mum having her house sold from under her. Given that I was the only government MP within cooee then it was all my fault. No matter the problem, the demand was the same. You helped create this goddammed mess. Fix it. Or we'll fix you at the next election.

I doubt if there's a more impotent creature than a backbench government MP. You have no role in any decision made by the Cabinet but you're responsible nonetheless. Despite having a reputation as a party rebel, the people I'd been seeing all day didn't give a damn. It was guilt by association. So after a full day of constituents shouting, pleading, threatening and crying at me . . . yeah, I'd had enough. I locked the outside door, pulled the curtains and poured myself a generous whisky.

There was a knock at the door. Loud. I ignored it. They could come back and bitch at me tomorrow. Again and this time loud enough to rattle the adjoining window. I took a sip of the drink and waited for whoever it was to give up and go away. Then a male voice from outside. 'Mis-ter Laws?' I sighed, put down the glass, and headed to the door.

A square, squat young Maori man stood in the door frame. He was wearing a short-sleeved shirt and tie and it somehow seemed incongruous — like he was the defendant waiting to go into the dock. Which, in a funny sort of way, he was. Because this was Norm Hewitt, Hawke's Bay's premier sportsman and captain of the Magpies. And he was in big trouble.

We had met only once before, briefly, at a civic function honouring the team for escaping the dreaded drop to the second division. He had a reputation as a bad bugger — not afraid to do some damage when the ref wasn't looking. Like most Bay supporters, I didn't care. He was on our side. A local hero. And probably the only one we had.

I smiled a nervous welcome. It struck me as odd that this young lion would come calling outside work hours. The conversation went something like this:

'Norm Hewitt. What can I do for you?'

'I'm in a bit of trouble.'

'What sort of trouble?'

'I've been sacked.'

'What? From your job?'

'From my job, from the captaincy and from the team. And they're talking about banning me from the game.'

And that's how we met. Nine years ago with me smelling of whisky and Norm looking as grey as a graveyard statue. He'd been driving around, he said, seen the office light on and decided to stop.

As it turned out I represented Norm at the consequent NZ Rugby Football Union disciplinary hearing. It didn't make a blind bit of difference. His job as the Hawke's Bay union's rugby co-ordinator was already gone, his captaincy stripped and it was only when his team-mates mutinied that the Hawke's Bay union rescinded his suspension. But the NZRFU had the last laugh. They banned him from the next month's NZ Maoris tour to the Pacific Islands.

Two things struck me about the episode. First, the farce of the NZRFU procedure. Second, the evidence at the hearing. It suggested that my client was a living contradiction. I was representing Dr Jeckyll. The NZRFU were trying Mr Hyde.

Over the years I came to appreciate that there were many shades to Norm's character. He could be brutal and grasping and mean. A fighter with the killer instinct and a need to physically intimidate and dominate others. And yet also a remarkably sensitive and shy man, with a genuine regard for the weak and the vulnerable. At times reconciling those extremes has not been easy.

As I came to know him better I slowly came to understand the environment, the experiences and the people who had helped shaped the man. And that the very violence and determination that upset others was also the reason why he was a top rugby player, an All Black and one of the true hard men of the modern game.

But then he needed to be. Because rugby is a kind of war. An extremely aggressive scrap that prizes brute force as much as it values skill, cunning and creativity. For rugby fans, it is the complete sport. The marriage of brawn and brain. Skill and strength. Even body and soul.

Yet most of rugby's leading players and stars are no more than cardboard cut-outs, caricatures of their true selves. Their public images have been massaged by their unions, managers and any number of media liaisons. They are no more real to us, than cartoon heroes. And maybe because we don't need to regard them as individuals, we find it easier to praise and jeer them, to cheer and curse. They may be our de facto champions, our gladiators, but they are also ours to denigrate and dismiss should they stumble or fall.

This is the story of one such player. Told from the inside. Of the boy who had a dream to be an All Black but who was equipped with no more physical talent than any kid of his generation. But what made Norm Hewitt unusual was that he possessed a remarkable will, a determination that bordered on unnatural. Particularly given his confused childhood and an adolescence that prepared him only for prison.

This could have been a book of one man's rise, fall and redemption. But life is not so simple. Instead this is the story of a complex individual who fashioned himself into an All Black — of a champion whose weaknesses can still strike him down at any moment.

And I hope this book is something more. The chance to look at rugby from the inside. To gain a view of the game as it really is. To see the sport through a player's eyes without being sanitised by PR or diluted by political correctness. This is no panegyric to the sport of rugby union. This is no bland biography where a ghost writer censors a player's nostalgia.

Instead, this is one man's truth. Warts and all. The truth of Norm Hewitt. Modern day gladiator.

Michael Laws
October 2001

CHAPTER ONE

Beginnings

I t was late and the Te Aute College senior was heading back into the dormitory block after a surreptitious night out with his mates. His seniority bestowed a variety of privileges and one of them was a measure of liberty from officious housemasters. So too did his physical presence — a square, muscled, young man with an air of menace. As he pulled open the outside door, he noticed the young boy crouching in the shadows of the building. He stopped and demanded to know what the kid thought he was playing at — it was past lights out and juniors were supposed to have been in bed hours ago. The boy kept staring at the ground as if deaf. So the senior persisted — did he want the bash or something? What the hell was he playing at, skulking around the dorm like some mangy dog? Finally the young boy looked up and for the first time the senior could make out the frightened face and dimly recognise the features.

'I can't go back in there.'

'You're bloody going in all right . . .'

'Not until everyone's asleep.'

'And why's that?'

The boy hesitated. 'It's not safe.'

The senior softened. He knew this junior — had cuffed him for giving some cheek a couple of days back. He reached out and pulled the boy into the light.

'What's the problem, kid? You can tell me.'

So the boy did. Told him everything. About the bullying, the violent rousings in the dead of night, the mindless beatings. And about one senior in particular who was making his life hell. A senior who had extended his repertoire in recent weeks to include a series of perverse humiliations that had left the third former confused and ashamed.

The senior listened with growing horror. Bullying was an accepted way of life at Te Aute but not this sort of abuse. He put his arm around the boy's shoulder and walked him inside.

'You bunk down in my cube tonight. As for the other, forget it. I'll put a stop to that crap.'

The next day senior Gavin Hinds made good his promise. He let it be known that he had adopted the young Norm Hewitt as his special responsibility. Anybody who touched the kid from now on would have to answer to him. And so the junior slept for the rest of that year on a mattress on the floor of Hind's cubicle. No reason was ever offered to the authorities for this arrangement, nor to anyone else for that matter. It just was.

But the senior considered his responsibility only partially completed. Removing the third former from the nocturnal predations of the older boy could only be a temporary solution. The kid had to learn to defend himself, so that even if he was overwhelmed he would have done enough damage to the attacker to ensure there was no repeat.

Hinds well understood the peculiar skills required to survive at the Te Aute hostel and physical intimidation was top of the list. So he taught the young Norm to fight, staged bare-knuckle contests that reverberated around the hostel walls as blow after blow was exchanged, blood flowing freely from skinned knuckles and cut faces. Night after night they fought — savage contests of adolescent strength — until the lessons had been properly absorbed. Until the kid was staunch, could absorb a beating and refuse to cower, no matter how bad the pain.

One night, the final test. The senior had insisted through all the months of fierce training that fights were won by the boldest and the toughest but not necessarily by the strongest. The young Hewitt would have to dominate his opponent from the first instant and strike without hesitation. He withdrew a carving knife from under his pillow, taken earlier in the day from the hostel's kitchen, and gave it to his charge.

'Now, stick me,' he commanded.

The young Hewitt did as bidden. He plunged the knife into Hinds' side, blood instantly spurting from the wound.

'Gavin wanted to show me that if I was going to win, then I had to hurt people' remembers Norm. 'And also that he was staunch enough to take a wound without flinching. That you never show pain to an opponent. Sometimes we would fight until we had nothing left — just lying on the ground, hurt and exhausted. But he saved my life. He didn't need to help me, or even take an interest. The fighting was his way of making sure I'd survive at Te Aute after he left.'

It's an episode in Norm's life that has caused a good measure of anguish over the years — initially regret at the abuse, then that Gavin Hinds died before he had a chance to properly thank him. Ironically, it would be one of Hind's best friends who would later help the adult Norm Hewitt begin a different journey. A journey provoked by a very different shame, but one that was no less intense nor influential.

FAMILY

Norm Hewitt was born in 1968 in Hastings, Hawke's Bay. His mother Mabel is of Ngati Kahungunu descent — the dominant iwi of the Bay. She was raised by her grandparents and took their surname, Tutaki. Norm's father Russell is Pakeha, the Hewitt antecedents emigrating from Lancashire at the turn of the twentieth century to escape the suffocating class and climate of Mother England. Mabel and Russell were introduced by mutual friends and had their first date in Hastings, where Russell worked as a machinist at the Odlins timber factory and Mabel as a knifehand at the Tomoana freezing works.

Their characters were and remain a study in contrast — Russell a fiery individual, obstinate and proud; Mabel a generous, kind-hearted soul who lives for her whanau. Most of their Hawke's Bay friends of the time considered that they would be 'good for each other' — each having children from previous relationships, and each having strengths that complemented. And so they started going out and fell in love at a time when Hastings was the economic heart of a prosperous Hawke's Bay and the farming community its landed aristocracy.

Not long after they met Norm was conceived and the family moved to Porongahau, an isolated settlement in central Hawke's Bay. Russell took up a position on the extensive Maungarapa Station, owned by Don Mouat and his family — a job that involved a mix of gardening and labouring work, with a rent-free house as part of the employment package. This would be the home in which they would raise their family — Robert from Mabel's earlier relationship, Norm, Tracey, Russell Junior (known as 'Skin' from the earliest of ages) and Louana. Russell would continue to work at Maungarapa Station until 1994 when their All Black son would help finance the purchase of the Wanstead Tavern some twenty kilometres away.

The Hewitt household that Norm remembers was one of extremes — one moment happy and carefree, the next consumed by the ugliness of domestic violence. Not surprisingly, this atmosphere created an indelible impression on the child.

'Dad had this jealousy thing — usually after they'd been out to a party and had too much to drink. Then Mum would cop it from the old man. Although I've always loved my father I hated what he was doing, what the violence was doing to the family. I guess we were a loving family, but we were also a scared one.'

There were nights that still cause Norm to wince at their memory — nights when he would lead his young brothers and sisters to the open paddock beside the farmhouse, so that they wouldn't have to hear or witness the beatings. Nights when he would cry himself to sleep from both fear and the frustration of not being able to reconcile the supportive, sober father and the drunken monster that would lurch home on too many nights. Neither could he reconcile that his mother stayed — that she didn't just scoop up her children and flee from this violent, drunken man. He promised himself that the moment he was old and strong enough, he would stand up and protect his mother and end the abuse. Years later he would see the movie *Once Were Warriors* and leave the theatre shaken. No matter that the story was fiction and the characters mere actors — he had just seen his own childhood, his own background brought to vivid life.

'It was weird. People around me were saying what great acting and direction and all that — although you could tell they thought it was all a bit exaggerated for dramatic effect. And I wanted to say 'No' — that's the way it was for me. That's exactly the environment I lived in.'

There was also the more subtle effect of his father's rages — the young Norm imprinting that women were somehow a lesser gender and were required to put up with such male excess. That domestic violence might well be a problem but it could also be a solution.

Maungarapa itself was a hard-working, hard-drinking station where the rural workers and shearers of the district regularly gathered for weekend parties. Inescapably, the farm kids were a part of such commotion and at one such gathering Norm was plied with beer by a few of the single shepherds. It was their joke, their night's entertainment, to watch the kid hoover the froth from their glasses. Soon the child was drunk, tripping over himself to the laughter of the company. The end result was that he missed his first day at primary school, unable to attend because of the hangover. All at five years of age.

But despite the various upsets Norm also remembers happy family times — endless games of rugby and bulrush with his brothers and the other kids at the school just over the back fence, helping his father with farm chores, a typical rural kid on a typical sheep station. From these earliest times he acquired an appetite for hard physical work, relishing the challenge and determined to overcome any lack of size or strength. However, despite this willingness to work, Norm was a far from perfect child.

'I was a stroppy little bugger — hated being told what to do. Resented authority no matter who was giving the orders. Whether it was because of what was happening at home or because I was just a bolshy kid fullstop, I don't know. It was something that was a part of my character from as early as I can remember. I never liked people telling me what to do. I'd do the opposite sometimes just to spite them.'

There was one exception. He would listen to anyone who would coach him at rugby. Whether it was his father or the school coach or 'Rusty' Allen, the Central Hawke's Bay primary schools coach, Norm was their most avid pupil. He had a desperate hunger to learn any new skill or technique — a desire to play better, to best an opponent and then to dominate. A hunger to win.

It was his father who first identified the latent rugby talent in his second son, but his was not a universal opinion. In refusing to allow his son to attend rugby practices with the neighbouring school, the Maungarapa headmaster informed Russell Hewitt that his son 'would never amount to much' — the kind of put-down that would antagonise any parent. He was on the verge of withdrawing Norm from the school when the decision was effectively made for him.

The rebellious youngster had given a teacher some defiant cheek and the man's patience had finally snapped. He picked up the young boy and slammed him against the side of the classroom, stunning the child and ripping his shirt. That afternoon all the Hewitt children were withdrawn from Maungarapa and sent down the road to Porongahau School.

But the rugby field was not quite so easily regained. While playing one-on-one scrag with his older brother, Norm tackled Robert only for the older boy to collapse squarely upon Norm's face. Mabel rushed outside in answer to her son's screaming and after assessing the damage rang the local GP. Give him two disprins and wait until the swelling goes down, she was advised. By the next morning Norm's right eye had swollen to the size of a tennis ball so his mother drove him into Waipukurau and sought a second medical opinion. The doctor took one look, rang Napier Hospital and advised them that he had a young boy in his rooms with a fractured eye socket, the eyeball having slipped down inside the cheek. The Napier surgeon's post-operation order was unequivocal — no rugby for at least a year or risk permanently losing the sight in his eye. So Norm played hockey that winter, and instead presented a danger to everyone within stick distance.

When he returned to the fields, his rugby skills were quickly appreciated by 'Rusty' Allen, the Central Hawke's Bay primary schools selector and coach. The boy had good ball skills but also an unusual determination and fearlessness — prime qualities for the annual Ross Shield, a sub-union competition that dominates primary school rugby in Hawke's Bay.

But despite possessing the requisite talent for the CHB team, Norm faced a seemingly insurmountable barrier. The Ross Shield applied a strict weight maximum on its players of eight stone and he was well over. To this day it remains at the 53 kilogram equivalent — a perennial difficulty for coaches to select players, particularly forwards, who fall under the limit. So the reverse would often occur. The coaches would select their respective squads and then diet those who were overweight down to the accepted maximum — the kind of practice that might invite the attention of the Commissioner for Children these days.

1981 was no exception, and the CHB coach asked the Hewitts' permission to put Norm on a special regime to drop the necessary pounds and make the team. They took one look at their son's eager face and agreed — initially unaware that this 'diet' comprised strenuous physical exercise, oranges and ice cream. That was it. No meat, no potatoes, no vegetables, no bread — just oranges and ice cream. A pre-'Zone' diet regime that had the young Hewitt retching after the worst of the training sessions. But he made it. On weigh-in day Norm snuck in just below the limit. One week later and he weighed a full stone heavier.

The extra weight was no impediment to his all-round ability, nor to his strength as a prop forward. Over the week long competition he played outstanding rugby and was rewarded with a starting position in the Hawke's Bay Primary Schools team for representative fixtures against Wellington and Horowhenua. Prop was not a position he especially enjoyed but as one of the heavier lads on the team he was marked down as a tight forward — an early prisoner of his physique.

To this day his contributions at Ross Shield level are remembered. Current organiser Errol Hantz recalls the young Hewitt as 'a short, stumpy little fellow and quite rotund. But he was also a tough little guy, strong and gutsy, and he loved taking the ball straight up the middle. And very fair — you never saw any dirt from the kid.'

Informed of this observation, Norm smiles. 'He must've confused me with someone else. I remember one dust-up with Simon Tremain [the son of All Black legend Kel Tremain] that stopped the game and almost had me sent off. I knew who he was so I made it my special job to niggle him and he reacted. It worked too — I think that was the only game CHB won.'

It was a measure of the young Hewitt that he went out of his way to upset the golden-haired boy in the opposing team although not simply to advance his team's prospects. Station life in rural Hawke's Bay had made him aware of the 'haves' and the 'have nots' and the young, privileged Tremain was an unwitting symbol for Norm's resentment.

The Ross Shield had a profound effect upon the young Norm. He came home from the tournament and announced that he now knew what he was going to do with the rest of his life. He was going to be an All Black. When reminded by his father that he needed to have a real job, Norm shook his head. No. All he wanted to be was an All Black. Nothing else mattered.

Yet this was no exceptional child athlete. There had been others at the Ross Shield who were faster, fitter, stronger and infinitely more skilled. All that could be said was that the young Hewitt had potential. But then so did most of the other boys he played against at this level. It would require other qualities to take him to the top.

TE AUTE

At the end of his form two year Russell and Mabel had to decide on Norm's secondary schooling, and there was no hesitation in their choice of Te Aute College. His older brother Robert was already at Te Aute, and Mabel wanted to see her son assert his Maori identity, an association that until then had lain largely dormant. From Russell's viewpoint, Te Aute had the virtue of being the nearest school to the isolated station, and he had no difficulty with its emphasis on Maori culture and language. It also had one other great asset. It was one of the country's most famous rugby schools — a reputation that clinched the decision.

Te Aute was like many other single-sex boarding schools of the time — Maori or mainstream, public or private. It had developed a distinct culture — a lifestyle distilled from generations of schoolboys being left to their own devices by masters who considered that a little Darwinian toughness was no bad thing. Te Aute had grafted its own adolescent traditions into this mix, its own mysteries of the dorm, an internal order free of adult influence or official restraint. William Golding may have written *Lord of the Flies* as fiction but at Te Aute it could have passed as anthropological study.

Consequently, the hostel had its own absurd traditions, translated initially from the public schools of England and adapted to local conditions and culture. At Te Aute, this hybrid of Maori and English tradition produced its own environment — peer respect earned by being 'staunch' — a no-nonsense machismo that took pride in physical strength and fighting ability. Despite the occasional bouts of temper he'd experienced at home, Te Aute's hostel life represented a shock to the young Norm — a child doted on by his mother and thus used to constant protection and support.

The bullying problem at the school in the late 70s and early 80s was worse than systemic. It was an endemic part of the school's culture, and principal Awi Riddell was in despair at how to be rid of it. Headmaster and hostel manager from 1977 to 1989, Riddell immediately outlawed the practice of school prefects being allowed to cane juniors. Henceforth, Riddell declared to one of his first school assemblies, all corporal punishment would be administered by the teaching staff.

That night the head prefect of the school called his own unofficial assembly. Responding to the outrage of his fellow seniors, the young man ordered the pupils to ignore Riddell's decree. It would be business as usual. Anyone who disagreed was asked to leave the meeting. Two juniors made the mistake of doing so. The next morning Riddell discovered them with 'their faces beaten to a pulp' — victims of a merciless beating by the same head prefect and his deputy. The police were called, and the prefects expelled, but the war was far from over. The boarding school intimidation would conspire to frustrate all Riddell's efforts at reform.

To counter the initial shock of separation from their families, junior hostel boys were unofficially assigned to a senior student — the theory being that this would provide them with a friendly mentor who would look after them in the often hostile environment. Te Aute had developed its own unique version of the 'fagging' found in private schools — it was called 'nodding', and a third former or 'nod' would make cups of tea or coffee on demand, wash his senior's clothes and generally run minor errands. It was a form of adolescent 'protection' — any junior refusing the senior's demands would be severely punished. The masters tolerated the tradition — it seemed the least of their problems compared with some of the school's other thuggish activities.

Unfortunately the young Norm was assigned to a senior who not only misinterpreted his responsibility but sought to use it for his own sexual gratification. Although the abuse was irregular it led Norm to take extraordinary precautions to avoid contact, including waiting outside the dormitory block until well past midnight. Then he would sneak back into his cubicle and snatch sufficient sleep to get him through the next day.

So it is that the late Gavin Hinds will always be a hero to Norm Hewitt. He had the courage to intervene. But the damage had been done, the young boy developing a self-loathing that would surface in adult years when least needed, and also affect his most intimate relationships for years to come.

For the moment though, the abuse was not so much forgotten as shelved away. There was sport to play, school lessons to ignore, and hostel hierarchies to absorb and understand. One of his finer moments in his inaugural year was to make the Te Aute cricket 1st XI — a ramshackle assembly of kids who played in red shirts, black shorts and bare feet, and who seemed out of place among the ironed whites of their Hastings and Napier school rivals. But their enthusiasm made up for their rough uniform, and young Norm proved a more than competent fast bowler and a useful fielder. His cricket coach, Richard Schumacher, recalls that the combination of a windmill bowling action (à la Lance Cairns) and 'awesome upper body strength' had an unsettling effect on most opposing batting line-ups.

'Especially in the nets,' chuckles Schumacher. 'Quite a few of the boys were scared — you were never sure if Norm's next ball was going to be fired at your head or bounce up off a good length. But there was no question he was a good little cricketer and could have gone on if he'd wanted.'

In his senior years Norm would turn his attention to softball and utilise that same strength as a designated hitter in Te Aute's representative side. In 1986 the school would contest and win the New Zealand secondary schools title at Blenheim, due in no small part to Norm's bludgeoning efforts.

TESTING THE EDGE

Things gradually settled down at school, with Norm assimilating the rhythm of the hostel and gradually coping with its various undercurrents. He still regarded schoolwork as the boring bit between breakfast and afternoon rugby practice, but he found a surprising application for his accounting and economics lessons. Like many his age he'd taken up smoking, but he discovered that a packet of cigarettes ensured an immediate market of equally desperate schoolboy smokers. Within weeks he'd set up an elaborate contraband operation, purchasing various goods away from the school and retailing them to his peers. The illicit trade broadened — first beer, then hard spirits, and finally cannabis. By his fifth form year, Norm was the school's primary dealer, trailing a black rubbish bag full of dope and finding any number of takers.

Later he would branch out in his 'commercial' activities, into money-lending and debt-collecting. On pocket-money day the first call of many hostel boys would be to the gruff Shylock who had appeared so generous days earlier but now required repayment plus interest.

'I ran "the shop" for a couple of years,' Norm says. 'Some weeks I'd literally have hundreds of dollars in my hands from all the various sales and lending. Alcohol and dope were the favourites — I was peddling booze at fifteen and dope not long after. Never gave much thought to the illegality of it all — just saw the opportunity to make some money. Then to make some more.'

Dope smoking was not uncommon among the boarders and, unlike President Clinton, Norm admits to enthusiastic inhaling. He would chain-smoke cannabis cigarettes for days on end, turning up in his classes stoned and blood-shot. If the school authorities noticed anything then they made no attempt to intervene. But he soon realised that his constant cannabis use was robbing him of his sporting ability and making him a listless student. 'I was becoming a dumb boy, and I didn't think I needed any extra help in that department,' he smiles.

One day he simply decided to quit. He wanted to be an All Black and the dope was destroying any talent he might possess. From now on, he would stick to the booze. From henceforth, dope would get the big swerve.

'If it hadn't been for the game, how much I wanted to play rugby and play it well, I would have kept on smoking the weed. It was everywhere and I had no problem getting it and selling it on at school. And if I hadn't have stopped I would've ended up joining a gang — probably the Mongies [Mongrel Mob]. Then sold harder and harder drugs and ended up in prison. I even had a bit of a fantasy about being a Mob hit-man. There were quite a few Te Aute boys who took that path, and the Mob and the [Black] Power were regarded as staunch at our school. In their own way, they were the real role models for Maori boys who weren't too good at schoolwork.'

Certainly Norm regarded the patched members who attended the Te Aute games with a reverential awe. He liked their swagger, their fuck-you defiance, their seeming freedom from any kind of societal restraint.

'For a lot of us boys, the gangs were role models. I could see myself joining one although it would probably have been Highway 61 because my Mum's brother was in that gang. I thought gangs were cool, and for a lot of Maori kids, they still are. I seriously thought about it — about getting patched one day. I was no academic and making a fair bit of money from running "the shop". I had no real values as such — all I cared about was looking after "number one". And boarding school wasn't too different from being in a gang. The strong ran the place, the rest took the orders and the whole lot of you enjoyed the thrill of doing something a bit suss.'

Remarkably, Norm credits the game of rugby for steering him away from that path.

'I wanted to be an All Black so much that even at that age I knew what was required to get there. Rugby ended that whole gang temptation thing for me. But we can't all be professional rugby players or All Blacks. There were a hell of a lot of guys who went straight into the gangs after they left school because they didn't see any alternative. It was the gangs or the dole. Usually both.'

Over 1983–84, Norm's fourth and fifth form years, the Te Aute College 1st XV was among the country's best — beaten only once and winning the prestigious Top Four competition in the latter year. Although the school had a roll of only 240 pupils, the whole of Te Aute regarded rugby as special, as more than just a game. It was an expression of the school's identity — a public statement as to the school's mana. In their traditional encounters against Wanganui Collegiate, New Plymouth Boys' High, Palmerston North Boys' and Rotorua Boys', Te Aute was feared as much as respected. And at home they were near unbeatable — the players supported on the sidelines by the rest of their schoolmates chanting fierce haka and joined by past pupils and cheering parents.

'In the games against the traditional schools there was always a bit of the old Pakeha versus Maori thing. And it was an issue, believe me. Us Maori kids hated being looked down on and we knew what those rah-rah types at Collegiate thought of us. But it was the other Maori boarding schools that you really wanted to beat — St Stephen's, Wesley, Church College. It wasn't just a clash of teams. It was Maori against Maori, mana against mana, tribe against tribe. You hated losing those ones.'

Because of the quality of rugby at Te Aute, Norm didn't make the 1st XV squad until his fifth year at the school — and even then he couldn't make the playing team. He was selected as the reserve prop to two boys from well-known Hawke's Bay Maori families, George Ormond from Mahia and Eddie Konia from Flaxmere.

Indeed, coach Awi Riddell regarded Norm's playing abilities as 'very limited. He was strong but had no vision of the game. Would just pick up the ball and run, head down. I can't take any credit for his later career. You certainly wouldn't have picked him as a future All Black from his days at Te Aute.'

It was only when first-choice tighthead prop George Ormond was concussed that Norm took his place in the Te Aute front row. Ormond would later return, but suffer another blow to the head and be warned off the game for good. Almost immediately after, tragedy struck the Konia family and the entire team.

Eddie's younger brother Walter was the team's halfback and the school was playing Church College at Hamilton. In the last minutes of the game Walter went in to tackle an opposing player and took a knee to the head. He picked himself up from the clash, heard the referee blow full-time, and started to walk from the field. Suddenly he collapsed. After being taken by ambulance to Hamilton Hospital he slipped into a coma. A few days later he died, a massive blood clot lodged in his brain.

'It shook us up real bad,' says Norm. 'He was a great little kid and he'd been one of my dorm-mates right through school. He was a generous and quiet boy — not at all your typical halfback. And then ... we just never recovered. His death was so wrong, so shocking — something that every one of us could relate to in the sense that it could have been us. We never dealt properly with it — Walter was there one day and gone the next. None of us could understand that.'

Te Aute lost most of its traditional games after that bleak June day in Hamilton — sometimes trying too hard in its bid to honour the young Konia.

Off the field, though, Norm's bullocking runs and general play had been noticed by the Hawke's Bay secondary school selectors, who picked him for their representative team to play Wellington. Despite the Te Aute coach's assessment of his skills, there was enough in the prop's play to attract wider interest and provide Norm with a good measure of personal satisfaction. His Hawke's Bay team-mates included three future All Blacks — wing John Timu, No. 8 Richard Turner and halfback Stu Forster. In addition a good number of the players in that secondary school team went on to be selected for NPC and Super 12 teams, including Mike 'Tyson' Edwards, Simon Tremain, Justin Cullen, Nathan Paewai, George Konia and Simon Halford.

At school Norm was now revelling in his mana as a senior, a 1st XV hero and an age-group provincial rugby rep. But the booze had become a problem, and his drink-affected actions were causing alarm. As well he'd assimilated the prevailing Te Aute boarding culture — so well, in fact, that he was constantly defying teachers and engaged in a series of running skirmishes with headmaster Riddell.

Around the boarding house he had a less savoury reputation than just that of an anti-authoritarian troublemaker. He had become exactly what he'd first feared — a strong-arm bully — intimidating weaker kids, imposing his physical authority on those around him. He was also a willing participant in any violence that was going and was exhilarated by his domination of his hostel mates and the cowering of those unwise enough to take him on.

'I was a thug,' he says ruefully. 'At times I could get really carried away — this whole black rage thing would take over and I'd go psycho. It wasn't just the other kids who were scared when that happened; shit, it was me too. But mostly I was just another Te Aute bully.'

But there was one important difference. Norm had become the bully of the bullys. Not content with frightening the living daylights out of the juniors, he imposed a reign of terror on the senior students as well. Ironically, he saw himself as a protector. If a junior had received a thrashing at the hands of an older boy, he would seek out the older boy and deliver his own brand of justice. When a couple of the dorm's juniors complained that they'd been 'touched up' by a senior, and after Norm had satisfied himself that the claims were true, he decided on a very personal payback. Norm beat the offender so badly that he thought he'd permanently injured the boy. When he looked up, all he could see was blood — every wall in the room smeared in red.

A furious Riddell demanded an explanation. Norm refused. Any examination must fall too close and his earlier humiliations as a junior had not been forgotten. The headmaster telephoned Norm's father, who at the time was deputy chairman of the school's board of governors, and advised him that he could no longer tolerate his son within the boarding establishment. Incredibly, a solution was proffered — Norm could private board with Te Aute's farm manager Peter Graham and his family. Graham was also the 1st XV's physical trainer, and so was considered to have Norm's general measure. The arrangement suited everyone — Norm and Awi Riddell would reduce their regular confrontations at the boarding establishment, and the young man could return for his second year as a sixth former and anchor Te Aute's scrum for the '87 rugby season.

Over the Christmas holidays Norm picked up his usual haymaking job — back-breaking, energy-sapping stuff that stretches the physical reserves of any adult worker let alone a teenager. Yet Norm relished the challenge and easily held his own. He was one of the workers — would head off to the pub with them after work, get pissed, go to the same parties. And if there were verbals with other patrons or any edgy physical disputes then the young Hewitt could hold his own. No one had any worries on that score.

Things had also changed at home. One night when Russell and Mabel were arguing and Norm regarded his mother as at risk, he stepped between the two and knocked his father to the ground. Then did it again. It was a critical event, altering the balance within the family home and providing a different reference point for his mother and his younger sisters and brothers.

'I dropped Dad a couple of times that night,' Norm says. 'I mean, I know people might find it a bit strange, but I wasn't prepared to watch Mum cop any more. The old man and me were too much alike I guess — get on the piss, get a bit silly. But that's the way it was then — that was the environment a lot of families lived in. Still do.'

Yet Norm's father continued to be his son's strongest ally. At the start of the 1987 school year Norm had wandered into school on a Saturday afternoon straight from the Te Aute pub. A junior crossed his path and Norm saw that he was carrying a plastic bag of cannabis and confiscated it. He was still debating what to do next — hand it over to the school authorities or sell it — when a teacher interrupted his progress. He could smell the booze on Norm's breath, spotted the bag, and duly reported the incident to Awi Riddell.

'By the standards of the time I had no choice,' says the former headmaster. 'Nowadays I don't think suspensions or expulsions work — you're not helping the student and you're transferring the problem to somebody else. These days I'd offer counselling, find out what the real problem was, try and help a kid overcome the problem.'

Instead, Riddell rang Russell Hewitt and advised him that he should withdraw his son from Te Aute or he would be suspended pending the next meeting of the Board of Governors. As deputy chairman Russell had his own views on the issue, convinced that the principal had singled out Norm for special attention. But after initially challenging the verdict Hewitt Senior bowed to the inevitable. In March 1987 Norm Hewitt was formally withdrawn from Te Aute to avoid the inevitable expulsion.

'There was a fair bit of shame for the family attached to that decision,' Norm now says. 'It was meant to be my crowning year at Te Aute and instead I left under the cloud of being a druggie. Which actually understated the reason because I wasn't so much a user as a dealer. I guess I was lucky to last as long as I did.'

And so Norm Hewitt's school career ended ingloriously. He'd spent two years in the fifth form, failed University Entrance at his first attempt, and had nothing to show prospective employers except an acknowledged appetite for physical work and the beginnings of a drinking problem. It was the kind of resume that could have consigned him to a life of manual labour, with his previous antics suggesting the likelihood of later scrapes with the law.

But Norm had two saving graces — one familial, one internal. His mother was determined not to give up on her son, and continued to look out for his interests — approaching family friends to find private board for him when he started work in the woolstores at Napier, showering him with a mother's love. And the second was a determination in her son to be the best rugby player he could be — to harness his ability and ride it as far as it would take him.

Whether that combination would be enough, no-one was prepared to guess.

CHAPTER TWO

Hawke's Bay

Having left Te Aute College in disgrace, Norm's immediate future was bleak. He had neither references nor academic credentials — only a couple of scratchy School Cert passes gained over his two years in the fifth form. In addition, the 'Rogernomics' revolution was still in full swing, and the body count was high. The massive Whakatu freezing works near Hastings had closed with over two thousand jobs lost, while the rural economy was reeling under the successive blows of high interest rates, low market returns and the withdrawal of farm subsidies. In such an environment an unskilled Maori youth was destined for an early introduction to the dole office.

Fortunately, the competitive club rugby scene in the Bay provided Norm with an alternative. Each year the Te Aute 1st XV played a Napier Tech Old Boys selection as part of an early season interchange, and the Tech coaching staff had previously admired the strong young prop who loved to run with the ball. When you leave school, they told Norm, come and have a chat. Suddenly that invitation had developed a currency.

Within a fortnight Norm Hewitt had become the latest recruit to the Tech Old Boys rugby club, with a labouring job provided for him at the Napier Port coolstores. Private board with the club's secretary was arranged, and he was allocated a starting place in the Colts side. Considering the circumstances, it had been a good save, and the Tech officials were equally delighted at having secured the promising youngster. By season's end Norm had repaid the club with a series of consistent on-field performances and selection in the representative Hawke's Bay Colts team.

'And if I hadn't been a half-decent rugby player?' Norm shrugs. 'Mate, I'd have been well and truly stuffed.'

Despite frequent protestations to the contrary, rugby clubs are not altruistic societies. They are interested in players for as long as they have value on the field. A sense of camaraderie may be offered to prospective players in return for their loyalty, but by the 1980s off-season recruitment drives were becoming vital if clubs wanted to stay competitive. Commercial deals were arranged for the better players — a job with a club supporter, subsidised accommodation, travel expenses. At higher levels, back-of-the-hand cash, or boot money as it was known to the players, after the northern hemisphere tradition of slipping a note into the players' boots while they were in the showers. No names, no pack drill.

Such inducements took on added importance for provincial players as local economies worsened. The official boast, that rugby was an amateur sport, had already been contradicted at the highest level by the 1986 Crusaders tour of South Africa and by the gathering exodus of young players to larger unions. While he might not have possessed formal qualifications, Norm well understood the new dynamic that ran through the game.

'I knew rugby wasn't just a game anymore, it was an entertainment business. And the public was the market, if you like, for that entertainment. People paid upfront cash and they demanded a certain quality. Although at that time rugby was my life. I played the game because I loved it, and it was the only thing that mattered. Nothing else. The footy field was the only place I felt comfortable. But I wasn't dumb either. I could see what was happening — that the better players were being paid. That you could make a living out of the sport.'

For the moment, though, such thoughts were secondary to the sheer thrill of getting on the field and playing. It was not just that he felt a rapport with the game, but rugby seemed to be the only thing he was good at. Sure, he enjoyed the physical clash and the fellowship of the after-match, but it was more than that. Rugby provided him with a measure of self-respect that he could find nowhere else. He fell easily into the club lifestyle of train, play and get pissed.

An early highlight was being called in to provide scrummaging practice for the Tongan international team before their World Cup pool match against Canada in Napier. But the initial excitement soon disappeared.

'I was scared. They were big, black men — they were huge. There were times when I thought I would actually hurt myself, the pressure they could generate through their front row was so intense. It was one hell of a shock. Here I was playing as a Colts prop and generally doing OK. And then I was up against these monsters. And they didn't give a shit how young or inexperienced you were — they just kept boring into you.'

It was a lesson that had an immediate impact on the 18-year-old. Norm might be strong for a schoolboy or even a club colt, but he was a mere sapling against adult competition, and no favours were granted for youth. He would need to be stronger still if he was going to play prop at senior levels. Though there was another solution.

'I'd played a couple of games at prop for the rep under-18s but the hooker they'd selected could only hook with one foot. And his throwing-in wasn't all that flash either. So the coach, Peter Loomes, said "How about it?" I didn't object. As long as I was on the field, that was OK by me.'

So while Norm continued to play prop for the Tech Colts, his continuing selection in the Hawke's Bay's Colts squad was as a hooker. Loomes' hunch was confirmed by the suggestion of his club coach that Norm make the transition permanent. He wasn't really big enough to play prop at senior level, while power scrummaging was becoming an important feature of the game. A converted prop could be an asset in the front row. All Black hooker Sean Fitzpatrick had set the example as a hooker who could scrummage powerfully but also pop up in the loose as a fourth flanker.

'Fitzy revolutionised the role of hooker. The All Blacks had picked mobile hookers before him — Hika Reid would probably be the best example — but Fitzy was something else again. He could scrum *and* he could run. Lineouts were also important — you had to have the ball thrown in with pinpoint accuracy. And tightheads were very rare — the way the scrum had developed meant fewer tightheads. No hooker should ever lose their own ball. So the scrum was being used more as a set-piece weapon — screwing a halfback away from his backline, and giving him dirty ball as his pack went sideways.'

The sudden move to hooker caused the young Hewitt no grief. He could understand the logic, and if he wanted to play prop at senior level it would mean growing another three inches and putting on another 20 kg. While he might achieve the latter, his genetics had already ruled out the former. Besides, he discovered that he enjoyed the new role, although there were also some unique hazards that took a bit of getting used to.

'The thing about the front row is that every scrum is a contest that's generally hidden from the spectators, the referee and even most of your team-mates. So you use every trick, every tactic to get on a roll, knowing you can't be properly monitored or policed. The reason it's so tough is that it's all about physical domination, and you use every advantage you can. If your scrum's stuffed then so is the tight five. If your tight five is on their heels you've got no show of winning a modern rugby game.

'It's an incredibly vulnerable position. I quickly learned where not to put my head. One of their locks could deliver a sneaky punch or their hooker knee you in the face as they stood up. It was real trial and error stuff — mostly error.'

It was also extremely claustrophobic as the forward packs drove into each other at scrum time and the power of the opposing packs was translated directly through the legs, backs, shoulders and necks of the two hookers. A couple of times Norm found himself blacking out from the pressure.

'It's like smashing into a brick wall at speed — you feel it most through your neck and shoulders. But I knew I couldn't give up. I had to guts it out or I'd stay at Colts level.'

He also had to learn new skills like throwing in to the lineout and running different defensive lines. But the greatest change required was physical. Because hookers are expected to be more mobile than props, he needed to be fitter and faster, to have both better aerobic and anaerobic capacity. But if he was really going to mix it at a senior level, he would also need to be stronger.

SETTLING IN

At Tech itself Norm was enjoying an active social life — part of any rugby club's attraction. It was train hard, play hard and drink hard, with the post-match revelries at the Napier clubhouse both boisterous and irresistible. One of the toughest hombres was Terrence Taylor, a hard-nosed prop and repo agent-cum-debt collector who occasionally represented Hawke's Bay at a representative level. He was ten years older than Norm but his no-nonsense style impressed the youngster and he came to regard Taylor as an unlikely role model, both on and off the field.

'"TT" [Taylor] was a legend at Tech, and when I started playing senior rugby for the club he made a point of looking out for me. On the other side of our scrum was Hamish Quinlavan who was one hard dude, despite being a schoolteacher. Being in the middle of those two was a quick introduction to all the traditions of the front row. They were hard men and that's what I wanted to be.'

Another young player at the Tech club was No. 8 Richard Turner, who had already played for the Hawke's Bay rep team while still only a student at Napier Boys' High. The Hewitt and Turner families met on the sidelines each Saturday to support their sons, and a friendship soon developed. On one such Saturday Norm's mother confessed that she was worried about her son. He was emotionally immature and she was concerned that he could be led astray too easily. In response, the Turners offered Norm accommodation with them and he eagerly accepted. Despite all his clubroom bravado and bluster, he was feeling pangs of homesickness. The new arrangement might help to ease those feelings.

'Richard and I were both at the coolstores and we'd been in a number of grade teams together so it wasn't surprising that we got on. The Turners were a fantastic family — warm, open, and Mrs Turner was one hell of a cook. No wonder Richard was so big! But it was good to be with a family again. I was a real mummy's boy in that regard. I needed to feel I was somewhere safe.'

Over that summer, Hawke's Bay's rep coach Richard Hunt pondered the region's abysmal rugby record. The halcyon days of the 1960s Ranfurly Shield era were but a distant memory and the Magpies were firmly rooted in the second division of the New Zealand rugby championship. It was an unacceptable ranking for the Bay's administrators, who remembered Hawke's Bay's former glory all too clearly.

But the metropolitan unions were now dominating New Zealand rugby like never before — the decline of the rural sector, the rise of the finance and service industries and the growing importance of tertiary education was having its effect on areas like Hawke's Bay, Northland and Southland. Where once a school-leaver would have found a job or an apprenticeship locally, the opportunities were now elsewhere. In less than a decade, rugby power had shifted irretrievably from the provinces to the main centres, and the move towards professionalism would do even more to entrench the divide.

The corresponding importance of tertiary education also favoured cities with a university — particularly Otago University, whose specialist Phys Ed School was attracting some of the best young players of the generation, including outstanding Hawke's Bay products like Taine Randell and Josh Kronfeld. Although for those who lacked the school qualifications to further their education, Hawke's Bay did have its own unofficial 'university — the Tomoana freezing works.

Current NZRFU councillor Tom Mulligan, a mainstay of the Hawke's Bay union, was then a foreman at Tomoana. He was also a proud supporter of the Clive rugby club which was regarded, along with the MAC club, as the natural progression for ex-Te Aute players. Norm received approaches from both clubs, but he had already pledged his allegiance to

Tech. Besides, the nature of his departure from Te Aute was not something that encouraged a continuing association.

Both Mulligan and Tomoana works manager Dave Guscott were avid Magpie supporters, and both served on the union's executive. It had become their unofficial role to secure promising players by providing jobs for them at Tomoana. Any number of Clive and Hawke's Bay players found themselves rubbing shoulders on the chains — Stu Forster, Paul Cooke, Gordon Falcon, Jason McDowell, and soon Norm Hewitt.

As Norm says, 'You only ever worked at the freezing works for the money. Anybody who's worked in them knows that it's messy, smelly, boring work. Quite a lot of people would get all doped up as well, so it's not the kind of place where you go to get job satisfaction. But I was unskilled, the pay was good and the boss was generous with leave for rugby games. It could've been worse.'

As Richard Hunt came to assemble his Hawke's Bay squad for the 1988 rep season his pool of talent would have been very much smaller but for Tomoana and its sympathetic management.

INTO THE REPS

One of the first calls Hunt made that season was to the 19-year-old Norm Hewitt. He had seen the young man play with the representative Colts team, and the hooking position was a troubled area. First-choice hooker Craig Brownlie was injured, and it was either take a punt on the promising youngster or select from the mediocre talent available on the club scene.

'It wasn't too much of a surprise because the Tech coaches had already indicated that I'd be playing senior that season, and I'd picked up that there wasn't much around. All the same I was only 19, and it's one thing to play Colts — entirely another to be selected for the senior firsts. Then the next thing I'm being told to turn up for rep training!'

In fact, Norm was to play his first rep game for Hawke's Bay before even making his senior club debut. A Bay team was selected to play a Supporters XV in a trial game on Napier's McLean Park — a typical scrappy, start-of-season affair that the Bay just won. But there had been enough in the young Hewitt's play for Hunt to be encouraged.

The next week Norm played his first game for the Tech Old Boys seniors. Their forward pack dominated the Hastings High School Old Boys opposition, and seconds before half-time a ball spewed loose and Norm charged down the blindside to find the opposing backs melting before him as he scored his first senior try.

'I can only dimly remember the action, but I can definitely remember how I felt. They'd come back at us and the try gave Tech some breathing space. There were the usual thumps on the shoulder as I ran back — y'know, the well-done-mate stuff you get — and I felt, I don't know, as if I belonged, I guess. That playing rugby was not only what I wanted to do for as long as I could but that the whole Te Aute business was now behind me. There were Mum and Dad on the sideline cheering me on — it was magic.'

The Tech club celebrated its season opener in the usual manner — with a noisy leer-up in the clubrooms, where the 19-year-old indulged in all the usual drinking games. He'd left school unable to know when enough was enough, and his nights at the Tech clubrooms only exacerbated the problem. He quickly became a binge drinker, trying to match his consumption against his older and more experienced clubmates, and failing dismally. He would stagger home pissed, a surliness simmering beneath the surface. At such times a different Norm Hewitt would appear — a snarling young beast who made others blanch.

'The Colts actually started me off. We'd have drinking sessions after training, another one after the game. It was just rugby . . . drink . . . rugby . . . drink. Teenagers think they're immortal anyway and I was no different. It was — still is — a booze culture. At least I'd had some training [at Te Aute] for the lifestyle. Some of the backs would be off their heads after the second bottle. Silly as chooks.'

Nevertheless, the constant diet of alcohol was beginning to corrode his self-control. There were mutterings about his off-field behaviour, but most hoped it was simply a phase he would grow out of. Such matters were not rep coach Richard Hunt's concern. His more immediate problem was that Hawke's Bay's promotion aspirations were already falling apart. In pre-competition games the Bay were defeated by Waikato, then hammered by third-division Wanganui — the midfield combination of John Hainsworth and Steve Gordon running riot against indifferent Hawke's Bay tackling. Hunt was furious at his team and let them know it, although the young hooker escaped the worst of his tongue. The forwards had won enough ball, it was the backs who had given the Keystone Cops impression.

'I was excited at playing rep rugby but I hadn't realised how tough it was going to be. [All Black] Richard Loe was in the opposing front-row for the Waikato game and that was plain scary. He loved confrontation and wasn't afraid to smack a few ears around. Against Wanganui I struck [Samoan international hooker] Tala Leiasamaivao and he was outstanding. After those first couple of games I knew I would have to step up or I wouldn't survive. I lost a bit of confidence about then too and

Russell and Mabel Hewitt with the infant Norm at Maungarapa 1968.

No larger nor more athletic than his peers. Norm (top right hand corner) in his first representative team — Central Hawke's Bay Ross Shield 1981.

Junior Norm in Te Aute's third form rugby team (front row, far right) —
already a victim of the college's perverse culture.

A Te Aute 1st XV
post-match haka.
Their season was
blighted by the
tragic death of
young halfback
Walter Konia.

Lord of all he
surveys.
The senior Norm
has meta-
morphosed into
the bully of
bullies.

The public face of Te Aute College. A helpful Norm escorts then Governor-General, Sir Paul Reeves, around the school during a vice-regal visit.

Left: *The young lion Hewitt prepares to defend. Hawke's Bay v Wellington, 1992. A significant win at McLean Park 32-22.*

Left: *Hard men — (from left) Terrence Taylor, Gordon Falcon, 'Boom' Graham and Norm in Hawke's Bay's alternative strip versus the mighty Auckland, Napier 1992. It was not these guys' fault that the visitors triumphed 40-9.*

Never bested. The Hawke's Bay front row of Orcades Crawford, Norm and Terrence Taylor. Taylor was the young hooker's early mentor.

wondered whether I was really good enough . . . if I wasn't just fooling myself that I could play at this level.'

A fortnight later Hawke's Bay were scheduled to play the touring Welsh team, but they suffered another loss in preparation — a 22-point drubbing by a very average Manawatu combination. It was hardly the kind of form likely to send a shudder through the Wales management, even if the Scarlet Dragons were having their own problems. After being spanked by a record 52-3 in the first test, the Hawke's Bay game represented a chance for Wales to put their tour back on track and give fringe players a chance to impress before the second test. So it was a decidedly useful side that Wales put onto McLean Park that brilliantly sunny Wednesday afternoon — led again by first-five Johnathon Davies and including the flier Ieuan Evans and an experienced forward pack.

'They were big, fierce-looking men — much bigger than our pack — and I was a bit overawed just looking at them as we lined up for the kick-off. It was the biggest game of my life up until then so my stomach was churning and I felt sick. It was like . . . this is it . . . this is my first taste of the big time. I can remember looking down at my arms, and there were goosebumps everywhere.'

The Hawke's Bay side that afternoon was one of the youngest the Bay had ever fielded — two 18-year-olds in halfback Stu Forster and fullback Jason McDowell (who was still attending Napier Boys' High), two 19-year-olds in Richard Turner and Norm Hewitt, and a backline still gun-shy after the Wanganui debacle. Prior to the game their coach Richard Hunt had sarcastically predicted a '50 points each draw', given both teams' propensity to regard defence as an unnecessary distraction. He was half right.

'They smashed us. Their forwards weren't as impressive as they looked but their backs were fast and bloody clever. By comparison, we looked like we were playing in gumboots. Davies was in brilliant form — a great runner. You wondered what he might do behind a decent forward pack. He had amazing vision and everything he did was class. For us, it was a disappointing game because it was a big crowd, great weather and a perfect pitch and the Welsh just wasted us.'

Making it doubly humiliating was the fact that the Welsh were regarded as the worst overseas team to tour New Zealand since the 'Awful Aussies' of 1972. The final score was 45 points to 18. In the end the Bay youngsters had acquitted themselves well, this time showing up their older team-mates. Norm's effort was typically honest and industrious and, despite his earlier apprehension, good enough to draw the attention of the national selectors.

GETTING NOTICED

The traditional North–South inter-island game had been cancelled the previous year because of fears the contest was becoming too one-sided. To offer a more meaningful contest, the NZRFU instead launched a tri-series competition with teams drawn from Northern, Central and Southern zones. In essence, the North Island was halved, with a line drawn through Lake Taupo, the upper half constituting the Northern Zone, the lower half the Central Zone, and the South Island renamed the Southern Zone. The sides would play each other for the George Nepia Trophy — the hope being that some of the great fullback's lustre might rub off on this otherwise tawdry creation.

However, there were some benefits for the All Black selection panel under their new convenor Alex Wyllie. Along with his assistants Earle Kirton and Lane Penn, Wyllie could watch the three zone matches as quasi-All Black trials, even if withdrawals and injuries robbed the games of any real meaning. In particular, the Central team lacked any cohesive structure or sense of identity, but it was still required to play a Northern team dominated by the champion Auckland side, and then front up a couple of days later and take on the Southern XV.

Norm had taken little interest in the zonal competition when it was first announced, and did not see that it had any relevance to his career. His concentration was focused almost entirely on the local club scene where he hoped to prove to Hunt that he should remain the Bay's top hooker.

'I came home from training one night and there's this phone call — some guy saying he's Alex Wyllie. So I said — yeah right, piss off — pull the other one. Thought it was one of my clubmates having me on. It must have taken Alex a good couple of minutes to persuade me who he was. And then he said he wanted me in Rotorua next week for the first Zone game. They needed a reserve hooker for the Central team — someone was injured. OK, I said. End of conversation.'

His immediate reaction to the call was to pick up the phone again and tell his parents the good news. But then he stopped midway through and replaced the receiver. No, he couldn't show he was excited, not even to his family. He had to be staunch — make like it was nothing. But his practised reserve was shaken at the team's first practice at Rotorua.

'I couldn't say a word. I was just blown away. Here I was practising with guys who were my idols — I even had posters of some of them on my wall at home and now here I was, eating at the same table, having a few beers and training in their company. I sat on the bench for both the zone games

— understudy to Glenn Fraser — but just to be among those men . . . it was something else.'

In some ways he was fortunate not to play. The Central side were thrashed 68-6 by a rampant North that included no fewer than twelve All Blacks and one of the great front rows of all time in Steve McDowell, Richard Loe and Sean Fitzpatrick. The loose forward trio was, if anything, even more impressive — Buck Shelford, Zinzan Brooke and Michael Jones.

'It was a massacre. I remember thinking, Glenn Fraser, don't you bloody get injured. No way do I want to face that lot.'

In their next game, against South, Central were also easily defeated, with former Hawke's Bay schoolboy star John Timu running in a sparkling try for the southerners. The talent trickle from the Bay to Otago had begun, with South fullback Greg Cooper another recent export. Soon, the trickle would become a flood.

Despite his unexpected selection for the Central team, Norm's general form was causing his rep coach Hunt real concern. Although the young hooker had promise, a tough second division campaign lay in prospect, and he needed a no-surrender forward pack. One that appreciated that lower division rugby might not have the same skill level but it had no less appetite for the rough stuff. Another year with Hawke's Bay out of the top flight and Hunt would be out of a job. Drastic changes were required.

Celtic hooker Alex Matthewson, a former New Zealand Colt, had returned to the Bay and was challenging hard for Norm's hooking spot. In a dour struggle between the Celtic and Tech club teams the duelling hookers clashed — the young buck determined to keep his place, the older man equally keen to win back his former rep position. They butted heads, barged each other off the ball and finally resorted to open fisticuffs, their team-mates having to drag them apart. But Matthewson had done enough — Hunt dumped Norm back on to the bench for the Bay's opening divisional match against Mid-Canterbury.

'I was so pissed off. No-one likes being dropped and I'd let the clash with Matthewson get real personal. And I reckoned if I was good enough to be the Central zone's reserve, how come I'm not good enough to front for the Bay? I hated being beaten and that's why we'd got into the stoush in the club game. We knew what was at stake.'

Also called into the rep squad were former All Blacks Mark 'Cowboy' Shaw and Graeme Higginson. Shaw was known as much for his withering straight right as for his skills as a loose forward, and Higginson was an equally abrasive character. Hunt made Shaw his captain, while Higginson was induced from his Wairarapa farm after officially retiring a couple of seasons earlier.

'The talk in the team was that money had changed hands. Higgie still had to satisfy residential qualifications, and there was a bit of newspaper talk about deals done down at the NZRFU by Kel Tremain and some of the others. As for Cowboy — he'd sat out the first half of the season and it was quite a surprise to see him pulling on the boots again. Although they were just what the team needed — some steel in the forward pack and some leadership for us younger guys.'

But despite the changes and the solidity of Shaw and Higginson the Bay floundered in their opening game against Mid-Canterbury, provoking harsh criticism from Tremain and other Hawke's Bay officials. The 20-16 win was achieved with the greatest degree of luck, even the locals confessing that the better team had lost. The second division campaign appeared doomed, with just three days before the next game against Southland.

Hunt made only two changes to his playing fifteen, but both were significant. Out went first-five Ross McLeod and hooker Matthewson — in came the two central Hawke's Bay lads, Ross White and Norm Hewitt. Both were outstanding in an impressive 38-27 victory against one of the division's top teams, with Norm the player of the day. Not only did he initiate most of the pack's driving play but he demonstrated a commitment that left his more experienced team-mates trailing in his wake. Now that he was back on the field he was determined not to give Hunt any opportunity to drop him again. The challenge had been met.

Only for a fresh one to be issued. It came in the form of the Bay's next match against the all-conquering Ranfurly Shield-holders Auckland. The champion team had decided to 'tour' the Shield against teams from lower divisions, its side stacked with All Blacks including Joe Stanley, Grant Fox, the Whetton brothers, Zinzan Brooke, Steve McDowell and Sean Fitzpatrick. The front row of McDowell, Fitzpatrick and Manu Samoa great Peter Fatialofa presented a particular fascination for the opposing 19-year-old hooker.

'I'd seen the North front row for the zone game, although that had been from the sideline. Now I was up against the best provincial front row in the world. No doubt about that. I tried my hardest in that game but I was a boy against men. I had no show. They were too strong, too skilled, too athletic, too fast. Even so, I was still annoyed with myself that I let Fitzpatrick get a tighthead off me. It really pissed me off. And he didn't give me any let-off because I was young or green or anything — I got the odd elbow or boot along the way.

'That was the thing I quickly discovered about the top players — they were aggressive all the time. They had the killer instinct, that Auckland team. Never give a sucker a break.'

Norm also discovered that the Aucklanders would use any means to unsettle their opposition.

'At one of the first lineouts, Fitzpatrick leans across and says, "I'm going to get you, you little black cunt." In that one instant I lost any respect I had for the guy. Although those kind of racial taunts were part and parcel of the game in those days, I couldn't believe that an All Black would use them. Stupid, I know, but it was like I thought the All Blacks were on a different plane — that they didn't need to get into the verbals because they were so superior. But they did — Jeez, did they what.'

Norm's reaction was immediate. He'd track down that prick Fitzpatrick and somewhere, some time, he'd deal to the bastard. 'But I never caught him, and I tracked him the whole bloody game. He'd succeeded in what he wanted to do. He'd put me off my game totally. Years later when [English prop Victor] Obogu claimed that Fitzy had racially taunted him in a test match, and the All Black management denied it, I knew who I believed. But that was Fitzy — any advantage, he'd use it.'

The final score suggested a rugby massacre — 62 points to 9; 10 tries to nil — and it was a fair summation of the gulf between the two teams. The locals seemed not to mind. They had come to see the greatest All Blacks of their generation at play and they had not been disappointed.

UP . . .

The rest of the Bay's season was aimed at accumulating enough points to escape the lesser status of the second division. The semi-finals and final format was still in the future; for now it was a straight round-robin contest, with the highest-placed team being promoted to the first division. There were grinding wins over South Canterbury, Marlborough and Poverty Bay, but the Bay's performance was being matched by their border rivals Wairarapa-Bush. It would come down to the last game of the season — the winner would go up, the loser remain rooted in relative obscurity.

For Norm the season had been like stepping onto an assembly line — one practice after another, one game after another. Even off the field rugby dominated — a few beers after the game with his rep team-mates, midweek sessions with some of his clubmates. It was rugby, work and alcohol, and each seemed to dovetail into the others perfectly. That he could drink a prodigious amount stood him in good stead with some of the senior players.

'It was a meathead lifestyle but it would be wrong to say I didn't enjoy it. I mean, I was having the time of my life. Last year virtually expelled from Te Aute, this year cheered on by ten thousand people at McLean Park. I was somebody, and I felt good for the first time in a long time. The Bay and the Tech teams were my tribes — I didn't need anything or anyone else.'

For all his burgeoning confidence, there were others who were determined he would not be getting a swollen head. Captain Mark Shaw singled the youngster out for some direct criticism.

'He used to say — how come you train like Tarzan and play like Jane? Why are you such a girl on the field? The teasing got to me — I couldn't stand having the mickey taken out of me. Down south — I can't remember what game it was after — we all got pissed and I responded with a few verbals of my own. So he decked me. A couple of times. They were good punches too — I didn't see them coming.'

The Bay team had adopted the notorious 'back of the bus' pecking order that rewarded senior players with an informal influence off the field. For Norm it was not much different from his boarding school days — the same principles, the same notion that age and experience bestowed automatic respect. The inner sanctum regarded it as their responsibility to slap down any young players who were getting too big for their boots. And the punching out reminded Norm of his position in the team order.

'Mark Shaw was an old-fashioned guy in that respect. Very black and white — you couldn't have fitted a cigarette paper in between. If you'd upset him, he let you know and quick. On or off the field. I remember him once saying that he was sick of us hairy-arsed schoolboys not putting our body on the line during games. He got really upset, and an upset Cowboy was not a pretty sight. But that was the guy — he gave his guts every game and he expected everybody else to do the same. I respected him for that — he spoke the kind of language I understood.'

Certainly Shaw was determined to remind his charges that the work still needed to be done. Their next game was against Wairarapa-Bush, and its outcome would effectively decide the second division title. Wairarapa had a good forward pack that was led by No. 8 Stu Cruden and included two former All Blacks in Brent Anderson and Brett Harvey. They would not surrender their title chances lightly — especially given that the game was to be played on their home patch at Masterton.

'It wasn't much of a game. Mark Shaw scored a try in the first couple of minutes but then they scored off a couple of our mistakes. It was good to have TT [Terrence Taylor] beside me in the front row that day because he settled me down after they scored from one of our scrums.'

At half-time the teams turned around at 10-all and the pattern of the first half was repeated — the pressure of the occasion creating mistakes on both sides and the opposition profiting. But it was Wairarapa-Bush who made the greater number of mistakes, and the final score was 32 points to 18. Hawke's Bay was back in the first division — the experience of Shaw and Higginson and the boot of fullback Matthew Cooper had secured the day.

'It was my first taste of victory and there's nothing that tastes as good. It's sort of like great sex except it's better because you're not just pleased for yourself — you're stoked that your mates and all your supporters are feeling just as good. And that you were a part of it — that's rugby at its best. A goal has been reached and it's been long and physically draining, but you and your mates have done it. It was brilliant. We got blotto all the way home — they had to pour us off the bus when we arrived.'

To cap it all off, it had been Norm's blazer game for Hawke's Bay — his twelfth rep game, leading to the formal presentation of the blazer. It was a proud moment at the after-match as he accepted the award, Mum and Dad looking on.

. . . AND DOWN

If 1988 had been an easy introduction to provincial rugby, the next season provided a truer lesson. Despite all the optimism that the glory days were about to be repeated, Hawke's Bay's officials failed to appreciate that rugby had entered a new and acquisitive era — transfers and judicious recruiting were required to make a team competitive at first division level.

'The move towards "shamateurism" was just starting in the provinces. I mean, everyone knew that the rebel Cavaliers had got big money to tour South Africa in '86, but everyone still lied about it. I talked to one guy later on who said he'd paid off his mortgage with the Bok money; another had set himself up in business.'

Institutional dishonesty became part and parcel of the modern game. So much so that provincial unions arranged for player payments and job inducements to be offered through clubs or sponsors. In that way, union officials could maintain a literal truth — that they were not paying players. But equally, they turned two blind eyes to the other calumnies and not only condoned the back-door arrangements but actively encouraged them.

The larger unions were a more potent magnet still. To be part of a winning first division team was to attract the attention of the national selectors. Ambitious players looked at Auckland's stellar line-up, noted the steady progression of their latest recruits into the All Blacks, and drew the obvious conclusion. Teams like Canterbury, Wellington and North Harbour also began to actively seek exciting young players, offering them the chance to train in better facilities under the guidance of better coaches.

Again the health of the provincial economy played its part. Without a reputable tertiary institution and with unemployment steadily increasing in Hawke's Bay, the only real jobs that could be offered to players were through the Tomoana works. For a player looking to maximise their off-field education and skills, it was not the most inviting of prospects. And yet without Tomoana's benevolence it is difficult to see how Hawke's Bay could have retained their players for as long as they did. Over a third of the province's top playing XV were employed as freezing workers in the 1989 rugby season.

Captain and All Black trialist Matt Cooper had a position specially created as a rugby club coordinator so that his services might be retained in the Bay, but the overall trend was ominous. There were also three farmers in the rep team — all loosies — including the dynamic Paul Renton. But things were so tough on the farm that many playing careers were cut short by financial necessity.

To make matters worse the Hawke's Bay team were again humiliated in their lead-up match by third division Wanganui. The programme cover for the home game seemed a sick joke. 'We're Back' it boldly declared. Most of the spectators agreed. Back in deep doo-doos.

The first championship game was a rematch of the previous year's Shield contest — Auckland at McLean Park. The Bay were swept ruthlessly aside 50 points to 12. Eight tries to nil. If anything the Auckland team were stronger than the previous year, so the Bay could take some heart. But a 60-point hiding from Otago soon quashed any remaining optimism, and a sound thrashing from Bay of Plenty completed the misery. Three games back in the first division and over 140 points had been conceded.

The abject performances infuriated Hawke's Bay's officials, and a 'council of war' was held involving coach Hunt, captain Matthew Cooper and various committee members. President Pat Sloane publicly criticised the team for their lack of commitment, although the problems were more deep-rooted than that.

'I'd just come back from playing for the New Zealand Colts when that comment was made. It was like stepping back into the Stone Age in terms of coaching, management, professionalism, the whole works — the Hawke's Bay union didn't have a clue. I might only have been young but it was obvious that Richard Hunt was getting it in the neck from just about everyone and was under a lot of pressure. I mean it wasn't his fault that we were out of our depth and that the union hierarchy hadn't properly prepared for first division rugby. And a lot of our team lacked confidence — they knew they weren't first division material and that affected their play on the field. But that didn't stop Hunt copping it.'

With the next game, against Taranaki, the rot was temporarily postponed — a 22-12 home victory, with Norm the outstanding forward on the park. '*The Bay's back in business*' screamed the headlines in the local paper.

Too early. Although the team had shown improvement against Wellington and North Auckland the gulf in standard and experience was obvious to all, including the players. Morale plummeted. A narrow loss to an off-colour North Harbour provided some hope, but Hawke's Bay still had to defeat a strong Canterbury unit boasting seven All Blacks if they were to retain their first division status. But there would be no miracle, and even with a game left Hawke's Bay's fate was sealed. The final loss to Counties, in front of a threadbare home crowd, was a funereal contest, the Bay pack capitulating long before the final whistle.

'No-one wanted to be there. We'd already been relegated and it was the coach's last game before the chop. We couldn't even get ourselves motivated by that — just went though the motions and got dicked again. It was so frustrating because we'd been sent up to do a job and hadn't been given the players or the backing to do it. And all those people who'd made a fuss of us the year before started looking sideways at us now. That was the first time I appreciated how fickle the public are.'

A plea was made before the Counties game, and again at the after-match function, for the outstanding players — Paul Cooke, Matthew Cooper, Stu Forster, Norm Hewitt — to stay in Hawke's Bay for the next season. Not to decamp to greener and more profitable pastures, but to restore the team's fortunes. It was a call repeated by captain Cooper himself. Loyalty, loyalty, loyalty . . . remember your roots. In the end, only Norm Hewitt would stay. Matthew Cooper would ignore his own pleas and join Waikato; Cooke and Forster plunge south and join Laurie Mains'

Otago squad. Richard Turner had already anticipated the exodus and joined North Harbour at the start of the season. To make matters worse, the Hawke's Bay under-18 star Josh Kronfeld was on his way down to Otago. It was not just current rep players that the Bay was haemorrhaging.

'I thought about it. Especially now that I'd been selected as a New Zealand Colt and drawn wider attention. But I was only 20 years old, and a young 20 at that. We also had the nucleus of a good team — Terrence Taylor and Orcades Crawford had become regulars in the front row, Gordon Falcon had made his debut, 'Boom' [Romana] Graham was a promising No. 8. I thought I should give it another year.'

But the real reason was more personal. Whatever his prowess on the rugby field, Norm lacked the social confidence to stray too far from family. Although his emotional development was stunted, he was not insensitive, and cities like Auckland, Wellington and Dunedin were too big and too different. Despite his rugby ambitions, his insecurities tethered him to the familiar.

Then the newly appointed Hawke's Bay coach, Graeme Taylor, made the young hooker a remarkable offer. One too good to refuse.

CHAPTER THREE

John Hart

Despite Hawke's Bay's return to the second division, Norm was relieved at the progress he'd made during the 1989 season. He'd cemented his role within the Bay team, attracted the interest of the national selection panel, and had been selected for the New Zealand Colts squad. There he had trained under the man who was to have a major influence on his future rugby career — John Hart.

Hart was highly regarded in rugby circles as more than just a good coach, but as a man with a rare vision for the game. He was a thinker and a motivator, someone who brought new and professional concepts to the traditional game and whose teams played winning, crowd-pleasing rugby. He was also an articulate man, too garrulous for most of the old guard, a striking contrast to the gruff exterior and monosyllabic conversation of so many other New Zealand coaches. In short, Hart was a man for his times — talkative, accessible, and possessing a clear understanding of rugby's role in the national psyche. But, like many intelligent, ambitious men, he could be impatient to the point of rashness, and took criticism personally.

For all that, his coaching record was extraordinary. He had taken over the reins of a disjointed Auckland team in 1982, and constructed a side that many regard as the greatest provincial team in the history of the game. Within three years he had made Auckland the dominant force in the land — winning the Ranfurly Shield in a breathtaking game at Lancaster Park and taking out a mortgage on the National Championship. An array of talent flowered under Hart's coaching and management — a pantheon of players that included Andy Haden, Joe Stanley, Steve McDowell, Sean Fitzpatrick, the Whetton brothers, Grant Fox and Zinzan Brooke. Two of Hart's brightest stars were John Kirwan and Michael Jones, who he had plucked from obscurity to dazzle the rugby world with their freakish skills.

There were those who suggested that any dyslexic, deaf dummy could make a decent team out of such talent, and Hart acquired a reputation in the envious south as an arrogant motormouth. But that's the nature of New Zealand. It doesn't so much chop down its tall poppies as dig them up and incinerate them. And, despite his diminutive physical stature, the ex-Waitemata halfback was one of rugby's tallest poppies — the country's first 'yuppie' coach.

After being selected as the All Black coach for the national team's tour to Japan, Hart was dumped in favour of Cantabrian Alex Wyllie. Although the two had worked together under Brian Lochore as All Black selectors, there could be no greater contrast in personality or style. Wyllie was a straight-up, no-bullshit coach of the old school — a former All Black loose forward of fearsome reputation who had more than earned his nickname 'Grizz'. The two men were like oil and water — they might flow in the same direction but they could never combine. That the NZRFU would later attempt to make them work together betrays the organisation's naivete.

But that would be in the future. For the moment, labyrinthine politicking had conspired to oust Hart from his position as convenor of selectors. The most vitriolic criticism had come from the South Island, where Hart was portrayed as a sharp-talking city slicker whose philosophies and style were alien. Worse than alien. Anti-rugby. Anti-New Zealand.

By 1989 John Hart had bounced back from this disappointment to replace Wellingtonian Earle Kirton on the All Black selection panel and be assigned selection and coaching responsibilities for the New Zealand Colts. Kirton's poor record with the Colts the previous year had been the primary factor in his sacking — failure at any international level had its consequences. Convenor Alex Wyllie continued his association with the All Blacks, while the other selector was Lane Penn, a shy and retiring man who was appointed Wyllie's assistant. It was a selection panel designed by a committee — the sum of its parts much greater than its whole.

NEW ZEALAND COLTS

The New Zealand Colts selection procedure was not an exact science — it was a hit-and-miss affair that often saw good players ignored and the mediocre attain national recognition. Provinces were required to nominate players aged under 21 years, most of whom were not playing senior representative rugby. From those nominations, the Colts panel chose 72 players to attend a week-long coaching school based at the Police College in Porirua. Four teams were then selected for the ensuing trials, which culminated in the announcement of the New Zealand Colts squad.

A year earlier Norm Hewitt had been nominated by Hawke's Bay and dutifully attended the trial week, only to miss final selection — ranked behind Wanganui's Tala Leiasamaivao and Counties' Andrew Roose. He had been mildly disappointed, but in his heart suspected he wasn't yet ready, and he still had another season in which to be eligible for team selection.

1989 was different. This time he was determined to make the squad, and he was duly chosen as the back-up hooker to Andrew Roose. Despite his delight at making the Colts squad, the most lasting impression he retained from the camp was meeting John Hart, and being perplexed by the man's effervescence and energy.

'The guy was amazing. Always talking, always waving his hands around, always had the "go" button on full throttle. All these bright new ideas spewing out all over the place, and you didn't have time to take it all in. He introduced a real excitement into training.

'It was the first time I'd struck the grids that are used for skills building and coordination. There was so much variation that your brain would start hurting because of the concentration required. But that's what Hart wanted. He wanted you to think your options under pressure. It was another planet.'

Certainly Hart had a special affinity for coaching the Colts. By nature the young men were eager and impressionable — willing to learn from an acknowledged master of rugby strategy.

'But Harty was also the dominant personality and that suited him. He was the king and we were his subjects. And he was such a perfectionist — there was a level of professionalism at his trainings that overawed most of us. I was totally blown away.'

Although it was not entirely a one-way street. John Hart had also been forced to take notice of the young Maori hooker from Hawke's Bay.

'My first impression was of Norm's physical hardness. It's something that has remained with him throughout his entire career — that real focused, hard-nosed approach that he brings to his rugby. Not just in playing but in training as well. I mean he's not a flashy player but he's a real, honest grafter. That's always been his strength, and I had no hesitation in selecting him for the Colts. We were going to be playing some tough provinces and some tough forward packs before the Colts "test" against Australia. We would need players like Norm and I knew he'd do the job for me.'

Although Andrew Roose was given the first chance to shine, in the Colts' opening tour match against Horowhenua, Norm was selected for the key Taranaki game. The provincial side boasted a formidable pack and an experienced backline marshalled by Kieran Crowley. They were generally expected to win, especially since they'd recently defeated a strong Wellington team.

But the Colts team that afternoon brimmed with talent — it was possibly the most talented under-21 team to have represented the country, boasting no fewer than ten future All Blacks — from Matthew Ridge, Va'aiga Tuigamala and Walter Little in the backs to Jamie Joseph, Craig Dowd and Norm Hewitt in the tight five. The side was captained by future Western Samoa star Pat Lam, and it was a measure of its strength that players like Richard Turner, Simon Tremain and Mike Edwards could only make the reserves. The result was a 48-18 thrashing of the first division team and the reselection of the playing fifteen for the match against their Australian counterparts on Eden Park.

A week later, the Colts' 'test' was played as the curtain-raiser to the sole Bledisloe Cup game of 1989. Again, the Colts proved irresistible — the forwards setting a dominant platform from which their outstanding back-line could launch raid after raid on the Australians. The loss of the previous year was erased — trans-Tasman pride restored with a 38-15 triumph, Tuigamala and Auckland flanker Mark Carter scoring two tries each.

The next year Hart's Colts team would be even more successful — thrashing the Australians by 60 points. But in a 'best of' combination taken from his three years with the youth team, the All Black coach would select no less than ten of the 1988 squad in his dream XV, including Norm Hewitt as hooker.

Yet for all Hart's undoubted ability and success, Norm felt uncomfortable in the man's presence. It was a discomfort that he could not articulate or rationalise, but it was there — a constant irritant that prevented him succumbing to Hart's charm.

'We were such different personalities, I guess, but that was only a part of it. He had his favourites — would always socialise with the Auckland guys — and that made them a clique in my book. Some of the Auckland players strutted around as if they owned the show, and that was resented by a lot of us — especially when they were the same guys who would hang around the coach.

'But I couldn't suss Hart out — couldn't work out what he wanted, what his angle was. He played mind-games with the players — I guess to motivate them better — but that just made me even more wary and suspicious. If anything I starting closing down whenever he was around because he was so different from anybody I'd ever struck before. I was just a Maori freezing worker from Hastings — there was not one thing about John Hart that I recognised from my world.'

He had a better relationship with assistant coach Graeme Williams — a former Wellington and All Black flanker of the old school. Tough and uncompromising. Direct to the point of rudeness.

'It was Graeme who ran the forwards and who told me I'd been selected to play the Colts international. I could identify with him because he was like the other rugby guys I knew from Hawke's Bay. And he was a bit of a legend because he'd been an All Black during the 60s and a real staunch captain for Wellington during that era.'

One of the most important lessons Williams taught the young Hewitt was to visualise the match and game scenarios before he confronted them on the field. David Yates, the Hawke's Bay rep squad's doctor, had also introduced Norm to the technique — the theory being that if something similar happens on the field then the brain has already prepared the appropriate response and will react accordingly. It was a technique that Norm began to experiment with during the Colts tour, and he was surprised with its success.

'The higher the level of rugby, the more structured the environment. You have to know your job and how best to do it within the team pattern. But you can't always simulate in practice the hundreds of scenarios that you'll confront in a match. So you imagine them, think about them ... what you'd do, how you might handle it. That Colts tour was the first time I used that approach and it worked enough for me to carry on with it.'

The Colts' 'test' also gave Norm his first real taste of big-time rugby — staying at a swanky hotel on Auckland's North Shore, sucked up by the surrounding Bledisloe Cup hype, running onto Eden Park in front of a big crowd. The night before he'd been so excited he could barely sleep — had finally dropped off just after two, only to be the first one down to breakfast.

The match itself was a blur, the adrenalin pumping so hard that he was genuinely mystified when the game ended — wondered if the referee hadn't made some terrible blunder and blown it up twenty minutes early.

'I'd played before crowds before but not before 40,000 people at Eden

Park cheering you on. There's always an amazing energy that a home crowd gives you, but this was the first time I'd struck it at an international level. And we were only playing the curtain-raiser.'

Those three rarefied weeks spent training and playing with the Colts had their effect on the young man. Rugby was more than a game now — it was a way of life, his vocation. Which made the return to the drudgery of the freezing works even more difficult than usual. He had tasted this higher rugby, had sampled the professionalism — the black uniform, the superior transport and hotels, the mixing and mingling with legends, stars and thinkers of the game. It was not just a giddy experience, it irrevocably affirmed Norm's devotion to the game — that every aspect of his life would be subordinate to the quest to become an All Black.

'The Colts experience opened up my brain like some sort of new drug. It was so awesome and then — bang — I was in Rotorua watching Hawke's Bay get dicked by Bay of Plenty. Next minute I'm back on the field, up against older guys who are kicking you on the ground, smacking into you from your blind side, punching you when the ref's not looking. If anything, because you've been a Colt you get singled out a bit. I was brought into line real quick, and had to fight to survive. There's no glamour getting rucked over.'

The contrast also taught Norm a lesson. Yes, he would need to develop his skills, work on his fitness and generally hone his abilities. But, again, there was no substitute for physical hardness. It was him or them, and if he flinched then he could forget about going any further.

'I wasn't a wing or a flanker or a first five-eight. I was in the front row, and unless you're as ruthless as the guys you're playing you just won't make it. Those older guys will spit you out sideways. Playing first division rugby after the Colts was not so much a shock as a reminder. Welcome back to the real world.'

RUGBY NEWS YOUTH TOUR

At the end of the regular season Norm was able to extend his playing pattern by touring overseas with the *Rugby News* youth team. It was a team organised by the popular rugby weekly, and aimed at promising youngsters who were sponsored by their clubs. Each participating club funded an individual player; Richard Turner had been Tech Old Boys' nominee the year before. This year the tour was to Hong Kong, Ireland and England, and Norm jumped at the opportunity when it was offered to him. It would be his first trip outside New Zealand.

Another attraction of the tour was the chance to train under the legendary Fred Allen — the genius who had presided over the all-conquering All Blacks of the 1960s. This time Allen would be acting as assistant to Sid Going, with former Counties and New Zealand Maori winger Peter Goldsmith as manager. The quality of the team itself was variable. Although there were individuals of genuine international ability in Craig Dowd, Oscar Iwashita and Shane Howarth, there were also players of a lesser club standard. Despite their aim of winning all eight tour games, the team quickly determined that having a good time was of equal if not greater importance.

'For most of us it was our first ever trip outside New Zealand and the first stop was Hong Kong. Culture Shock 101. Flying into the airport was bad enough — between all these rows of apartment blocks — watching people eat their dinners just metres away from your window . . . I was petrified.'

Although breakfast and lunch were provided during the tour, the players were left to get their own evening meals. These excursions generally provided the highlights of the trip — in Hong Kong, trying to steer clear of the rat, dog and cat menus; in Ireland, powerless against the charm of the Guinness and the local Colleens; in England, discovering that pubs and the players' remaining spending money bore absolutely no correlation to each other. The tour was a ceaseless diet of training, playing and drinking — with the occasional horizontal experience thrown in for boasting rights — and no-one was complaining. For these young men it was a satisfying mix of sport and recreation, with few able to discern any appreciable difference between the two. After the last blow-out party — the team consuming sixty dozen cans of Budweiser on their stopover in Los Angeles — Norm could only confirm that he had chanced upon the perfect lifestyle.

He had also celebrated his twenty-first birthday on the *Rugby News* tour and could no longer claim Colt status. If he wanted to play international rugby again he would need to earn that right against the competing demands of senior provincial players. Other Hawke's Bay players had deserted the region for first division opportunities elsewhere, recognising that national selection depended on having a national profile and a healthy exposure to the All Black selection panel. To play second division was to beg obscurity.

And yet, for possibly the first time in his life, Norm was feeling a measure of peace — with both the world and himself. Rugby had treated him well over the past couple of years, Hawke's Bay rugby in particular.

Although the job was still a hassle. If he didn't work he didn't get paid, and there had been plenty of interruptions over the past season. But even as he was working through these issues, other top Bay players were already on their way to points north, south and west.

Coach Richard Hunt had also resigned, and his successor was the Bay's coaching coordinator, former policeman Graeme ('GK') Taylor. Taylor's job description was clear: he had to create a playing squad that would take Hawke's Bay back into the first division.

But first he would need a captain. Someone to provide on-field leadership when the practice strategies and coach's commands were lost in the fog of battle. Someone who would lead by example, be good enough to command a permanent place in the team, and who could make tough decisions when required.

So, at 21 years of age, a half-formed hooker was offered the position. To follow in the footsteps of Graeme Higginson, Mark Shaw and Matthew Cooper and lead the Bay out of the wilderness. It was more than a gamble on the part of the new coach — it seemed a reckless throw of the dice. Norm had never captained any side in which he'd played — either at age group or club level.

To outsiders the young Hewitt was not just unready for such responsibility, he was incapable of it. He would never command the team respect or develop the management skills necessary for such a role. Too much of a front row meathead — his grunting conversational style misinterpreted as a lack of smarts rather than as basic insecurity. There was much head shaking among the Bay's administrators. Taylor had just made his first mistake. And the season hadn't even started yet.

CHAPTER FOUR

Leader

When Graeme ('GK') Taylor was appointed Hawke's Bay rep coach at the end of the 1989 rugby season, he was well placed to appreciate the scarce resources at his command. As the union's coaching coordinator over the previous two years he had been a helpless witness to the bleeding of talent to other provinces. Over the summer months this bleeding had developed into a haemorrhage as Cooper, Cooke and Forster made their respective choices. They left behind a young and inexperienced team who lacked depth in the forwards and ability in the backs. Restoring the Bay to the first division had suddenly become a task of heroic proportions.

But Taylor's background didn't suggest the kind of man given to panic. As a senior player he had been one half of a potent midfield combination for Counties, teaming with the legendary Bruce Robertson. They were an unlikely partnership — Robertson tall and blond, with an almost ethereal quality; Taylor short and dark, an honest artisan. Although it was Robertson who would go on to achieve international recognition, Taylor's record deserves its own respect. He played 147 first-class matches for Counties, became its most capped back ever and acquired a reputation as a no-nonsense doer.

After graduating from Ardmore Teachers' College, Taylor joined the New Zealand Police, working as a detective with the South Auckland CIB. He was later posted back to his family home of Hawke's Bay, but the disruptive nature of police shiftwork and his daily exposure to the criminal underworld took their toll. Finally, the Teresa Cormack inquiry, a harrowing investigation into the molestation and murder of a five-year-old child, eroded any remaining empathy for the job.

Taylor's resignation from the police coincided with the decision of the Hawke's Bay Rugby Union to appoint its first full-time coaching coordinator. Although the position represented a significant drop in income, it promised less stress, and a chance to develop a new career in the game that he loved. Ironically, Taylor's later selection as coach of the Bay rep team meant he lost his job as coordinator — a ludicrous consequence of the sport's amateur regulations. He was thus required to find a new job to support his rugby 'habit', becoming executive director of Napier's YMCA.

Together with his assistant, Graeme Weber, Taylor planned for the new rugby season with just one goal in mind: to return the Magpies to first division football. The first division guaranteed crowds, coverage and cash. In contrast, player and sponsor loyalties would soon evaporate if Hawke's Bay continued to languish in the lower competition. Public support would soon follow.

There was also an underlying feeling among many Bay supporters that their team deserved a place at the top table almost as of right. One of the more suffocating aspects of rugby in the region was the collective memory of the 1960s Ranfurly Shield era. It was as if this memory of halcyon days stood as a ready reference point against which any present rugby achievement must be judged. It was a nostalgic hankering for the days when the Magpies dominated provincial rugby and when the world seemed a better and simpler place.

THE NEW CAPTAIN

One of Taylor's first tasks was to choose a captain. The Magpies had had some strong on-field leaders during the 80s, only for them to be lost to other provinces or attractions. First and foremost Taylor needed a captain who would commit himself to Hawke's Bay. But he was looking for much more than just loyalty — he required a captain who would command an automatic place in the team and help him develop a specific team culture.

'There was no real choice,' Taylor recalls. 'I needed a long-term captain whose own rugby skills would command the other players' respect. Norm impressed me as being keenly motivated and being an obvious investment in the team's future. Captaincy is very important in the modern game. You need someone who can instantly size up the on-field situation and not just know what to do but make the other players respond as well. Sure, Norm had some rough edges, but I reckoned that the responsibility would soon smooth those over.'

However, his initial impressions of the young Hewitt, as both a player and a man, had been less than complimentary.

'When he was playing for the Tech Colts, I would have rated him as only a slightly above average player. Likely to be good at club level, with maybe an outside chance of getting selected for the reps. But no more than that. He didn't stand out to me as a particularly athletic or commanding player on the field.'

Off the field too, Norm was poorly perceived. The Tech Colts boys had established a reputation for often riotous partying and, as a policeman, Taylor had been required to deal with the aftermath of some of their excesses.

'There was one night, when I was the duty sergeant at the Napier watch house, when a call came in — around two in the morning. There was a big, dead, yellow chicken lying in the middle of Emerson Street. As you can imagine, the call caused quite a stir in the station so I dispatched a car to check it out and went with them. As we were driving there I recognised some of the Tech boys cutting across Clive Square, at the top of Emerson Street, and one of them was Norm. And when we got to the scene, there was a yellow chicken lying in the street all right. A tall, lanky guy dressed in a "Big Bird" fancy dress costume — the character from off "Sesame Street". Out cold.'

Further investigation revealed that the Colts had tried to gain admittance to a private party, only to discover that the guests included a good section of Napier's gay community. Big Bird had barred the Colts' entry, and the young Hewitt had taken umbrage at both the intervention and the event. Fortunately the victim refused to press charges, and the police let the matter drop. There was little sympathy for Big Bird around the watch house — being gay in provincial New Zealand was considered a crime all of its own.

At the time the whole incident was dismissed as a bit of over-the-top fun — the kind of yobbo excess that attends drunk young men. The others in the Colts party knew that Norm had a temper when drunk, but even they must have been surprised at the ferocity that accompanied the punching out of Big Bird. And there was no way Norm was going to explain that being confronted by a large gay guy triggered all sorts of unsavoury memories.

Certainly the incident was forgotten by the time Taylor entrusted the Hawke's Bay captaincy to the 21-year-old, even if concerns at his appointment were raised in more traditional quarters. Some in the Bay's administration considered the young man unready for such responsibility — others doubted he'd ever be ready.

A curious dichotomy arose. On the one hand, Norm Hewitt was the Bay's only star player, highly respected for his playing prowess. On the other, he was perceived as an uneducated boor, too ill-mannered to appear in public as the face of Hawke's Bay rugby.

Indeed, Norm's early attempts at after-match speech-making only seemed to confirm this criticism. He would shuffle uncomfortably up to the podium, mumble a few desultory words, then slink back to his seat. Hardly surprising, given that he'd never spoken in public before and that the audience of grey-haired and tut-tutting reefer jackets seemed as alien as creatures from Mars.

Norm's shyness was also obvious in other social situations. Like many young Maori he avoided eye contact with strangers, particularly Pakeha strangers, and this reinforced the unfavourable judgement that emanated from some quarters. In addition there were those who had already judged Norm before meeting him.

In their match programmes for the 1990 rugby season the Hawke's Bay Rugby Union listed their captain's occupation as 'repo agent'. It was an entry that did little to advance his public standing, although as far as Norm was concerned any job was better than nothing. And with the Tomoana freezing works closing for the off-season, it was either repo work or the dole. A couple of weeks on welfare convinced him that regular cash in the hand was a mighty persuader.

It was his old Tech mate TT who had offered him the job. Terrence Taylor had bought the business, 'Hawke's Bay Commercial Recoveries', from a private investigator and he needed a working partner. Most of the recovery contracts came from finance companies and local businesses, and usually just the sight of the two burly front-rowers was enough to make a defaulter surrender the goods.

The intimidation factor was not lost on Norm — he and Terry only received payment if the debt was immediately discharged or the goods seized; front-door politeness didn't win any prizes. Initially it was easy work and Norm might pocket $300–400 a day, although as the recession began to bite further and credit tightened that soon became $300–400 a week.

But it was not just the diminishing income that made Norm uneasy. He would visit the same neighbourhoods day after day, week after week. Increasingly he was repossessing goods that belonged to friends and acquaintances, even whanau, and he became uneasy at the additional hardship he was causing such families.

'There was one particular job that really made me stop and think. We knocked on the door of a family of Islanders and just marched in and took every scrap in their house. From the lounge, the hallways, the kids' bedrooms — the lot. I mean, there were young kids running around everywhere, crying, and Mum was on her own and also crying and obviously frightened . . . I felt like a total shit.'

'Sure, they'd got themselves in the crap and if it wasn't me then someone else would soon take my place. But that justification wore off. I felt bad, totally empty.'

So he quit and took up a job as a millhand at a timber plant near Waipawa. Not much more than a labourer's job, and certainly no more than a labourer's pay — but at least he could look at himself in the morning.

BOUNCING BACK

The grumblings over the young Maori hooker's uncouth manners continued, although the early performances of the Hawke's Bay team delivered a fresh villain for local critics. After trouncings by Counties and North Auckland, and a shock defeat by the lowly rated Poverty Bay, Graeme Taylor's coaching ability became a matter of open debate.

Some of that criticism hit home and was reflected in the message Taylor wrote on the whiteboard prior to the team running out onto McLean Park to play a non-championship game against first division Wellington. *'Defend as if your life depends upon it and attack as if your future depends upon it. BECAUSE IT DOES!!!'* He might well have added, 'and so does mine'.

The result was a stunning 38 points to 19 victory — six tries to two and Hawke's Bay's first win over Wellington in thirteen years. As it transpired, it was the team's most important game of the season, because it gave the young players a confidence they had previously been lacking. They then carried this resolve through their entire NPC campaign.

By mid-season, and after some useful wins, only Manawatu and King Country stood realistic chances of thwarting the Bay's return to the first division. Then a convincing 23-15 home victory over King Country provided the team with a vital break over the rest of the competition. It seemed that with each game the team was developing further, and so too was Norm's captaincy. Although his commands rarely strayed beyond the 'get stuck in' variety, he led by example, hurling himself at opposing forward packs and physically imposing himself on his front-row rivals. Any trick was used to gain the upper hand — the flying elbow or knee, the stamping on hands, the sly back-hander when the ref wasn't looking.

'The forward battle was a real jungle in those days. It was like a form of street-fighting, and if you didn't take them out first, they'd take you. There were a lot of talented players who couldn't handle that side of things. So if you whacked someone really early on, you could put them right off their game. I mean, the forwards are about physical domination, and you do anything you have to do to get it. That's what I was taught by people like Mark Shaw and Graeme Higginson, and they were right.'

The King Country win was capped by Norm being named in the New Zealand Development Team to tour Canada at the end of the season. It was additional confirmation from the national selectors that he was now firmly in the frame for higher honours. He had already played in the All Black trials at Palmerston North, even though it was clear that he was a distant fourth in the selectors' rankings for hooker. The incumbent Sean Fitzpatrick was the undisputed number one, while Waikato's Warren Gatland and North Harbour's Graeme Dowd contested the role of understudy. Norm was there to make up the numbers.

'Getting to that trial was a huge buzz — making me even more determined that I just had to be an All Black. I wanted that jersey so bad that I could almost taste it. Every day I would get up and think about getting selected — sit on the side of the bed and dream of putting on the black jersey. It filled almost every part of my day until it developed into an obsession, I guess. Nothing else mattered and no-one else mattered. I was totally blinkered — my focus was that narrow, that intense.'

However, there was still the more mundane task of securing the NPC second division title. Norm recognised the importance of returning the Bay to the first division elite — not just for the union, but for his own ambitions. Only in regular competition against the Fitzpatricks, Gatlands and Dowds of the first division could he improve his play and impress the national selectors.

Hawke's Bay's cause that year was actively assisted by the erratic performances of the powerful Manawatu team. The green-and-whites featured any number of top players including All Black Kevin Schuler, a mercurial Lee Stensness, and tough veterans like Stu Cruden, Adrian McKenzie, Robbie McLean and Bruce Hemera. But while Manawatu would blow hot and cold — brilliant one week, awful the next — Hawke's Bay kept on their unspectacular but winning way. With two rounds left to play, the Magpies needed only to defeat northern rival Poverty Bay to secure the NPC title.

Ironically, Norm missed both this winning revenge and the final round loss to Manawatu.

In the first of many injuries that would inhibit his career, he'd broken his thumb in training — accidentally smashing into prop Greg Halford during a lineout drill — but he was determined to play the next game against Wairarapa. The win was achieved at the cost of further damaging his thumb, and it was a bittersweet experience to watch from the sideline as his team-mates clinched their promotion.

'I remember watching Andy Dalton looking on as David Kirk raised the World Cup that first time in 1987. The guy looked sick. Well, that's how I felt that day. I was really pumped because we'd won but it was, like, I was the spare part.' It was a feeling that he would later be able to study from an infinite variety of angles.

However, there was the compensation of the Canadian tour with the development team, a young squad that included no fewer than twelve past or future All Blacks. Provided that his thumb came right.

The development team was a happy mix of old and new friends — Richard Turner was a familiar face, and Norm found that he 'clicked' with Taranaki prop Mark 'Bull' Allen as soon as they met. The team also comprised a host of other players with equally overwhelming ambitions to win the silver fern — including Robin Brooke, Shane Howarth, Mark Carter and Jon Preston — and was coached by All Black selector Lane Penn, with 'Cowboy' Shaw as his assistant. The latter drew ribald guffaws from the squad as their plane touched down in Vancouver. 'Let the great Canadian cunt hunt begin!' Shaw declared, an indication that a fair measure of off-field success was also expected.

'I loved Canada,' Norm recalls. 'Along with Ireland it was the best country I've ever visited in my rugby career, and I think most players would make the same judgement.

It's such a vast place, with incredible contrasts in scenery, weather, people, cultures. And then there was the chance to experience a genuine north American Halloween — magic stuff.' He smiles. 'The ladies were pretty friendly too. There's a real groupie culture surrounding Canadian rugby.'

The team won all five of its games and as the only hooker selected, Norm played in all of them. Promising prop Olo Brown was expected to provide cover if required, although his tour was cut short when he was called into the All Black team then touring France. Norm had been hiding the fact that his thumb had still not healed properly, and although Brown's departure reminded him of how close an All Black call-up might be, he regretted the Aucklander's absence. Now he would just have to grin and bear it — play through the excruciating pain as a punishment for his earlier deception. But the brutal lessons he had learned from Gavin Hinds at Te Aute had been well learned. Pain needed to be confronted and defeated. It must never be allowed to win.

By year's end Norm could reflect on a period of solid progress, although the respected *New Zealand Rugby Almanack* noted the ever-growing quality of first class hookers. In its review of the 1990 season it ranked Sean Fitzpatrick 'in a class of his own', then listed Warren Gatland and John Buchan of Canterbury next in its imaginary ranking order. Hewitt's abilities were considered no greater than those of Graeme Dowd or a host of others, including North Auckland's Con Barrell and Bay of Plenty's Jesse Ranui.

Besides there were more immediate difficulties at hand. As Norm flew back from Canada he faced the prospect of going back on the unemployment benefit. His rugby duties for Hawke's Bay and the New Zealand Development Team had only demonstrated to potential employers that they would be carrying an often absent employee, and there was an automatic recoil at the prospect. It was another of the ironies of the time — the more-market economy disinclined to surrender its 'no-free-lunches policy' despite dining out on the exploits of its sporting champions.

So Norm hit on an alternative strategy — one learned from his 'shop' days at Te Aute. The art of the bluff. He suggested to the Hawke's Bay Rugby Union that he was being courted by other first division unions.

'I think there were a couple of minor conversations [with other unions] — but nothing serious. I didn't threaten to leave — just noted I might have to. That sort of thing.'

The tactic worked. Desperate to keep their leading player and captain, the Hawke's Bay Rugby Union offered him Graeme Taylor's old job of coaching coordinator. Bay officials saw it as a shrewd tactic to retain talent without breaching the game's amateur standards. Although, unbeknown to them, the shrewder ploy had actually come from the young Hewitt.

REALITY CHECK

In some ways, Taylor regretted that his team had taken the step back into the top flight quite so quickly. For all their enthusiasm they were still a young squad, prone to dips in mood and confidence, and the backline was a ponderous affair that would struggle against the fliers from other unions. Like many provincial unions that would yo-yo between the lower rungs of the first division and the upper rungs of the second, Hawke's Bay's forward planning was utterly reliant on each season's success. For every step forward, there appeared an equal reaction backwards.

Because immediate results were important, the Bay recruited two Auckland players of Samoan extraction to bolster the backline — To'o Vaega and Edmund Fuiava. But nothing could really prepare the squad for their first NPC game of the 1991 season, against the all-conquering Auckland.

The Auckland team that ran out into the brilliant sunshine at Napier that May day had fifteen All Blacks on the field, and another four sitting in the reserves. But this time the Bay team was not overawed by either the occasion or the competition. Led by captain Hewitt, and with Gordon Falcon and 'Boom' Graham in the vanguard, the forwards tore into their opposition like berserkers, niggling and harassing at every opportunity. The early exchanges were brutal as the Aucklanders met fire with fire — captain Gary Whetton king-hitting Norm at one break-down, the blow opening a wound under the hooker's eye, requiring immediate stitches. Meanwhile Auckland halfback Jason Hewett had his ear ripped open by flailing Bay boots, anybody who went to ground in palpable danger.

In the end it was the sheer class of the Auckland backline, steadied at first-five by the unflappable Grant Fox, that set up a comfortable 49-18 win. As an introduction to the realities of first division football, the match had made its point. Skill could only flourish if certain physical fundamentals were attended to. On that score at least, the Bay had not been cowed. But against the sheer class and pace of the Auckland backs it was always going to be an unequal struggle.

Two weeks later Hawke's Bay played the touring Romanians and, in a close and exciting contest, ran out 24-17 winners. After a fifteen-year drought it was the first of three international victories Hawke's Bay would enjoy in the early 90s — the others against the Lions in 1993 and the French a year later. Some of the touring team would later be involved in the overthrow of Romanian dictator Nicoli Ceaucescu, although not necessarily on the side of the democrats. The Romanian captain, Hralambie Dumitras, would be killed in fighting to protect the despotic regime, and many of the players had links to the dictator's security forces.

The week of the Romanian game had been an exhausting one for Norm. In between the Auckland and Romanian games he had played in the early All Black trial at Rotorua, a game that was considered critical in determining the composition of the 1991 World Cup squad. Still feeling the effects of the Auckland game three days earlier, particularly the Whetton injury, he allowed himself to be outplayed by his opposite Graeme Dowd. In the later trial Sean Fitzpatrick comfortably resisted any challenge from Warren Gatland, but the Waikato hooker had played well enough to secure the reserve berth. In the space of one week, Norm's All Black aspirations had vanished.

It could have been worse. Earlier in the month, the Maori selectors had encouraged All Black prop Steve McDowell to pack down as a hooker in the annual Prince of Wales clash with Southern Maori. The experiment had proved a disaster, with Norm hooking for the Southern Maori team and teaching his opposite that, no matter how able a prop he might be, the position of hooker required specialist skills. That point was confirmed by the New Zealand Maori selectors in their choice of Norm Hewitt as rake for the team's match against Wellington — McDowell returning to the loosehead.

It had been an exhausting and exhilarating month for Norm but, ultimately, it had ended in failure. At least failure by his definition. He had captained Southern Maori to an upset win over Northern Maori, gained selection for New Zealand Maori, led Hawke's Bay in exciting matches against Auckland and Romania — the latter the Bay's first international win since 1976 — and played in the All Black trials. And all at just 22 years of age.

But that All Black jersey was as elusive as it had ever been. Fitzpatrick was only 27 years old and destined to be the All Black captain no matter what happened at that year's World Cup. Gatland and Dowd were no older. And then there were all the other useful hookers coming through the provincial ranks.

For the first time, Norm began to doubt. Began to wonder if he had the right stuff, the right mix of talent and tenacity to ever become an All Black. He knew he was not a naturally gifted athlete — and that at 1.74 metres (5' 9") and 98 kg he didn't have the height or size of some of his competitors. Indeed, it had only been through a successful ruse that he was listed in all the match programmes and rugby guides (including the *Almanack*) as 1.78 metres and over 100 kg. Nor was he an expert enough scrummager to push the Fitzpatricks, Gatlands or Dowds from their higher national rankings.

'I did quite a stocktake. Looked at my game and tried to work out where I was going wrong — what I could do to make myself a better player. I decided that one of the things I definitely had to do was get stronger — essentially become the third prop in the scrum. Rugby is a *very* physical game — especially in the tight five. I needed to be as big and as intimidating as my opposition, although I knew I wasn't going to get any taller! I was going to have to make up for that in other ways.'

In consultation with coach Taylor, Norm mapped out a strategy to keep his claims at the forefront of the All Black selectors' minds. He began to concentrate on increasing his upper torso strength, improving his speed over the first twenty metres, and hitting the jumper at lineouts. The modern game had evolved to the point where each player had a defined range of on-field tasks that were designed to have the team performing at maximum capacity. Captain and coach would thus set goals before key games — the number of times Norm might hit the ball up in general play, accuracy percentages for lineout throws, even a target number of tackles.

A year later the new national selectors, under former Otago coach Laurie Mains, would draw up a detailed job description for every position in the All Black team to guide them in their selections. For the role of hooker, the four key requirements were listed as:

◆ an accurate lineout thrower — the key forward at the lineout;
◆ to pressure the opposition's scrum;
◆ play the 'fourth' loose forward role as required;
◆ tackle like a loose forward and act as cover on the blind at the lineout.

Their skills list matched the Taylor/Hewitt prescription almost to the punctuation.

GETTING STRONG

While Norm realised that he might not have the raw talent or athletic instinct of some of his rugby peers, he had no intention of regarding these shortcomings as a barrier to his All Black dream. That one singular goal had sustained him for much of his life — through the domestic crises at home, the bleakness of Te Aute, the subsequent expulsion, the various injuries and selection setbacks. If he didn't possess the natural ability to play rugby at the highest level he wouldn't abandon his dream — he would acquire the requisite skills.

He had already made Graeme Taylor a partner in this quest, but the strongest influence on his adult rugby career would come from someone who was not connected to the sport at all — 55-year-old power lifter and ex-TV wrestler Joe Fau. A square brick of Samoan muscle, Fau became both a physical trainer and a mentor, forcing his young charge through a series of pain barriers as he exhorted Norm, in his halting English, to 'get bigger, get stronger'.

'As I look back now I realise that a good number of people had positive influences on my rugby career. Each held a particular piece to the jigsaw, but Joe was something else again. He not only impressed me with his incredible toughness but he was also a father figure. He had simple ideas, simple instructions. The most important was never to give up. If you quit, you'll always lose.'

Fau introduced Norm to heavy weights and concentrated on the staple exercises of the power lifter — squats, dead lifts and bench presses. Always the aim was to lift more.

When Norm started training at the YMCA gym he could barely bench-press eighty kilos — after a year with Joe Fau he'd set an astonishing personal best of one hundred and eighty kilos. He also followed Fau's instruction to eat more, and after a morning weights session would go back to his flat with a parcel of fish and chips before eating a kilo of steak, six eggs and a loaf of bread. Then he would go to sleep in preparation for another weights session later that afternoon. Not surprisingly, Norm tipped 120 kg in the off-season, before playing at around 110 kg.

Such were the rapid gains in both strength and size that rumours began to float around the Hawke's Bay club scene that Norm Hewitt was on steroids.

'But it was just down to all that hard work in the gym. Joe hated steroids — hated drugs of any kind. Reckoned that people who needed drugs to get strong were just cheats. And that's the way I've always seen it too. You're robbing yourself as much as anybody else.'

But there were other costs to the strength gain, including being less mobile around the field. So Norm began to introduce a balance to the weight sessions, combining them with aerobic work-outs and sprint training. It was very much seat-of-the-pants stuff, but through trial and error, and with Joe Fau's active encouragement, a happy medium was eventually found.

But it was not quite such as happy medium off the field. All other aspects of his life were subordinate to acquiring the silver fern, which made it particularly difficult for Norm's partner of the time — Keri Neho. The two had met through Norm's sister Tracey, when the two girls were boarders at St Joseph's Maori Girls' College at Greenmeadows. Even though Keri and Norm were now living together, the order of precedence had never changed. Rugby first, everything else — including Keri — a distant second.

'Sometimes she would ask if I was embarrassed with her. Why I'd be going out to functions alone, not involving her in things. But it wasn't that. It was just that I was more comfortable with the rugby scene — drinking, socialising with the guys. And Keri had her own friends and whanau. The more I got into rugby, the more I grew away from her — the more selfish I became. I mean I definitely liked her, but obviously not enough.'

STAYING UP

Despite Hawke's Bay's promising start to the 1991 season, four successive NPC losses confused even the most benign optimists. The gloom was temporarily lifted by a convincing 23-nil win over Counties, but settled in again after further losses to Bay of Plenty and Otago. With three games to play the one-win, six-loss record suggested a hasty return to second division rugby. The survival odds had been further lengthened by the bizarre decision of the NZRFU to reduce the number of first division teams from eleven to nine. This was supposedly to provide a symmetry to the NPC by having an equal number of teams in each of the three divisions. The two bottom teams were to be automatically relegated — the third last team would play the second division winners for the final slot.

Taylor addressed some of the more obvious deficiencies in the squad by recruiting the experienced Gordon brothers — prop Huia from Wellington, and second-five Steve from Wanganui. Steve Gordon, in particular, provided the Bay backline with much-needed stability, teaming well with another Te Aute College product, teenager Murdoch Paewai. But the most important change came at fullback, with the promotion of Havelock North freezing worker Jarrod Cunningham. His was a genuine talent — defensively fearless, a skilled attacker and a champion goalkicker.

But the miraculous would need to become commonplace if Hawke's Bay was to avoid the dreaded drop. And it did. First, they drew 31-all against Canterbury at Lancaster Park, then they upset Waikato 22-13 at Hamilton — results that had the rugby public scratching their heads. All would come down to the final game against Taranaki at McLean Park.

With only a quarter of the game gone the Bay were down nil-16 and looking a ragged mess. But, leading from the front, Norm settled down his forward pack, the possession stakes started to even, and with just three minutes left the teams were tied at 19-all.

But it was not enough. News reached the ground that Bay of Plenty had just inflicted a shock defeat on Canterbury; if the draw held, the

Magpies would be automatically relegated. Gordon Falcon charged out from his 22-metre line, the Bay forwards churning after him, and a penalty was awarded 50 metres out. Jarrod Cunningham, aware of the Bay of Plenty result and thus the kick's critical importance, coolly slotted the goal. But still it was not over — the Taranaki team laid siege to the Bay goal-line before fullback Kieran Crowley steamed into the backline on a switch move and headed for the winning try. But Steve Gordon, who recognised the move from having played in countless Wanganui–Taranaki games, drifted back and crunched the All Black fullback, then hung on as a fierce ruck formed over the two of them. The whistle blew — and then it blew again.

There were unforgettable scenes of jubilation and relief at McLean Park that Saturday afternoon, and deserved plaudits to captain Hewitt for marshalling his troops after Taranaki's explosive start. Yet there was also a sadness to the victory. At the after-match function Crowley openly critic-ised the NZRFU's nine-team edict and rightly prophesied its destructive impact on provincial rugby.

'Let the fish-heads [officials] near anything, and they'll screw it up,' says Norm. 'But it was a particularly incompetent bunch in charge then. Too many old men.'

The Hawke's Bay's collective relief could be gauged from the civic reception accorded the Bay squad in the wake of the Taranaki victory. That evening, addressing the various mayors and MPs present including myself, Hewitt emphasised the uncertain nature of his players' futures and challenged them to provide a tangible demonstration of the community's gratitude. He didn't beg for special favours or cash hand-outs — just the chance for some of his team-mates to have regular work.

It was not so much a conscious act of duty as an instinctive belief that a captain's status carried responsibility — that his official mana established any number of reciprocal loyalties. There was nothing I could say to Norm that evening — I just nodded politely and smiled — the insincere communion of the politician when faced with the impossible request. But one thing I did learn from the exchange. I was sure dealing with no meathead.

CHAPTER FIVE

Otago

The failure of the All Blacks' '91 World Cup campaign provoked a tsunami of recrimination. Part disappointment, part depression, part *Schadenfreude*, this outburst of national anguish would be repeated eight years later with, if anything, even more intensity. Indeed, the similarities would be striking — media-whipped favouritism, stuttering performances in the pool matches, and then a convincing defeat in the semi-final. And in both cases there would be the same salt to the open wound — the spectacle of jubilant Wallabies hoisting the William Webb Ellis Trophy to international acclaim.

In the wake of the 1991 failure, Otago's Laurie Mains defeated the World Cup co-coach, John Hart, for the top All Black coaching job. It was an ugly and partisan contest with outrageous bias, scurrilous whispering campaigns and the sowing of even further division. The end result was a new All Black selection panel, convened by Mains, with North Harbour's Peter Thorburn and Wellington's Earle Kirton as his lieutenants. There was also the promise of new strategies and fresh styles — a nod to previously rejected players that they were back in the frame.

Another important innovation at this time was the decision by the International Rugby Board (IRB) to increase the value of the try from four points to five. There had been growing frustration that the penalty goal had become the prime source of point-scoring — that ten-man rugby was being tacitly encouraged. Although the saner option of reducing the penalty goal's value to two points — half the value of a try

— was rejected. Too much like rugby league, one suspects.

The motivations behind this official encouragement of the 15-man game were not entirely altruistic. The World Cup had introduced the IRB to the entertainment business, and they were duly flattered by the potential of huge profits and the international marketing of the amateur game. But TV audiences and sponsors preferred a game of constant action — open running, big defensive hits, tries being scored — and not a game that relied solely on forward packs trudging from set-piece to set-piece waiting for the inevitable shot at goal.

About the only thing holding the game back now was the game's administration — amateur in all senses of the word, including the non-payment of its star attractions. Although there was a general recognition that top players should be compensated for time spent away from their employment, there was strong resistance to actually paying them a salary. But it was all too late. Even at provincial and club levels, 'shamateurism' had taken over. Illegal, under-the-table payments were a fact of life as clubs, provinces and national unions sought to retain or recruit leading players. No longer was this dodgy practice confined to Italy or France.

The Hawke's Bay coaching coordinator's role was just one such device — a commercial arrangement to keep Norm in the Bay. His sole focus was now on improving his own rugby ability — training with Joe Fau at the YMCA gym in the morning and then heading upstairs to discuss strategy and tactics with Graeme Taylor.

'BORIS'

Despite early promise, Norm's 1992 season proved disastrous. Instead of making progress, his career stagnated — a direct consequence of his heavy drinking. There were binge sessions with his Tech mates and leer-ups after the rep games where he would knock back can after can and watch all the wannabes drop like flies. But he possessed not the slightest inkling that there might be a correlation between his alcohol intake and the decline in his on-field performance.

'I was also getting out of control when I drank. Some people have a kind of character when they're pissed — y'know — happy, silly, depressed, sex-pest — that kind of thing. Mine was just hard out. I didn't give a shit about anything. I was one staunch bastard.'

His rugby mates called him 'pure evil' — a moniker that Norm wore with a cockeyed pride. Generally amiable, he could mutate into a physical bully — dominating any other 'hard man' who might be showing off or flexing their machismo. There were mindless contests of strength, the occasional fight, the intimidation of pretenders, the wanton destruction of property.

'And I could *hate*. Really screw myself up and hate whoever was in my way. Dominate the prick — want to do him real damage, just like on-field.'

Graeme Taylor created a special character, a doppelganger, to explain these drunken outbursts.

'We'd say "Boris" was on the loose. It was like Norm became another person. People knew that when he got drunk he could become violent, and it frightened them. A lot of us witnessed those incidents and a hell of a lot more rugby people knew about them. It was scary stuff. I saw rugby guys break down and cry because he'd frightened them so much. At the time, I believed I was immune — that if he performed in front of me then I could settle him down because of our relationship. But later ... no. "Boris" was all consuming. And he wasn't pretty.'

Yet these episodes did not seem to affect the relationship between coach and captain. They continued their close association — meeting almost daily to plan the team training, discuss team selection, organise sponsorship, arrange any publicity.

'We were doing everything,' recalls Norm. 'The team had a manager [former All Black Ian Macrae] but he was a manager in name only. More of a figurehead really — someone to impress the other unions. I guess GK and I took on too much — trying to plug all the gaps — but if we hadn't then it wouldn't have happened. The union hierarchy were hopeless.'

Even at a provincial level, the game's amateur code was proving inadequate against the increasingly professional demands of the sport. Both Taylor and Macrae relied on outside employment to support their voluntary rugby duties, and for a real estate agent like Macrae the burden was doubly harsh. The nature of his job entailed a considerable amount of weekend and after-hours work, and the management of a first division rugby team must have been a considerable distraction. And vice versa.

One of the more pressing problems confronting the Hawke's Bay union was the retention of its leading players. To help with this a special trust was formed to raise funds to assist reps who might be experiencing financial difficulties. As an example, one of the key tight five was on the dole and his partner was due to give birth to their first child. The trust helped by paying some of their household bills. In addition, the trust aimed to raise a pool of money which would be divided between the team as an end-of-season bonus — an incentive for members of the team to stay. Of course, the union could not be officially involved, hence the formation of the shadow trust.

To further the trust's aims, Graeme Taylor began calling on various political and business leaders in the Bay. Remembering Norm's entreaty from the previous year, I reluctantly agreed to my electorate office organising a celebrity dinner series. The first celebrity was Wallaby skipper Nick Farr-Jones, who spoke of the aftermath to their '91 World Cup win and the team's reception back in Australia. How they'd expected a muted response, given the predominance of league and Aussie rules, and instead flown into Sydney to find airport fire trucks spraying their aeroplane in tribute, while hundreds of chanting fans waited in reception; he told of the ticker tape parades and tears, of finally understanding the nature of their achievement and its importance to all of Australia. And then he concluded by saying that rugby was a family, and donating his speaking fee to the Hawke's Bay players' fund. The standing ovation lasted for minutes.

Unfortunately such generosity was not demonstrated by any of the leading All Blacks who were invited to speak. Farr-Jones and Wallaby coach Bob Dwyer might fly over from Australia (Dwyer, a year later, in the middle of a test series against the Springboks!) in the belief that rugby's top personalities owed the game that had created them. But countless All Blacks declined invitations because they deemed the speaking fee of $750 plus expenses insufficient. The only New Zealander who was prepared to forego his fee was coach Laurie Mains. In the end, a $6000 profit was made from the first series but $6000 would go nowhere between a Magpies squad of 22 players.

The trust's aims were not helped by the tragic death of the charismatic Kel Tremain — not only a rugby legend, but a successful Bay businessman and a member of the NZRFU's executive council. An indication of Tremain's influence was that the All Black trials were to be hosted by Hawke's Bay the next month — an early chance for the new selectors to assess the available talent and pick a squad for the coming series against the invitation World XV.

The announcement of the four trial teams reflected the different thinking of the new selectors as they jettisoned the Whetton brothers and first-five Grant Fox — three mainstays of the World Cup effort. Fox's kicking talents would eventually secure his recall, but it was an inglorious and premature end to the All Black careers of both Gary and Alan Whetton. Also missing were another pair of Auckland brothers — Zinzan and Robin Brooke. Accusations of Mains' anti-Auckland bias swirled around the northern media.

Although Norm had been named in the early trial it was obvious from his placing against Otago's David Latta that the selectors regarded him as no more than an apprentice. Despite captaining his Probables team to a 43-26 victory Norm's name was missing from the final trial, with Sean Fitzpatrick, Warren Gatland and Graeme Dowd the favoured hookers. Gatland, in particular, played superbly in the Saracens' shock 20-15 win over the shadow All Blacks combination — the upset inspired by the coaching of Graeme Taylor and Graham Mourie.

For Norm though there was little to take from the week. He was no closer to his dream than the year previous and the hooking triumvirate seemed as secure as ever. After the trials, Taylor encouraged his captain to instead concentrate on the long-term — to look to the 1995 World Cup as his All Black target. But it was a bitter pill for Norm to swallow and his reaction was to drink even harder the next time the opportunity presented itself.

SACKED

However, there was some consolation. After captaining his Southern Maori team to a good win in the annual Prince of Wales match, Norm was selected for the New Zealand Maori team. His delight increased when he found out that his good mates Gordon Falcon and Romana Graham had also made the Maori team, and that a tour of the Pacific Islands had been arranged for October. Sun, surf, kava — an ideal way to finish off the season.

Back in the Bay, the Magpies' NPC campaign had begun well, with traditional rival Wellington defeated by 32 points to 22. There was loose talk at the bar about this being the Magpies' year — about getting into the final four and nabbing one of those Super 10 spots for next year. And then the wheels fell off. Big time.

The signs were all there in the Bay's dismal performance against the newly promoted King Country. On a sodden ground at Te Kuiti the team struggled to find their earlier rhythm, and were embarrassed by the energetic hustling of their unfashionable opponents. A week later there was a narrow escape against fellow strugglers North Auckland, but even in this win it was obvious that the backline lacked the pace and vision required for first division rugby. On the other hand the forward pack was ruthlessly efficient — with the accent on ruthless. In Norm Hewitt, Terrence Taylor and Orcades Crawford the Magpies possessed a front row that could hold its own against any and was intimidated by none. The loose forward trio of Falcon, Graham and former Natal rep John Plumtree was similarly outstanding, the locks useful. But once the ball entered the backline a conspiracy seemed to take over — dropped passes, missed tackles, slow service — each bumble further eroding the players' confidence.

The two NPC wins had at least assured Hawke's Bay of first division survival, so the southern games against Canterbury and Otago lacked their usual urgency. It was a testing itinerary, with three away games in a week — Canterbury on the Saturday, Otago on the Wednesday, then up to Takapuna to play an in-form North Harbour. After a nondescript 9-34 loss at Lancaster Park there were drunken hi-jinks back at the team's hotel, with chairs and tables ending up in the swimming pool. But the incident was overlooked — a little high-spirited vandalism was part and parcel of most touring teams' after-dark repertoire — the unspoken tradition that rarely attracted hotel complaint or press coverage as long as the damage was paid for.

And so down to Dunedin and another loss at Carisbrook on a bleak winter's afternoon. Then the usual after-match bunfight and back to the Shoreline Motor Hotel with a couple of Otago players in tow — those with family links back to the Bay.

'We had our usual "court" session once we got back to the hotel,' remembers Norm. 'Court sessions are a traditional part of most senior teams make-up — especially at the higher level and especially if you're touring. They're very much a part of that rugby camaraderie when you get together with your team-mates, enjoy yourselves — take the piss, get pissed, have a good laugh. It's the only time really when players and management are equal — all the labels are left at the door.'

The punishment at these parodies is uniform — 'scull' a good-sized beer, refill, repeat. A raft of drinking games accompanied the court sessions and as the alcohol took over, and reflexes became slower, the rate of 'offending' would increase.

'There are tons of games to accompany the court — speed sessions, "next", always drinking with your left hand, pointing only with your elbow . . . the idea is to get as much alcohol down your throat as quickly as possible. Actually the most inventive sessions were those with the All Blacks. Some of those guys must have spent weeks dreaming up new games. And each team had their own twist — the Otago boys borrowed quite a few from their scarfie mates.'

The court sessions were usually conducted with in good humour, although the unstable mix of strong young men and vast quantities of alcohol would sometimes provoke the occasional flare-up. Or worse. Norm recalls the '91 Divisional Team's tour of Australia — players selected from the second and third divisions after the 1990 rugby season.

'There was some appalling behaviour on that tour — even by our standards. Players spewing up in public, urinating in front of the "civilians", picking fights — that sort of thing. I mean it was generally accepted that there would always be a bit of damage when a team toured. Mix the booze, the boredom, the pack mentality, and the outcome is pretty obvious. It needs a strong manager at those times — a strong hand to keep things from getting out of control.'

It also required senior players to exercise some self-restraint — to draw the line and set an example. But in their captain, Hawke's Bay had one of the hardest of party animals. Discipline was also not improved by Ian Macrae and the rest of the Hawke's Bay management being accommodated in a separate wing to the players. That evening Taylor and Macrae had a few drinks with Otago coach Gordon Hunter at the Shoreline house bar and then retired to bed. But in the annex across from the main hotel block no-one was allowed to sleep. The partying had begun in earnest.

The next morning Graeme Taylor lined up for the 8am bus call to take the team out to Momona airport and home. Stops in Christchurch and Wellington were planned, and a refreshed Taylor intended to use them to finalise the team selection for Saturday's match against North Harbour.

'I was just about to get on the bus when Ian Macrae comes rushing over — face flushed, obviously agitated. He said there'd been some damage over the previous night, but I have to confess, I wasn't all that interested. As far as I was concerned, that was his problem to sort out. My job was to coach and, off the field, the manager's in charge. That's the way it works in New Zealand rugby — that's why we have travelling managers.'

Unbeknown to Taylor, the Otago union had received a serious complaint from the Shoreline Hotel about the state of a number of rooms over in the annex. In turn the union drew up a formal list of the Magpies' transgressions — and presented copies to both the Hawke's Bay union and the NZRFU. Led by Dunedin-based councillor John Dowling, Otago demanded that the vandals be identified and strong disciplinary action taken. Their demands were further fired by the prospect of the likely collateral damage to rugby's reputation if the media got wind of the incident.

On the bus Macrae demanded the names of those responsible. Despite some half-dozen players being involved, only Norm put up his hand.

'I said that I broke a door. Although I also said I would take responsibility because I was the captain. Macrae nodded but didn't say anything else. I thought that I'd be paying for the door, maybe get a bit of a reprimand, but didn't think much more of it. I mean that was my mentality at the time — it's happened, I've confessed, how much do I pay in restitution? I knew I was in a bit of trouble but I didn't have a clue as to how much.'

During the Christchurch stopover, Macrae again approached Taylor and told him that Hewitt needed to be punished. Again Taylor shrugged his shoulders.

'As far as I was concerned, it was Mac's call. I knew he was getting some heat from above although whether it was from [Hawke's Bay chairman] Tom Mulligan or higher up, I still don't know.'

When they finally arrived at Napier airport, Macrae gestured to Norm to come outside.

'We were waiting for our luggage and he said that he wanted to see me in his car, just over in the carpark. I got in and all he said was, "You're out of the team." That's all I remember . . . "You're out of the team." I was stunned. I can't remember saying or doing anything — just sitting there and thinking "Oh, no. What have I done? My career is over." '

In a daze, Norm collected his bags and immediately drove to Graeme Taylor's place, hoping that a less drastic solution might be found. On the way over the Te Aute expulsion flashed through his mind. Not again.

But Taylor was unsympathetic.

'GK told me that I'd made my bed — now I had to lie in it.'

End of conversation. And the end of their friendship.

'I felt — oh, I don't know — betrayed, I guess. GK was a really positive influence on my life at that time. He'd always been there to talk to — share a laugh, help me with my All Black ambitions, give me advice. And then it was all over and he'd walked away. I didn't know what to say, where to go, who to turn to.'

The hooker was devastated. He had done no more damage than anyone else but he was being hung out to dry as if he was the only culprit. And the powers-that-be had stripped him of his one passion — his reason for being. The capacity to play rugby. Within an hour of arriving back in the Bay, Norm Hewitt's world was in tatters.

MUTINY

Worse was to follow. In the aftermath of the incident, he was informed that he would be excluded from the New Zealand Maori team to tour the Islands. And, to compound the misery, that his contract with the

Hawke's Bay Rugby Union was to be terminated. At which point the story of the hotel damage and his suspension broke in the national media. Not content with punishment, the NZRFU seemed determined to set an example.

'I was shit scared. Couldn't sleep, couldn't talk — I was stunned at how quickly everything had happened. A few of the boys — Steve Gordon, TT, 'Boom', Gordy Falcon — dropped round to offer their support but there was nothing they could do. Someone suggested I get a lawyer — that there was still an official NZRFU disciplinary hearing even though they'd already found me guilty and decided on the punishment. And then I thought — Jeez, what else are they going to do? Ban me from the game? And that really freaked me.'

On a whim, he got in his car and drove over to Taradale and called in at the electorate office of the MP for Hawke's Bay.

As Norm tells it, 'I knew Michael from the civic reception the year earlier and then the celebrity dinners. He had a reputation as a bit of a scrapper but seemed genuine enough, although you never can be sure with politicians. Anyway ... what did I have to lose? I needed someone and maybe he could shake up the fish-heads. Although the reality was that I had no-one else to turn to and nowhere else to go.'

Unfortunately, there was little that could be done. The Otago union had presented Hawke's Bay and the NZRFU with a long list of complaints — the terrorising of hotel staff; vomiting in rooms and hallways; the systematic destruction of doors, telephones, TVs and fridges; urinating over bedclothes; setting fire to a duvet; spraying the fire hose over furniture and carpets. And Norm was deemed the sole responsible party.

'The door was mine,' he admit, 'but most of the other damage was down to others and some was just plain bullshit. I reckoned some bugger was loading the claims for insurance purposes.'

At the disciplinary hearing, conducted under the ageing McKenzie Stand at McLean Park, Norm's case was presented. It seemed obvious, at least to this outsider, that the Hawke's Bay union had been prodded into action but were embarrassed that their hearing was now the subject of independent scrutiny. It was therefore my intention to separate the NZRFU's punishment of Norm from his employment as the Hawke's Bay coaching coordinator. I was assured that the matters were not related — a complete lie, as it later transpired.

Neither the NZRFU nor the Otago union had representatives at the hearing, and there was no opportunity to cross-examine the complainants or test the validity of the charges. The Hawke's Bay union listened to my submission, listened also to the confessions of the other players, and promised a just conclusion. By week's end, all previous actions were confirmed — Norm was sacked as captain, suspended from the Hawke's Bay rep team for the rest of the season, his coordinator's job was forfeit, and there was an directive to the NZ Maori selectors that one N. Hewitt not be considered for the end of season tour to the Islands.

At which stage the players determined on their own course of action. At the next practice, Graeme Taylor was informed by Terrence Taylor that if Norm wasn't playing against North Harbour then neither was the rest of the Magpie squad. Faced with open mutiny, the coach suggested a compromise. Perhaps Norm could play, but not as captain. His good mate TT could take over — a clever choice given Norm's respect for his fellow front rower. But it still required the coach to sell the compromise to the administration.

The Hawke's Bay union were not of a mind to be blackmailed. Taylor was informed that the 'B' team were ready to be flown up to Onewa Domain should the 'A' team carry out their threat.

'I told them straight,' says Taylor. 'You do that and you do it without me. They'd be humiliated by a hundred points and the union would be a laughing stock throughout the country.'

Faced with the defection of the province's top 21 players, and their coach, the Bay executive backed down. The compromise was agreed — Hewitt would only be suspended from the captain's responsibilities, although he would still lose the coordinator's job.

There was a sour atmosphere on the flight up to Auckland, and the team was duly thrashed. A week later it was Waikato's turn to twist the knife. A rift had now opened between players and management, and it was one that would never be properly closed. And of the 'fish-heads' that had inflicted the punishment, there was a universal contempt.

'There's a code in this game. You look after your own. Sure, I was a bad bastard down in Otago but the NZRFU chose to turn a blind eye to the other incidents and also to the role of some of the Otago players. The punishment didn't fit the crime.'

And how does he feel today?

'I never forgot how I was treated. And when it came to finally leaving Hawke's Bay — and some of those same officials accused me of disloyalty — well, I remembered all right. Loyalty is a two-way street in my book.'

It had been an appalling year. The new All Black squad had been selected and Norm was no closer than under the Wyllie/Hart regime. If anything, he was even further away, with a big black mark against his name. Dropped from the Maori team, shunned by his own union, and back on the dole queue.

But his reaction to these reverses was not to slink away nor to feel sorry for himself. The ambition still burned. His desire for revenge would need to be leavened by the greater desire to wear the black jersey.

'I was going to show the bastards that if they thought they'd seen the back of me, then they were in for a big disappointment. You're only beaten if you allow yourself to be beaten. And I wasn't beaten. Not in my own mind. I was going to make them eat their words — prove that I couldn't be written off or ignored.'

And so he returned to the gym. Started lifting even heavier weights. Running even longer distances. Straining harder at sprint practice.

'I knew things were bad. But at least I'd learned who I could count on — and who I couldn't. There's nothing as motivational as trying to ram your critics' words back down their throats. And it suited me to play the victim because to have admitted any responsibility myself would have lessened my anger. It was that anger which spurred me on — I was ready to take on the world in the only way I knew how. Straight up.'

CHAPTER SIX

The word

O ver the Christmas break and well into the New Year, Norm brooded. Even though he had been the architect of his own misfortune, he still considered the loss of the coordinator's role as excessive punishment. The loss of the captaincy and his non-selection had surely been enough — why were they determined to rob him of his only income as well?

Maybe it would be best just make a clean break, start afresh somewhere else. He'd received an offer from the Wellington club to shift to the capital, and had had some preliminary discussions with the rep team's new coach, David Kirk. It was either that or accept the daily discomfort of being un-employed and under a cloud. And even if he chose to stay, what would he do for work — would it be back on the chains at Tomoana? He hovered between the tug of the familiar and the seemingly brighter prospects in Wellington.

'I was really pissed off with the Hawke's Bay union. As far as I was concerned they didn't deserve my commitment. Down in Wellington David Kirk was putting together a new NPC team and the Super 10 competition was starting. I thought I'd have a better chance of resurrecting my career where I could be a bit anonymous — where I could concentrate a hundred percent on my rugby.'

The new Super 10 competition comprised the elite unions of New Zealand, Australia and South Africa, and was to be held in April/May — at a time of the year when most players were still playing club rugby. But with the international season beginning soon after, the Super 10 also gave participating players a better chance of staking a claim for higher honours. It didn't take an Einstein to work out that the bigger the competition, the bigger the opportunities. And the bigger the money. Smaller unions like Hawke's Bay would be on a hiding to nothing. From now on it would be the Aucklands, Canterburys and Wellingtons who would skim the cream.

Yet for Norm an even more powerful influence was that of home. He had bought a house in Greenmeadows the previous year, moved in with Keri, and was enjoying the security and comfort of his own place. In contrast, Wellington would be new and foreign, and he would be in rented accommodation a long way from whanau.

There were other reasons to stay. The team-mates who had stuck by him during the Otago affair didn't deserve to be repaid with his desertion — even though he loathed the union's fish-heads. And despite the strain of his relationship with Graeme Taylor, at least GK was still picking him as the Magpies' No. 1 hooker. In Wellington he would have the immediate competition of Tim Mannix and no guarantee of automatic rep selection.

However, he had to balance that against accepting an uncertain financial future and a measure of notoriety — not eased by his decision to switch his club allegiance from Technical to Taradale. And so the internal debate swayed back and forth. Some days he would decide on Wellington, others on Hawke's Bay.

'I was becoming a bit schizo about it all. Although the change in clubs was an important factor, as it turned out. There'd been a scrap at the Tech clubrooms the night we won the Maddison [interclub trophy]. I was getting hammered with the rest of the guys and a bit of silly stuff started. Not too aggro — just people chipping each other, that sort of thing. Suddenly it's all on and even my old man's swinging away. No bastard was going to touch his boy!'

After this incident an atmosphere developed. Far from being feted, a discernible sourness greeted the players when they stepped into the clubrooms. Especially Norm.

'People would look at me sideways, make snide remarks, that sort of crap. I'd been no angel, but I didn't start the scrap. So I thought — "Stuff you".'

Besides, Taradale would be a fresh challenge. The Tech pack had become the dominant force in the Napier–Hastings interclub competition and, if anything, the team was too strong.

'So I went to Coops [Taradale president Ian Cooper] and told him that if I joined his club I reckoned I could almost guarantee the Nash [Cup] and the Maddison [Trophy] next season. And that other Tech players would come with me, and Taradale would soon be up there again.'

But there would be a price. $5000. Cash. Under the table.

'I didn't have a job. I had a mortgage and I needed the dough. As far as I was concerned, it was what they call a market opportunity.'

Ian Cooper didn't blink. It was not uncommon for metropolitan clubs to induce players with offers of jobs and assistance with accommodation, and these larger clubs had taught provincial New Zealand a lesson. Despite the game's supposedly amateur code, success on the field was more likely if it was actively assisted by the cheque book. And there were direct commercial gains to be made from such 'investments'. Success delivered better sponsorship deals, bigger after-match functions, more money through the bar, higher club profits. It was proof of the old adage: to make money, first you've got to spend some.

Norm was not the only player to leave Tech over the off-season. Coach Keith Price and rep players Peter Davis, Aaron Hamilton and Des Morris completed the mini-exodus. Along with former Manawatu centre George Konia and Maori All Black Romana Graham, Taradale now possessed a team that could challenge clubs like Tech, Havelock North and Clive for supremacy.

Tech officials screamed foul — long and loud. Norm was pointedly reminded that it was Tech who had provided him with sanctuary after the Te Aute debacle, and funded his youth team trip to Canada. In return, Norm considered the club had extracted its fair pound of flesh. He pointed to his past playing efforts and the full trophy cabinet as a handsome dividend on their outlay. He was ready to go. End of story.

In hindsight, it's impossible to escape the symbolism of Norm deliberately closing a door. If he wasn't going to leave Hawke's Bay, he needed to leave somewhere. Change the environment. And the Tech club was an unwitting part of a past that he was determined to escape.

A NEW JOB

Others had also been giving Norm Hewitt's job prospects a great deal of thought over the Christmas break — including me.

The previous year I'd established the Flaxmere Development Trust to attack the suburb's high unemployment rate. Given the Hastings Council's wilful neglect, Flaxmere was woefully underdeveloped and many community projects were begging for attention. It became a simple case of marrying these needs with the government's Taskforce Green programme and providing an administrative umbrella to prioritise and supervise the work.

I was also conscious that 1993 was election year. And that my work in Napier had been less prominent than in other areas of the electorate. Which was a problem, because I would need every scrap of support I could muster if the national polls were any indication. This survival instinct meshed with the professed intention of Napier mayor Alan Dick to give his council a stronger welfare focus. I reasoned that if I could extend the development trust concept into Napier then a happy synergy might be achieved. Napier would get various civic projects completed on the cheap, unemployed people would be provided with jobs, and I stood to reap the combined benefits at the ballot box. There are none so altruistic as politicians in election year.

But I needed someone to give the fledgling Napier Community Work Trust a quick and public profile. And to convince the council that they should donate ratepayers' money to the trust's cause. I suspected that if I approached the councillors direct my ulterior motives would become clear and the project stymied. It was while I was pondering on these matters that Norm Hewitt walked into my Taradale office.

I'd decided during the NZRFU hearing that Norm possessed an array of talents beyond the rugby field. There was a winning sincerity to his personality, along with some very real leadership qualities. He also possessed the kind of background with which trust employees might identify — a mediocre formal education, very recent experience of the dole, and an obvious Maori heritage. Norm Hewitt — Napier Community Work Trust. It seemed the perfect match.

But I would need 'seeding' finance from the Napier City Council, and some of the councillors had strong links to the Labour Party.

Leave it to me, Norm said. He would meet each of the councillors and petition them personally. A fortnight later mayor Alan Dick handed over a council cheque to the trust's newly appointed director — Norm Hewitt. And by the end of that year over seventy people had gained full-time jobs under the trust's management.

However, the director's salary was not a princely sum — $15,000 a year. But it was all the fledgling organisation could afford. And the director's responsibilities were far from simple — he would have to negotiate contracts with the Employment Service and the council; deal with the often suffocating red tape of officialdom; market the trust to job sponsors and the media; draw up individual employment contracts for the workers; ensure that the workers received on-the-job training, and supervise the various administration staff. Norm took it all in his stride, even when the trust's chairman — me — suffered regular (and very loud) anxiety attacks.

'I guess I put into practice all the things I'd picked up over the years. The "entrepreneurial" skills running the Te Aute shop, the organisational skills from being captain, the promotional skills from being in regular contact with the media and the union's sponsors. And Hawke's Bay was a first division rugby team. Local people wanted to associate themselves with that success and, in a funny sort of way, the trust gave them that opportunity.'

To further brighten his bank balance, Masonic Hotel proprietor Tony Crosby asked Norm to manage his new sports bar, 'The Sin Bin'. And so, through the unlikely combination of trust salary, Sin Bin wages and a Taradale backhander, Norm ended up better off than when he'd been employed by the Hawke's Bay Rugby Union.

'Yeah, it was ironic all right, but that was only one part to it. Here I was managing a bar but not drinking — helping unemployed people find jobs — mixing with the various movers and shakers in the Bay and earning respect for things other than playing rugby. And I enjoyed what I was doing — especially at the trust. Helping people to help themselves and giving them the chance to turn their own lives around. It was good stuff.'

His new status certainly turned heads. Halfway through the '93 season one of Hawke's Bay's senior officials — a man known for his trenchant criticism of Norm's antics — came up to me at an after-match function and shook my hand. 'I want to congratulate you on our captain's remarkable transformation. Can't believe it's the same man.'

As much as parliamentarians love receiving praise, I was forced to demur. Norm had done it all himself, I replied. And they were quite possibly the truest words I uttered that entire election year.

ON THE WAGON

The key to Norm's 'rehabilitation' was his decision to abstain from all alcohol — to give up the booze entirely. It was a choice he made without lecture or prompting, and one that stunned those around him.

'I didn't regard myself as having a drinking problem. Not at all. I stopped because I didn't want anything to get in the way of being an All Black. And the booze had let me down. Or rather the booze had helped me let myself down. So I thought if that's what it takes to get back in the game then it doesn't seem such a big sacrifice. And I stopped. Simple as that.'

Many saw Norm's decision as a tacit confession to an alcohol problem. Nothing could have been further from the truth.

'It was only ever intended to be a temporary thing. I was out to improve my athletic ability through more efficient training and recovery. If the fish-heads took notice and thought I was a reformed character then so much the better. At least I wouldn't be getting myself into any more embar-rassing situations like at the Shoreline.'

There was another part of the jigsaw that Norm had put in place. He suspected that the All Black selectors made subjective evaluations of players' abilities — their choices automatically included personal and political preferences. Selectors could and did play favourites, selecting or rejecting some players on nothing more than a whim. And Norm still had a reputation problem. A past that hung around his neck like the proverbial albatross.

One night when Norm and I were talking about trust matters, he mentioned his All Black aspirations, about how coach Laurie Mains came from Otago, and how the Otago union had kicked up all the fuss after the Shoreline incident the year before. I suggested he write to Mains, let him know what training he was doing, that he'd given up the booze — ask him the sort of qualities the selectors were looking for in a hooker. It was a glib response to a problem that I had no idea how to resolve.

'It sounded sort of dumb, but then I thought — why not? What have I got to lose?'

Norm road-tested the idea on Gary Sye, the Napier physiotherapist who moonlighted as the All Blacks' physio during the international season. Sye was enthusiastic, adding that Mains was a straight-up-and-down guy who hated all kinds of bullshit but recognised sincerity when he saw it. That night Norm sat down and wrote to the All Black coach — a painful process, given his literacy. Within days the All Black coach had replied — detailing the skills the selection panel were looking for and noting Norm's decision to go on the wagon.

'I couldn't believe it . . . Laurie Mains had replied. It was a huge boost to my confidence. Laurie said that what had happened last season wouldn't be held against me. Provided I stayed out of trouble, the slate was clean. I was buzzing — it was just the sign that I'd been looking for. Now I could concentrate on my game. Forget all the other bullshit.'

And concentrate he did. His improved levels of fitness were immediately apparent as the Taradale pack began churning its way through the local club competition, and again as the Magpies blitzed their neighbouring provinces in early season hit-outs. Within weeks Norm learned that Laurie

Mains was indeed a man of his word. The All Black trial teams were announced and Norm was selected as one of four hookers. Although Sean Fitzpatrick and Graeme Dowd would contest the main trial, Norm would oppose Warren Gatland to contest rankings three and four.

He was back in the game.

THE BRITISH LIONS

For All Black fans, the most anticipated event of 1993 was the tour of New Zealand by the British Lions — their first in a decade. Four years earlier the home unions had triumphed 2-1 in their series against the Wallabies, and a good number of that winning unit were again selected to make the trip downunder. The remainder of the All Blacks' international calendar involved one-off home tests against Australia and Western Samoa, and an end-of-season tour to Scotland and England.

Although Laurie Mains' tenure as All Black coach had started with series wins over the World XV and Ireland, there had also been a series loss to the Wallabies and an unconvincing victory over the renascent Springboks. The jury was still out on whether Mains possessed the right stuff, and his critics were not pacified by the recall of Grant Fox and Zinzan Brooke, or his reluctant appointment of Sean Fitzpatrick as All Black captain. As far as they were concerned, the Aucklanders should never have been dropped in the first place.

Mains' answer to his critics was clear. The 1995 World Cup was the prime objective and he was building a team with that goal in mind. However, the public were far from conditioned to the idea that the All Blacks would have to lose the occasional game to achieve this greater end. Win the World Cup *and everything else* was the fans' directive.

Norm also had his eyes squarely set on the 1995 World Cup. That was the long-term goal — to get selected in the squad to go to South Africa. But two years was a long way away — still in the never-never. He needed a firmer objective. Something closer, more tangible.

'Getting selected for the end-of-season tour to the UK became my new target. And that meant making the most of every chance that came my way. The first step was the Rotorua trials in May. I had to perform there and create an impression. Because there were some very good players who hadn't made the trials and they would have the whole of the NPC to impress.'

Unfortunately both the early and late trials were affected by torrential rain — a storm that lashed Rotorua and its quaintly named International

Stadium. If anything, the longer the rugby went, the worse the storm. By the end of the afternoon the ground resembled a small lake, with players aquaplaning everywhere, the ball like an orange pip squeezed under pressure. Which was doubly unfortunate for the Hawke's Bay hooker because he had played an absolute blinder in the early trial, with determined runs in the loose, a committed game in the tight and some deft handling touches despite the atrocious conditions. However, the late trial resembled an extremely vigorous game of water-polo, and Norm's earlier efforts were overshadowed by a general view that the weather had reduced the entire afternoon to a slippery lottery.

'It was all a bit disheartening. I'd played my guts out — been really happy with what I'd done — only for everybody to say that the trials didn't really count. Which was nonsense because you've got to play in all sorts of weather conditions. And England in winter isn't exactly known for its sunny skies and beach umbrellas.'

But Norm didn't have time to dwell on his disappointment. Two days later he led the Magpies to a 20-10 win over Wellington in a non-NPC clash at Napier. Again he was in dynamic form, leading from the front and channelling a forward pack that dominated its larger opposition. The experienced Wellington front row of the peripatetic Huia Gordon, Tim Mannix and the 135-kg Fijian 'Bill' Cavubati lost its battle against the Bay's aggressive scrummaging and the rot soon spread through the rest of the capital's team.

'Orcades Crawford had come back to Hawke's Bay the previous season and with TT and myself we'd developed a good front row. Orcades was a big, no-nonsense Maori guy — a sort of young Huia Gordon or Graham Hurunui I guess. One of those hard-nosed provincial props that never let you down. He'd been round a bit — East Coast, Waikato, Manawatu — but lucky for us he settled back in the Bay. Later I was pleased to see him get a go with the New Zealand Maori team and in the Super 12. He always gave 100 percent.'

A few days later Orcades Crawford and Norm teamed up again — this time in Southern Maori's narrow loss to Northern Maori at Levin. The game was a scrappy affair, all the players desperate to impress before the match between New Zealand Maori and the Lions the following week. That evening, step two in the rehabilitation of Norm Hewitt was completed, when he was named hooker for the warm-up jaunt against Manawatu and in the 'test' team to play the British Isles.

'The Maoris had a good set of forwards that year. Arran Pene was captain, and our loosies were Arran, Jamie Joseph and Zinzan Brooke. All of them were current All Blacks and all in good form. The tight five wasn't bad either — Kevin Boroevich, me and "Bubbles" Hurunui in the front row, with the Counties boys Jim Coe and Mark Cooksley as locks. It was a team that would have beaten most international teams — especially with Stu Forster at halfback. Although our backs weren't quite as experienced and, in the end, that turned out to be the difference.'

The British Isles had started their tour with solid wins over North Auckland and North Harbour, even if their playing style won them few friends. In marked contrast to previous Lion teams, they adopted a ten-man approach to the game, relying on their big, experienced forward pack and the tactical kicking of their halves. It was a swapping of traditional roles. In the past the tourists had usually been starved of possession by dominant All Black forward packs and sought compensation through sparkling back play. But now the northern hemisphere game had changed — forwards held their own, and backlines were underutilised by design rather than by circumstance.

But any negative thoughts were swept aside as fifteen scarlet jerseys ran out onto Athletic Park on a brilliantly fine day to confront the fearsome Maori haka. Certainly the Lions' faith in their forwards seemed misplaced by half-time as the Maori pack monstered its opposition and provided the platform for a commanding 20-nil lead.

'We were totally focused and really hyped up. There'd been a lot of dressing room talk about getting right up the noses of the Poms — restoring mana not just to the Maori jersey but to our people as well. And I don't think they knew what hit them.'

Norm's own performance was outstanding — belligerent, accurate and capped by a sweetly timed pass that saw Nelson winger Allen Prince haring away for a Maori try. Spectators nudged each other and pointed, checked their programmes to confirm the name of this dynamic No. 2.

But the half-time break gave the Lions the chance to catch their breath and reassess their game plan. In the second half they began to employ their experienced backs — Scotland's Gavin Hastings and Wales' winger Ieuan Evans particularly impressive with their incisive running and opportunism. Gradually the Lions edged themselves back into the match, the forwards getting sufficient ball for the outside backs to score three tries and snatch the game 24-20.

'We ran out of puff,' remembers Norm. 'It was still early season for most of us and we'd expended a lot of energy in that first half. A lot of nervous energy too, I think. When Evans, Underwood and company started running wide we eventually ran out of cover. Although their forwards weren't bad either. The Lions' No. 8 Ben Clarke had an exceptional game and Irish prop Nick Popplewell was a great scrummager. They would have walked into any All Blacks team had they been Kiwis — that's how good they were. But their real ability was out wide, and the crime was that they practically ignored the speed they had out there for the rest of the tour.'

Which was just as well for the struggling All Blacks. It required the outstanding kicking talents of Grant Fox to rescue the All Blacks in the first test of the series — an unconvincing 20-18 sneak in the last minutes of the game. After breathing a collective sigh of relief, the rugby public shrugged its shoulders. It was traditional for the All Blacks to stutter in their first international of the season, they reasoned . . . look at Ireland, look at the World XV last year. But what happened in the second tests of those series? Smacked 'em for six. She'll be right.

Four days before the second test Hawke's Bay were to have their crack at the tourists, and they too fancied their chances. They knew the Lions' best combinations would be rested ahead of the international, and there was no doubting the Magpies' ability to score tries. In their Ranfurly Shield challenge against the mighty Auckland team a fortnight earlier they had scored five tries and 31 points — a record against the shield-holders. Unfortunately, they had also conceded double that ratio of touchdowns to lose 31-69.

'That Shield match was a bizarre game. They had twenty points on us in about fifteen minutes — Eroni Clarke waltzing through the backline every time he touched the ball. But then we decided to chance our arm and the points just came. Gordon Falcon had an incredible game and Aaron Hamilton on the wing carved them up wide. Believe it or not, we actually had the winning of the game early in the second half but the referee missed a Gordy try that would have given us the lead. Then Eroni Clarke went mad again and it was all over.'

Despite this loss, both Graeme Taylor and his captain fancied their team's chances. And when the day dawned warm and sunny, and a crowd of sixteen thousand locals surged into McLean Park, the scene was set.

'I knew it would be a huge match. All the TV cameras and national press were there, McLean Park was packed, the guys were pumped. And GK pointed out that no Bay team had ever beaten the Lions, not even the legendary Shield team of the 60s. We had the chance to make history. I was really primed to perform when I ran out that day — it was as if this was my moment. And I knew it. Could sense that it was special.'

But despite Norm crashing over for a try in the twelfth minute and the team enjoying sustained periods on attack, the half-time whistle suggested otherwise. The Bay was down 5-17. Jarrod Cunningham was having a shocker with the boot, and the Lions were slowing the game down to suit their bigger forwards.

'I got the boys together at half-time,' recalls Taylor, 'and told them that we had to speed the game up — run them around the park with short lineouts, quick taps, spread the ball wide — that sort of thing. Norm barrelled some of the forwards for being a bit soft, urged them to lift their intensity level. I was providing the analysis and tactics while Norm rarked them up. We were a good team that day. But gee, he was motivated. He was on fire.'

The second forty minutes are now, rightly, part of Hawke's Bay rugby legend. At its completion Norm Hewitt would be rechristened 'Stormin' Norman' by the national media — a one-man whirlwind as he ran around the field like a man possessed, crunching into the increasingly timorous Lion backs, smashing over scarlet jerseys and stunning hard-bitten rugby reporters with the ferocity of his play.

One particular incident early in the second half left an indelible impression on all those watching — particularly the British media. From broken play on the Bay 22 the ball was worked clear to Norm on the blind and he dashed ahead as if shot from a gun. As the Lion backs came across in cover the crowd expected the hooker to turn and wait for support, but instead he veered infield — directly at the closing cover. The first unfortunate to cross his path was English winger Tony Underwood. The impact could be heard in the stands, as Underwood was dumped on his backside, Norm momentarily inspected the result, then plunged ahead again like an enraged bull. Eventually the hesitant Lion backline took him down in numbers, but the charge had set the tone. It was the game's defining moment — from then on the Magpie forward pack was rampant, with Norm continually in the vanguard.

'We had to intimidate them. Make them hang off us, give us enough time to put people into gaps. So I took the direct approach. You tackle me and it's going to hurt.'

As the game sped up, the Hawke's Bay loosies came into their own — Falcon, Simon Tremain and Dustin Watts were not just first to the break-down, but often second and third — picking up and running the ball around the fringes until the Lion forwards were committed, then spinning the ball wide. As the Bay's momentum increased so too did the enthusiasm of the local crowd as an improbable victory suddenly materialised before them.

'The Bay crowd are usually a bit reserved,' says Taylor. 'Sometimes you'd have the main stands full but you could swear they were all asleep. And crowds are important in motivating players — that roar of support has its adrenal influence on the pitch, believe me. Well, that afternoon the crowd really got into it — kept the boys going — and you could actually feel it. It was as if huge surges of electricity were running all over McLean Park — it was an amazing feeling, the crowd and the players feeding off each other.'

As referee Paddy O'Brien blew the final whistle an ecstatic McLean Park saluted their heroes. The game had been won 29-17 — Hawke's Bay scoring 24 unanswered points in the second half. The Lions had not looked like scoring — forced to defend against wave after wave of frenzied attack.

The occasion had been heightened by two sentimental touches. The first was the match-winning try by Magpies flanker Simon Tremain, son of Kel, who was playing in his father's memory. It was both an exhilarating and a poignant moment that was lost on none. The second was Hewitt's decision to recall Jarrod Cunningham for a last-minute penalty attempt. After failing to convert an easy opportunity at the start of the second half the fullback had been replaced as goalkicker by first-five Simon Kerr.

'Jarrod had saved us many times in the past and his general play that afternoon was excellent. But some of the crowd were jeering him and I just thought — "Stuff it, the guy deserves to be a part of this win. I'm not going to let any bastard take that away from him." Time was up on the clock and we were awarded another penalty — the Lions were deliberately fouling to slow play down. The crowd were screaming for us to run it — finish them off. But I thought — nah, this is Jarrod's.'

Cunningham duly kicked the goal — the last act of the game — and the pitch was invaded by hordes of delirious spectators.

The next day every news report hailed Norm as the chief contributor to the Magpies' outstanding victory. New Zealand's *Rugby News* claimed that Hewitt gave 'the best all-round hooker's performance in first-class rugby this season ... Whether cajoling his players into action, scoring a try, stealing a tighthead, throwing inch-perfectly to the lineout, or bouncing off countless Lions, he was simply an inspiration.' Napier's *Daily Telegraph* headlined its match report 'Norman's Conquest', while England's *Rugby World and Post* was similarly effusive: 'There were times when [Hewitt] twice and thrice became involved in the same attacking move, and when he had the ball in hand British backs, who had rather enjoyed the prospect of having an afternoon when they did not have to try and tackle Va'aiga Tuigamala, suddenly found an even more potent bomb on their doorstep.'

Graeme Taylor was in no doubt. Norm Hewitt was All Black material, he declared. And not just as a back-up to Sean Fitzpatrick. He was the All Black captain's equal in scrummaging and lineout accuracy, but in a class of his own as a ball carrier. Many around the country were inclined to agree — particularly after the first Lions test.

And so, overnight, a new 'Stormin' Norman' was born. The nickname, originally accorded to US Desert Force General Norman Schwarzkopf, was appropriated by the New Zealand press to salute a new warrior. But, unlike the original, this 'Stormin' Norman' did not take prisoners.

'THE WORD'

Despite Hewitt's exceptional form, the All Black selectors showed no inclination to shift from their preferred hookers — Fitzpatrick and Dowd. A winning team is rarely changed no matter how pressing the contenders, or how unconvincing the status quo. As long as the All Blacks kept winning test matches, Norm would remain on the outer.

And then the world changed.

Four days after their Hawke's Bay defeat, a superbly disciplined Lions team defeated the All Blacks on Athletic Park by a record margin — 20 points to 7. The Lion forwards had secured the win, with Martin Bayfield and Martin Johnson dominating the lineouts, flanker Peter Winterbottom outstanding, the front row of Jason Leonard, Brian Moore and Nick Popplewell shading their All Black opposites. Behind them Dewi Morris and Rob Andrew had controlled the pace of the game with astute kicking and a no-risks approach. The New Zealand rugby public went into shock.

But the man who felt the loss most was captain and hooker Sean Fitzpatrick. He had played poorly — being penalised for petty infringements, messing up lineout calls, being out-bustled in the loose and then coughing up the ball that had given flying Lion winger Rory Underwood the winning try. In the aftermath of defeat, Fitzpatrick suffered the most vociferous criticism of his entire rugby career.

'We expected criticism,' he wrote in his autobiography. 'But the situation developed out of reasonable proportion. This wasn't criticism — this was out and out character assassination . . . In the papers, on TV, on talkback radio . . . everywhere we turned we were slammed . . . Personally, I felt it was open season on me. I hated it.

'I thought back to all the praise lavished on me before my 50th test. That was only two weeks before — a lifetime ago. Suddenly, I was the worst player in the world. The public were in no doubt at all: I had to go.'

Within the All Black camp a general depression settled. And not all of it could be put down to the Athletic Park debacle — many of the players were anticipating the swing of the selectors' axe. To err may be human, but to forgive failure when a test series is at stake has never been a part of the New Zealand rugby psyche.

Even Fitzpatrick fretted. Despite being All Black captain, there would be no shield if Mains, Thorburn and company decided on drastic measures. And Norm Hewitt was the name of the moment — he was 'the word' — the reminder that there is always someone else out there waiting for the incumbent to fall, eager and hungry to claim their jersey. The Sunday and Monday that followed the second test were among the worst of Fitzpatrick's long playing career.

The All Black captain was not alone in his self-doubt. Coach Laurie Mains questioned his own role in the defeat. Maybe he'd overtrained his players . . . undertrained them . . . failed to press the right buttons . . . pulled the wrong ones. His career was also on the line. If this series was lost he could forget about taking the team through to the next World Cup. John Hart would be back in business.

It is now part of All Black folklore that the selectors responded to the crisis by pushing aside their initial panic. Only three changes were made for the crucial third test — Eroni Clarke dropped and Lee Stensness to debut at second-five, Arran Pene and Ian Jones preferred to Zinzan Brooke and Mark Cooksley at No. 8 and lock respectively. The players repaid their selectors' confidence by defeating the Lions 30-17 — Fitzpatrick leading from the front and scoring a try. Despite his outstanding form the Hawke's Bay hooker had not even been able to find his way into the team's reserves.

'Quite a few people were upset on my behalf. Saying that I should be in the team — if they'd been selecting on form then I would've been a shoo-in — that sort of thing. But I knew it didn't work like that. Sometimes it's harder getting out of the All Blacks than it is to get in. A coach wants to keep his squad together so that they can get the experience, build the patterns, grow their confidence. I knew I just had to keep on playing until they couldn't ignore me any more.'

In the meantime he concentrated on his duties with the community work trust and on playing for his new club. Taradale clinched the first-round Nash Cup competition — a good measure of payback in their 50-point thrashing of Tech Old Boys. And Norm was provided with another opportunity to impress when he was named in the New Zealand 'A' team to play the touring Samoans.

The coach of the 1993 'A' team was one of the All Black selection panel — North Harbour's Peter Thorburn — but far from this assisting his cause, Norm found Thorburn a remote and taciturn individual. Privately he wondered if some of the coach's reserve was down to Sean Fitzpatrick's international understudy being North Harbour's Graeme Dowd.

'I guess it was an instinctive suspicion rather than anything considered. I was becoming aware of how political All Black selections were — how every selector has their personal favourites and how provincial loyalties affect selections. At the time I just made the connection — thought it might explain why the guy was so stand-offish. Anyway, whatever the cause, we just didn't connect. Simple as that.'

Norm's regard for Thorburn was not increased by what happened at their first training run at Rotorua.

'He pulled me aside and said that there was a problem down in Dunedin [with the All Black preparation against Australia]. That Graeme Dowd was injured and that I'd have to pack up my kit, get down there to cover Fitzy and then fly back for the Samoan game on Sunday. And that was it. No congratulations, no here's your chance, no welcome to the ABs. It was just get your gear and bugger off south.'

It's an anticlimax that rancours with the burly hooker to this day.

'I'd wanted to be an All Black since I was five — had dreamed of pulling on that silver fern almost every day and every night from the time I played my first game of footy. I'd played hundreds of games for primary school teams, age group teams, clubs, reps and Maoris, with the sole motivation of one day being good enough. One day being chosen to represent my country. And then . . . here it was. I was going to be an All Black.

'Except that I wasn't. I was going to be an AB reserve, and these were the days before tactical substitutions. I was going to put on the All Black jersey, train with the team, sit in the grandstand — and hope like hell that Sean Fitzpatrick pulled a muscle or something. It was such a weird feeling, and the way Thorburn told me made it all seem like it was just nothing.'

To make matters worse, Thorburn made it obvious that Dowd's injury was the sole cause for his unexpected elevation — not anything that he might have done on the rugby paddock that year. The moment Dowd recovered from his injury, Norm would be back on the outer.

CHAPTER SEVEN

All Black

Bittersweet though his elevation might be, the Hawke's Bay hooker's more immediate worry became whether he would survive the trip south. Otago utility back Marc Ellis had also been called into the All Black reserves, and he too had been training with the New Zealand 'A' team in Rotorua. Ellis had something of a reputation as a playful larrikin — the typical Otago university 'scarfie' — and Norm would be given the chance to check out the reason for this reputation at close hand. The pair were provided with a rental car for the short trip to Taupo, where they were to catch a flight to Wellington and then on to Dunedin for the Bledisloe test. Ellis volunteered to drive, and less than three-quarters of an hour later they were in Taupo, Norm the colour of a starched sheet.

'When we got to Taupo there was a problem with the connection so Marc suggested we carry on to Wellington. I wasn't quick or smart enough to say "No." Big mistake — the guy drove like a maniac. But he had this constant series of one-liners going and all the jokes distracted me from throwing up. I had no time to think about becoming an All Black. Jeez, I just hoped I'd live.'

By the time they reached Dunedin, it was a different story. The weight of the call-up had begun to sink in, and Norm was a jitter of nerves. He joined the team in a city restaurant, where most of them came over, shook his hand, and welcomed him into the fold.

'I sat there, quiet as a mouse, trying not to show how awed I was at being in their company. I mean these guys were not just All Blacks — they were some of the greats of the game — Grant Fox, John Kirwan, Michael

Jones, Olo Brown . . . and here was the little Maori boy from Maungarapa, rubbing shoulders with them. I was blown away.'

There was a notable exception to the welcome. All Black captain Sean Fitzpatrick virtually ignored the new arrival — an attitude he would maintain throughout their respective playing careers. Unlike predecessors Gatland and Dowd, this latest understudy posed a real threat for the hooker's job.

'Initially I was surprised by [Fitzpatrick's] reaction. It was like he was reminding me that he was the king around here and I was some oink from the country. But after a while his attitude started to piss me off — that he wasn't man enough to acknowledge me as part of the All Black family. As I've got older, I think I understand a bit better. He didn't want to give me any advantage, no matter how small, that would affect his chance of staying the top dog. And if he could intimidate me off the field as well, then so much the better.'

However, other All Blacks made an immediately favourable impression on the young hooker. Particularly the strapping winger John Kirwan.

'He would have to be one of the most open and honest men I've ever met. I mean, here I was overwhelmed by all this star company and John comes over, goes out of his way to have a chat and explain how things are done. There was no bullshit about the man — he was a regular, upfront guy. When he came out and publicly admitted to his struggle with mental illness, it was so typical of his honesty. He was a breath of fresh air.'

At training, Norm was required to learn the new lineout codes, the new scrummaging calls, the set-piece tactics in case the unthinkable should happen. But what was happening off the field affected him more.

'When you're in the All Blacks — and especially in the lead-up to a test match —there's an incredible pressure that builds within the team. It becomes a force all of its own — a spirit that gets stronger and stronger until on match day you can almost cut it with a knife. It wasn't just that we were playing the world-champion Aussies, it was much more than that. It's all the ghosts of all those who've gone before you. And it's mixed up with this incredible expectation that the Kiwi public lays on the team. I mean I can look back now and rationalise the kind of pressures that build up, but at the time it was so over-the-top. Suffocating. I just wanted to get out of the hotel, go for a walk . . . breathe. But even then there would be someone shouting out "Smash those Aussie bastards".'

His surroundings certainly offered no relief. The All Blacks were staying at the same Shoreline Hotel that had been witness to the wrecking incident of the previous season.

And at no point did Norm actually feel a part of the team or the All Black set-up. He was, quite literally, the last minute ring-in, and coupled with being in the reserves, this induced a strange melancholy in the Hawke's Bay hooker.

'I wanted to be there but I didn't. I'd wanted to be an All Black more than anything else in my life — hell, it *was* my life — but not like this. When they gave me my All Black kit I went back to my room — laid out the jersey, the shorts, the socks on the bed and just stared at them for ages. Here it all was — right in front of me — and yet it wasn't. I knew the only way I would be an All Black would be if I took the field in the heat of battle. Otherwise I was just another pretender. Not the real thing.'

The game itself proved a triumph for both Laurie Mains and his beleaguered captain Sean Fitzpatrick. Despite the All Blacks' series win over the Lions there were still those who maintained that Australia was the No. 1 team in the world. As holders of the Bledisloe Cup and the World Cup, the Wallabies represented the truer challenge. Although something of that challenge had dissipated with the unavailability of stars Michael Lynagh, Willie Ofahangaue and brilliant youngster John Eales. Wallaby coach Bob Dwyer was forced to gamble and called in recently retired scrum-half Nick Farr-Jones, and 19-year-old Queenslander Pat Howard at first five-eighth. Farr-Jones worked, Howard did not. The youngster tried to run himself out of trouble in the first few minutes, was nailed by the All Black loosies, and went downhill from there.

'Michael Jones was everywhere that day. Every time the Aussies looked like having a sniff of an opening — wham — the "Iceman" would take them down and come up with the loose ball. "The Bus" [Inga Tuigamala] made [Wallaby winger David] Campese look a prize chump — went past him or through him all day.

'I don't remember much else about the game except feeling a bit weird. At one point I found myself cheering like a spectator and then I had to tell myself to get a grip, adopt the staunch AB poker face — look like I wasn't excited.'

That touch of the surreal was heightened when, after the final whistle blew to confirm a comfortable 25-10 All Black win, Norm had to scramble to catch a taxi to Momona airport so that he could catch connecting flights back to Rotorua for the New Zealand 'A' team's game against Manu Samoa the next day.

'I can remember thinking to myself that I was glad I had my AB kit in my bag otherwise I might have thought it was all a dream. I mean here the boys were back in Dunedin celebrating regaining the Bledisloe Cup, and here's me at 20,000 feet having to think about tomorrow's game. It was not the greatest introduction to All Black rugby.'

In contrast, the New Zealand 'A' team welcomed him back to Rotorua with genuine warmth. They were not only pleased for Norm, but also at what the sudden call-in signalled to the entire squad. Getting into the big time was not a forlorn hope — Norm Hewitt's selection proved it. And with an All Black tour to Scotland and England in the offing, the current AB squad would need new recruits. The Manu Samoa game the next day was a collective and individual trial, especially with selector Peter Thorburn as their coach.

The touring Samoans might have lost Frank Bunce and Steve Bachop to the All Blacks from their World Cup squad of two years before, but they still boasted a solid core of the team that had set the northern hemisphere alight during that tournament. Their backline boasted two more future All Blacks, Alama Ieremia and Ofisa Tonu'u, but their forward pack, despite containing several provincial reps, lacked both height and mobility. The New Zealand 'A' forwards blasted them off the park.

'We had a solid Waikato core to our pack — Graham Purvis, Steve Gordon, Richard Jerram, Duane Monkley — and then there was my old mate Richard Turner at No. 8, and former ABs like Blair Larsen and Kevin Boroevich. We beat them in the scrums, targeted the lines, drove from rucks and mauls — it was old-fashioned but effective.'

After eighty torrid minutes Manu Samoa were looking at the wrong end of a 13-37 scoreline, and their pretensions about challenging for a top rung in the rugby hierarchy had taken a severe battering.

'Players hate being in 'B' teams. I mean, however the fish-heads dress it up — whether it's a 'New Zealand XV' or 'New Zealand A' or whatever — there's a mongrel resentment that you're not considered No. 1 material — that the selectors say you're not good enough. So you work on that in the days leading up — you tell the players that if they want to be No. 1 then here's the opportunity to set a standard the ABs will find hard to match and that the selectors can't ignore.'

Two weeks later and New Zealand 'A' considered their case well made. Against the same Manu Samoa combination, the All Blacks relied on the boot of Grant Fox to kick seven penalties for a 35-13 win at Eden Park — scoring just two tries despite leading 22-6 at half-time. Once again Norm had stripped, put on the No. 21 reserve jersey, sat on the bench and watched the team play. Although by game's end there was a curious smile on his lips. The 'B' team had proved its point.

At the end of the test, Samoan captain Peter Fatialofa challenged the

All Blacks to play the next international between the two countries back in the Islands. Despite two further home tests against Samoa in 1996 and 1999, no All Black team has yet accepted the challenge and played a test in Apia. Or anywhere else in the Pacific Islands.

'I've toured the islands — Samoa, Tonga, Fiji — with Maori and divisional teams and it's an incredible tour — a chance to soak up the Polynesian culture as much as the sun and surf. They kill you with kindness off the paddock and then, almost as if to make up for it, try the more direct approach on the field.

'But the New Zealand Rugby Union have treated the Island unions pretty shabbily over the years. So too has Australia. Both their national teams should be doing the full Pacific Islands tour, say, once every four years. That way the Islands would be getting either the Wallabies or the ABs every two years and it would really lift rugby in the South Pacific. Up until now we've just colonised them — flogged their best players without giving anything back in return. The NZRFU have been right bastards to the Island nations.'

RELEGATION

Despite not feeling a 'real' All Black, Norm returned to Hawke's Bay to be feted as one. Wherever he went people would stop to shake his hand and congratulate him on his elevation to the black jersey. In some rugby circles, though, this was mixed with a measure of disbelief that the unruly front rower with the drinking problem had now joined the game's elite.

He also returned to take charge of an expanded community work trust — now responsible for projects throughout the Napier/Hastings area. It was a job he enjoyed, and his new status provided the trust with further sponsorship opportunities and a raft of new work contracts. Although the trust gained by the association, it was also having its effect on Norm.

'I guess there was a part of me that thought that, without rugby, I would probably be unemployed as well, and that made me work a bit harder for them. And it was good work — for the first time in my life I was helping others and discovering what a buzz you get out of watching people take the opportunities you provide them with, and how some of them make a real go of it. And in a job like that you have to use your brain too. In any given week there will be problems, either administrative or with personalities, and it was my job to resolve them and find a solution that worked.'

A later Department of Social Welfare report to the Minister of

Employment showered praise on the trust and its leadership. It also noted that over half the trust's employees went on to find full-time jobs, and Norm's role was seen as vital in that success. The effect continued to be reciprocal. For the first time in his life Norm was required to shrug off his Te Aute staunchness, and to balance the selfish pursuit of his All Black dream. He was required to give something of himself to others, and there was a significant change in both his character and his demeanour. Although that fierce core of determination still burned, Norm had come to appreciate that a smile and a cogent argument were more convincing than 'giving the evils' or threatening violence. His self-imposed ban on alcohol was also having its effect.

'I'd look at people in social situations who had once been hard-out drinking buddies, see them get all pissy-eyed and unco, and I'd think ... "Hell, that was me last year." And rather than get into trouble I was actually stopping people get messed up.

'But I still had the thirst. I mean that never left me. No doubt about that. After a big game you still wanted to be leering up with your rugby mates and instead here I was on the OJ or water. It wasn't easy, that's for real.'

But the greater thirst was to put on the black jersey with the silver fern, and his brief foray into the All Black camp had only whetted that desire. The booze could wait: the dream could not.

At the end of that year an All Black party was to be selected to tour Scotland and England, and Norm kept a nervous eye on any rugby literature he could lay his hands on for news of Graeme Dowd's injury. It wasn't so much that he wished the North Harbour hooker ill; rather that he needed to know who the competition would be for the No. 2 jersey and how they were playing. He had already anticipated a climactic showdown with Dowd later in the season when Hawke's Bay were scheduled to play North Harbour at Napier.

But the more immediate task was to help Graeme Taylor get the Hawke's Bay squad ready to survive another year in the NPC first division. Their win over the touring Lions had heightened expectations, and the team had also picked up 1992 All Black Dallas Seymour on transfer from Canterbury, and live-wire Wellington halfback John Bradbrook. In George Konia, Jarrod Cunningham, Murdoch Paewai and New Zealand Sevens speedster Aaron Hamilton, the Bay backline had a mixture of youth and pace.

However, the Bay forwards were too small to foot it with the larger provincial packs and the loss of English import John Fowler and the tough Romana Graham to overseas clubs rocked Taylor's preparations.

Despite that, the Bay played with rare elan and proved to be one of the most attractive teams in the whole of the NPC. But they kept losing. Always narrowly, but losing all the same. Finally, as it had in the two previous seasons, it came down to the last game of the year on McLean Park. Defeat King Country and they would stay up. Lose and they would be back in the second division.

'Man for man we were a better team than King Country and we knew it. We were at home, it was another perfect sunny day, the ground was packed. Maybe we thought it was ours of right, maybe we choked. But, Jeez, it was bad. Nothing worked and they closed down our backs all day.'

The final score was 16-12 to the visitors.

'I was devastated . . . just walked off the field shaking my head, unable to believe that we'd played so badly. And unlike the Lions, we hadn't been able to turn it around — nothing I said or did made it any better. As we headed back into the changing sheds, old GK took it pretty tough. He thought it was the end for him.'

And so it would prove — at least in Hawke's Bay. Despite urging Taylor to reapply for the coach's job, the union decided on a radical change. To complement their head-hunting of former All Black Wayne Smith as the Bay's new chief executive, the Hawke's Bay Rugby Union selected another Canterbury stalwart, John Phillips, as their 1994 coach, and named Dallas Seymour as captain. It was a Canterbury trifecta that would cause considerable resentment in club circles and, ironically, contribute towards Hawke's Bay remaining in the second division.

With Taylor gone and the Hawke's Bay union under the effective management of Wayne Smith and a group of local businessmen, including Peter Roebuck and John Buck, Norm decided to re-examine his association with the Magpies.

'I could see the way the game was going — the first division unions got the lion's share of the selectors' attention, the TV coverage, the crowds and the money. In the '93 All Black team that went to the UK only Ian Jones [North Auckland], and "Ginge" Henderson [Southland] played second division — and both were established ABs. Besides, Ginge was a favourite of Laurie's [Mains] and Ian Jones soon transferred to North Harbour. But I wasn't anything. I was on the fringe, and without first division rugby I was going to drop out of sight. So I made a mental note to have a chat with Laurie and sound him out about whether I should stay in the Bay or leave.'

The opportunity soon arose when Norm was confirmed as the second hooker in the touring party to Scotland and England. The announcement was not unexpected given Dowd's continuing unavailability, but it was still a relief to hear his name read out.

'I was going to be a real All Black! That's what I thought at the time — "I'm going to be a playing AB, not just a reserve." I would get the chance to play in the jersey instead of keeping it warm. So I didn't have much time to worry about the King Country loss or next year's prospects or whatever. I was just this bundle of nervous energy counting the days down to when we assembled in Auckland and flew out. It was such a buzz that I would wake up in the middle of the night and fret about not getting injured, staying healthy, eating the right foods, staying away from the booze.'

And his selection also had an unexpected financial reward. The All Blacks would be paid just a hundred dollars a day while they were on tour, but a series of fundraising events by the Hewitt whanau, the Taradale rugby club and other well-wishers meant that he left with $1500 in additional spending money.

'The people around me were great — the Taradale club, the trust who kept my job open — but it was the Porongahau whanau and the Pakipaki marae who really humbled me. They raised around $4000 from a variety of functions, and these were people who could barely afford it. It made me realise how proud other people were of my achievements — that they were as excited for me as I was.

'Sure, everyone likes being associated with success, but this was more than that. It was like I was representing all those people who had given their time and their money to make my path in the UK a bit easier. So no way was I going to be a spare part on tour — I was going to play every game to the max and put as much pressure on Fitzpatrick as I could.

'Man, was I ever pumped when I got on that plane.'

CHAPTER EIGHT

Tourist

Although Norm had been to the United Kingdom four years earlier with the *Rugby News* youth team, that was no preparation for the sheer scale and hype that accompanied a fully-fledged All Black tour. This time he would be contained within 'the bubble' — a group of privileged young men and their entourage of coach, assistant, doctor, masseur, manager and media liaison. It wasn't so much the new chores and responsibilities that perplexed the young traveller as the opulence of the surroundings and their almost hermetic containment from the commonplace.

'I couldn't get over how flash everything was. We had the best of hotels, the best food, we travelled business class everywhere, and there were heaps of free things from your training kits and clothes down to your daks and hankies. Even the smellies were free. I was amazed.'

For the first time Norm appreciated that the All Blacks were not just an illustrious, even revered, rugby team but an international sporting icon. Wherever they went in the UK they were feted as champions and, within some rugby quarters, treated as demi-gods. From the moment their jumbo touched down at Heathrow an air of unreality took over, as they encountered the often servile attitude of hotel staff, gaggles of young groupies at social functions, and the often lurid reporting of British sports journalists.

'It took me a long time to get used to the way the Brits treated us. The reputation of previous touring teams was grafted onto us immediately — especially the '91 World Cup squad, who had been perceived as unsmiling, arrogant arseholes. I mean this was a new team with a new coach and a new playing style, but to the media we were the same dark guys they'd hated two years earlier.'

But whatever the outside perceptions, Laurie Mains was determined the All Blacks were not going to be distracted from their mission. The public relations niceties were left to media liaison Ric Salizzo, and training became the immediate priority, with a practice scheduled as soon as the squad reached their London hotel. The aim was to acclimatise the players quickly and lessen any effects of jetlag, although Norm suspected a more demonic intent behind Mains' gut-busting demands.

'Laurie loved to see you broken [from training] — that you had nothing left. The killers were the sprint 150s — run, drop, run, drop. He loved to test you mentally — see if you could take it. There was no great science involved — I mean, we got aerobically very fit. But sometimes he overdid it, even if I was determined that he wouldn't see me beaten. I'd have had to fall down dead before I'd let him see that he'd got me.'

At an All Black camp back in New Zealand the squad had been tested and put into three separate fitness groups, with '1' the lowest and '3' the superior athletes.

'I was a definite "1". Which didn't worry me to start with because I've always been a bit cunning about these sorts of things. Never go hard out to start with: that's my rule. That way you have plenty of room for improvement and the coaches and fitness trainers can be conned a bit as to how well you've come on and responded to them. You get brownie points because they think you've got better by heaps.'

But Mains' fearsome reputation as a taskmaster soon had the hooker reassessing his strategy. Along with the other 'fatties' — props Graham Purvis, Olo Brown and Bull Allen — Norm was required to stay after practice and perform further speed and sprinting drills. And it was not unusual for winger Va'aiga Tuigamala to join them on these 'hell cycles', the strapping Samoan a notoriously indifferent trainer.

'You'd stagger back to the showers and your whole body would be quivering. Sometimes I wondered if Laurie hadn't been reincarnated from some concentration camp guard somewhere, because he seemed to have no "off" button, no ability to know when we'd had enough. But it worked, I guess. We did get fitter and faster and more able to play the mobile 80-minute game he wanted. It was always Laurie's aim to have us fitter than our opposition, although I didn't necessarily appreciate that at the time. I just thought — "You sadistic shit".'

Even more of a shock to his system than Mains' training methods was the attitude of some of his All Black companions.

'I knew Bull and Craig Dowd from some of the earlier Colts and youth teams, and Bull and I had become really good mates. We were in the same sort of position, I guess — both provincial boys, youngish, new to the ABs, a bit overawed by it all. And because it was so difficult at times we relied a lot on each other, lent on each other for support.

'But the attitude of some of the senior All Blacks was really stink. There was a huge, and I mean huge, gulf between them and us and they made sure we knew it. Right from the start of the tour it was obvious who the "test" team were and who the midweekers were, and Bull and I were definitely among the latter. So the team divided on those lines and some of the "test" players treated us like shit. Their arrogance was unbelievable.'

Despite the selection of some exciting new talent in Otago winger Jeff Wilson and Norm's former Hawke's Bay team-mate Stu Forster, the team developed an inner fragility that Norm insists had as much to do with attitude as the players' talents.

'There were a whole lot of us who didn't really feel a part of the tour. We were the midweekers — the "dirty dirties" — and it was a bit like being back in the third form at the Te Aute hostel. There were the "back of the bus" boys, who were the senior ABs, and they determined who did what — from the seating order to the court sessions to the various chores. You could handle that if they treated you OK and respected you as another player, but they didn't. We were beneath them, and that was that.'

On the rugby side of things the tour started well with a comfortable 39-12 victory over London & South East Counties, the manner of the win earning a standing ovation from the Twickenham crowd. But the next match was an entirely different affair, with most of the new boys — Shane Howarth, John Mitchell, Liam Barry, Richard Fromont and Norm — making their All Black debuts. Against them were pitted a rugged and experienced Midlands selection, led by English international Dean Richards, and not in the least overawed by their opponents or the occasion.

'I'd put my AB kit in my bag [in preparation for the bus drive to the ground] and then I took it out again, put it at the end of the bed, and just kept staring at it. I rubbed my fingers over the number 2 on the back, turned it over, ran my hand over the silver fern. I must have done that a hundred times. It was finally going to happen — this was it. I was so keyed up that I was back and forward from the toilet until there must have been a groove in the carpet. And then Zinny [Zinzan Brooke] comes in — he was captaining the team that day — and says, "Norm, you're leading the haka with Rushie," so that got me going even more. First game, first All

Black haka, and I'm the one to lead it. I've never been so nervous in my life.'

On the bus Norm tried to keep his mind focused on his allotted rugby tasks — the lineout and scrum calls, his positional play, making his tackles count. But inevitably his mind drifted back to his family and friends in the Bay, to the faxes that had come through to the hotel, and to their support and expectations. While there are some sportspeople who use such nervous energy to their advantage, for others it becomes a burden, a weight of expectation that they carry around with them.

'I was really worried about how I'd go, but after the haka and then the first clash at the maul I was fine. It was a tough game and both sides were pretty evenly matched. It was obvious that their combinations were more experienced than ours, and if it hadn't been for Matthew Cooper coming on as a replacement and landing a couple of penalties we might have only drawn the game, maybe even lost.'

Although both the British and the Kiwi media stressed the narrowness of the 12-6 win, all were agreed that hooker Hewitt had been impressive with his accuracy to the lineout and aggression in the loose. But any satisfaction he might have taken from this first game was dwarfed by the next, to be played at the headquarters of the Liverpool Football Club, the famous Anfield ground.

'We were to play the Northern Division there but I would have played in a fifth grade team to run out onto Anfield. It was a magic place, a sort of huge Wellington Stadium but with everything coloured in Liverpool red. Except for the field which was as green and smooth as a billiard table. You can understand just why soccer is so huge if you look at grounds like those — they create an atmosphere all of their own, even when they're empty.'

After the midweekers had established an early lead, including a barging Norm Hewitt try, the Northern Division came back fiercely, narrowly losing 21-27 despite being outscored four tries to nil. Unfortunately the game took place in the media shadow of an incident from the previous Saturday, when the 'A' team had defeated South-West Division, in which England international centre Phil de Glanville had his cheek sliced open by an All Black boot. This was the sort of incident the English press had been waiting for — proof positive of typical All Black thuggery. By the time the team reached Anfield, there was a perceptible cooling in the public reception.

'In a funny kind of way the de Glanville incident brought the team closer. The reaction of the British press was so over-the-top that you couldn't help but resent the attention. I mean rugby is a physical contest and already most of us, including me, had felt the tap-tap of a stray Pom boot. And, to be fair, All Black teams hate players lying on the wrong side of rucks trying to slow their ball down. So if the ref doesn't do his job, we remind the offender that there are other types of justice. Although the de Glanville injury was just an accident — nothing evil about it at all. Of course, he screamed blue murder, and that only made it worse.'

The de Glanville incident lingered on the sports pages for weeks, exacerbating the mutual antipathy between the English press and the touring All Blacks. Some of that dislike found its way onto the field.

'I've played against Australia, South Africa and Wales, but the team you really hate losing against are the Poms. There's something about the whole English class system that affects your perception of them, and rugby is very much a game for the sons of the nobs over there. I hate losing to the South Africans because so many of their fans and administrators are ignorant Afrikaners, but the English . . . it's not just on the field they consider themselves superior. It's an attitude that puts your back up as soon as you meet them.'

Norm's instinctive dislike was shared by most of the touring party — although he could hardly have been said to have assisted cordial Anglo-Kiwi relations. Before the first game there had been an official welcome at the Royal Lancaster Hotel where Norm, still exhausted from the morning's training and having missed lunch, was intercepted by a man 'looking like a Tower of London beefeater'.

'I thought he said: "Go over and make it known that you want something to eat," and he pointed me towards this old guy, dressed to the nines, who had a long nose and was smiling at everyone. So I stroll over there, tap him on the shoulder, and say: "So where's the food then?" Well, this old guy does a Homer — goes gulp-gulp like a fish — and looks at me as if I've just farted in church. Anyway, he waves somewhere over his right shoulder and I head off in that direction. It wasn't until afterwards that it was pointed out to me that the beefeater had actually said: "Go over there and introduce yourself to [former Prime Minister] Sir Edward Heath." Just as well the press didn't get hold of that one.'

Not that Norm was the only player to suffer ribbing from his teammates. Robin Brooke had been selected to complement the lean Ian Jones in the middle-row of the All Black scrum, but had aggravated a calf muscle early in the tour and would not play a game on the entire tour. Nevertheless, he remained with the squad and drew the unwelcome nickname of 'Bill' for his efforts, short for 'Food Bill'.

One of the highlights of the tour came early, when Norm was

introduced to the late Princess Diana at an official reception for the All Blacks at Buckingham Palace.

'The Queen and Princess Anne were there, but it was Diana who attracted all the boys. She was the most beautiful woman I've ever seen in my life. She had this magnetism, the X-factor and, believe me, a lot of it was definitely sex. All the boys milled around her and we were smitten. The poor old Queen and Princess Anne were left talking to the management team because none of us wanted to leave Diana. When she looked at you or talked to you it was as if the whole world stopped. She was an awesome lady.'

The next game against an England A selection officially confirmed the division between the test team and the midweekers, with Mains naming a shadow test line-up for the Scotland international only a fortnight away. After an experimental run at Anfield, Marc Ellis supplanted Steve Bachop as the first-choice first five-eighth, while young Southland star Jeff Wilson nailed John Kirwan's old spot on the wing. Arran Pene was preferred to Zinzan Brooke at No. 8, Zinzan reverting to the open side flank given the tour unavailability of either Michael Jones or Mike Brewer — Jones through injury, Brewer through work commitments.

But despite indifferent efforts against both England A and Scotland A, and an outstanding 84-9 display by the midweekers against the South of Scotland, Mains and his assistant Earle Kirton were intent on persevering with their choices in the belief that the new players would finally click. And in the first international against Scotland, those hopes were realised — the 51-15 thrashing seeming to confirm that Marc Ellis was the dashing successor to Grant Fox and that the youthful Jeff Wilson had the Midas touch — 'Goldie' scoring three tries on debut, Ellis two.

'At the time we all thought that this was one of the most complete All Black performances ever. But the truth was that Scotland weren't a patch on England and that the Scots' open play suited our style. I mean we were all pretty stoked after the win, and maybe that led to some overconfidence or maybe we forgot that the English play a much tighter, tougher game based around a big beefy pack. Whatever the cause, we got spanked the next Saturday [losing 9-15 against England] and that put the dampener on what had already been a pretty traumatic past few days.'

THE BREWER AFFAIR

Team relations soured dramatically in the week between the Scottish and English tests with the shock decision of Laurie Mains to call former Otago loosie Mike Brewer into the test reserves to replace the injured Ginge Henderson. That North Harbour's Liam Barry and Waikato's John Mitchell were both fit and already in the All Black squad was deemed irrelevant. The selection caused an uproar, both in Britain and back at home.

'I always thought Mike Brewer was a Grade A prick from the first time I met him. He personified all that was worst about the All Blacks — all the seniority and arrogance crap that I detested. He gave the impression that he was "the man" and that all dirt-trackers were just a bunch of nobodies. So when he was called into the ABs I was pissed off. The problem was that he was Laurie's boy — they went way back together at Otago — and All Black coaches do play favourites. Brewer was in Europe on business for his employer, the Canterbury clothing brand, but Liam had been playing OK — not brilliant, but definitely OK. He was young, it was his first tour, no-one else had gone much out of their way to help him — anyway, the next thing Mike Brewer is in the reserves and neither Liam nor [John] Mitchell are anywhere.'

To Norm the whole Brewer affair seemed to contradict the All Black camp talk about sacrifice and loyalty and sticking by your mates.

'We were supposed to be a "family" of thirty players on a mission to stuff the Poms. In no time at all there's this division line running down the team, with the senior ABs looking down on the rest of us. Then we have the de Glanville incident and the UK press going ape; we lose the main test against England — young Jeff Wilson bawling his eyes out in the dressing room because he thought he'd lost it for us — and then the Brit press go mad again after Jamie [Joseph] tramples all over [English halfback] Kyran Bracken. And, bang, right in the middle of this, the Brewer affair blows. I tell you — it wasn't happy campers. I couldn't wait to get home, but then I know a lot of the others felt the same way.'

The Brewer issue worsened. The flanker stayed with the team after the English test, was named in the All Black reserves against the Barbarians and took the field in the Cardiff match to replace an injured Blair Larsen. Despite many of the team's misgivings, they had no option but to accept the selection judgements of Mains and his assistant Earle Kirton. But then the affair turned sharply personal.

It had become a tradition for All Black touring parties to sell their pool of free tickets to each game and add the money to any other cash received from unofficial promotional activities. These included things like speaking to various UK clubs, or attending select functions as All Blacks and charging the organisers an attendance fee. There was a 'black market' in

All Black duties, with all the money pooled and divided equally between the players at the end of the tour. Now the pool was deemed to be divisible by 31, not 30. Ring-in Mike Brewer had been added to the list.

'Some of us objected strongly to that. Brewer wasn't selected as part of the original team and wasn't selected as back-up like, say, Blair Larsen had been. He was only playing because Laurie Mains went troppo. End of story. It wasn't like the Tabai Matson issue of a year or two earlier when Matson just happened to be in France and there was a crisis due to injuries to the touring backline. There was no crisis: Brewer shouldn't have been there. End of story. And he certainly wasn't entitled to the pool. After all, he'd done nothing to contribute to it and was still being paid by Canterbury.'

But the objectors were overruled by the team management. Brewer took his share from the pool, leaving an even sourer taste in the players' mouths.

'I came away from that tour pretty disillusioned with the whole AB set-up. Quite a few of the others felt the same way, and I think Laurie Mains probably realised what a goof he'd been. Unfortunately it was never made up to Liam Barry and we lost him way too early to Japan.

'But whenever NZRFU officials go on about loyalty and teamwork I think back to '93. It was not a good lesson to send to all us young guys, but I reckon we learned it all right. So when professionalism came along two years later, we all knew no-one was going to look after us except ourselves. And that UK tour played a good part in teaching us that lesson.'

Despite being lauded in the British and New Zealand rugby press as one of the stars of the tour, Norm had also absorbed another lesson. And, ultimately, a self-destructive one. That no matter how well he played, no matter how good his form, as long as Sean Fitzpatrick was an integral part of the All Black management team Norm would never claim the No. 2 jersey as his own.

'I used to think the only way I'd get to play a test would be if Fitzy broke a leg. And even then it would require traction to keep him from playing. There was an element of "poor me" to that view, but it was also bloody true. Fitzy was a legend. He was probably the most important part of the All Blacks' on-field strategy and tactics. He was a hooker, a player, a referee and an enormously combative and irritating opponent. He was worth two players sometimes. I knew that. But that didn't matter. No matter how much better I got than him, he was always going to be wearing that No. 2 jersey.'

Norm was also aware that Fitzpatrick's previous understudies, Warren Gatland and Graeme Dowd, had between them spent five seasons on the reserves bench, including every game at both the 1987 and 1991 World Cups. Only Dowd had ever taken the field in a test and that was as a replacement prop when Richard Loe was injured against Ireland in 1992. Sean Fitzpatrick's incredible record was that he had played every test from the start of the 1987 international season to the end of 1993 (indeed, until the pool section of the '95 World Cup) and never once had he left the field injured or been unavailable for selection.

GROUPIES

A certain level of aggression had always been part of the rugby experience for the All Blacks, but not all of it was confined to the field. Each tour involved the traditional 'backseat challenge', where younger team members would try to overthrow the bus seating order, with the senior players steadfastly defending their backseat status. Occasionally blood would be spilt and clothes ripped, but on the more extreme days a black eye, a split lip or a cracked tooth might also accompany the affray.

'I often wondered how many injuries that were passed off in the media as training injuries really came out of a backseat challenge. I mean, there was a line and generally we didn't cross it, but there were stresses in any touring party and sometimes the challenge could get a bit nasty. When the Mike Brewer controversy was on, for example, there was a real division between the top All Black fifteen and us midweekers. I can remember Jamie [Joseph] getting all upset when he played a game with us, saying that he wasn't a midweeker, that he was a test player. So a bit of an edge came into the camp and, yeah, it could find its way into the backseat challenge.'

There were other incidents in the tour that left a sour taste. At an official dinner after the last Barbarians game on the British tour, the English flanker Neil Back upset the new hooker with his comments about All Black great Michael Jones.

'Back boasted that he was a much better player than the Iceman and that even if Michael had played [in the English test] it wouldn't have made any difference to the result. Well, I let him have it with a few verbals until Brewer came over and told me to piss off — that I was just a dirt-tracker and who did I think I was? I thought about hitting the guy for a second but instead buggered off to a nearby hotel, caught up with some Kiwi supporters, got on the piss, and had a great night. But it seemed weird — here was I defending an AB against some wanker and here was another AB kicking me out for my efforts. That incident really highlighted the senior/junior divide for me.'

Another feature of the tour — indeed, of all Norm's touring experiences — was the groupies. Young women determined to have sex with and share in a star's status, if only for a few amorous moments. As All Blacks the team possessed a reputation well beyond New Zealand, so their attraction to groupies was similarly international.

On one of his first tours, with the *Rugby News* youth team, Norm had discovered the ambiguous delights of the groupie for himself — although the experience was more memorable for its interruption than its consummation.

'We were in Ireland, and that's one place that every touring team loves. It's a very friendly place and the countryside is so lush and green, while the pubs have the Guinness and the colleens. I ended up in this car in the carpark with this ultra-friendly lady and it's just starting to get a bit passionate when this policeman wanders over, knocks on the car window and says, "Sorry, matey, but you can't be doing that in there!" We weren't allowed to take girls back to the team hotel either so I didn't get to be doing it anywhere. And the next day I was still in a blur . . . young men's emotions and all that.'

But it wasn't until his return to the British Isles with the All Blacks in 1993 that he understood the genuine potency of the All Black jersey.

'It was like the beer. Sex was always there and always available if you wanted it. Mostly the girls would be the extrovert young types, but there were a lot of older women too, which surprised me. Apart from personality, groupies tended to come in every size, shape and colour. It was like wandering into a sweet shop. Take your pick.

'Actually I wasn't too keen during that UK tour because — and I know it sounds a bit wet — but because I was still with Keri. And it was my first All Black tour, and for me the tour was all about playing well in the black jersey. I was so preoccupied with rugby that not much else existed, including women. But some of the others really took advantage.

'There were basically three kinds of rugby tourist. There were those who'd decided they wouldn't indulge because of a relationship or marriage back home; then there were those who strayed no matter what was going on at home; and then there were the "yellow jersey" types. They would be racing each other to see how many birds they could screw while they were on tour — like winning stages in the Tour de France. The yellow jersey boys would push all sorts of boundaries . . . sex in public, sex with more than one chick, sex in front of an audience, all that kind of stuff . . . The point is, there was no shortage of women willing to oblige them. It was all very mutual. Some of the public sex girls were real exhibitionists.'

Over the years, though, Norm has become more cynical of the groupies' motivations.

'Sure, it takes two to tango and all that sort of stuff, but some of the girls had their own designs. Some really wanted to bag an All Black for good — start a relationship with them and then get the guy to pay for them to get them out of their personal circumstances or even the country they were in. Others were just silly fluff. And some just wanted the taste of something different. So when some of the guys thought they were scoring, they were actually being scored against.'

Team parties were also organised on tour to ensure there was no lack of female companionship.

'That was the job of the "dirty dirties". Those were the guys who weren't playing and weren't in the reserves either. We would go to quite elaborate lengths — like getting invites printed, having a room in the hotel done up, arranging the DJ and the booze. It was also their responsibility to act as a sort of quality control checkpoint. I mean, that's how detailed it could get. And there'd never be any shortage of women. In fact, the chicks always outnumbered the ABs. On later tours I was so much into the booze that I rarely took advantage. Given my state at those parties, even if I'd wanted to indulge, I couldn't have.'

Such antics finally came to a screaming halt once John Hart took over as the All Black coach in early 1996. There were no more dirty-dirties piss-ups, no more team-only parties, no more shag-a-thons, no more backseat challenges. At first sight, Hart's attitude appeared laudable. The All Blacks needed to be professional both on and off the field. If they were going to be portrayed as positive role models then their behaviour needed to match the expectation. But the banning caused massive resentment within the All Black camp, particularly from the party animals like Norm Hewitt.

'Everybody needs to blow off steam some time. And these were our outlets, our ways of coping. We were a bunch of young, fit men always in the public eye, and with the sort of hormones you expect fit young men to have. And, boy, it was mutual — we didn't have to impose ourselves. We also weren't children. We were old enough to make our own moral judgements. But suddenly it became like I was back at boarding school, back at Te Aute. There were new rules and regulations, and no-one was doing any explaining as to why. That was just the way John Hart wanted it.

'To start with I think he got away with it because rugby had just gone professional and we were unsure about what new demands that would bring. And also he was the new coach and you don't want to piss the coach off. Laurie Mains would play favourites with some of his selections and that was pretty well understood. Well, I considered that Hart had a preference for his Auckland boys, so if I rocked the boat or challenged him on non-rugby matters then I might not find myself selected again.

'But a real resentment grew up within the team and it accumulated over the months and years. We were men, not kids. We had a right to something of a private life. But John Hart seemed to be saying that once we were an AB, we belonged to him. At one stage he told us of a top AB getting a blowjob in an alley. He said that player would never play for the All Blacks again while he was in charge. And he didn't either.'

But that was for the future. For the moment, Norm had been on his first All Black tour — his first overseas crusade — and his eyes had been well and truly opened.

OFF THE WAGON

Norm came home to Napier to rest and recuperate over the summer months, and also to a deal with the Hawke's Bay Rugby Union that would make a mockery of the game's amateur regulations. As Norm remembers it, he was asked to meet with local businessmen Peter Roebuck and John Buck on McLean Park, and they were joined by Hawke's Bay Rugby Union chairman Tom Mulligan. He was asked directly — what would it take to keep him in Hawke's Bay for the 1994 season? Especially now that Hawke's Bay were in the second division?

'I said I had a $75,000 mortgage on my Greenmeadows house, and they said — "OK, we'll give you $25,000 a year for three years." So we shook hands on it and I received the first part of that instalment for the '94 season. $25,000 direct into my bank account.'

In fact, Norm had already decided to stick with the Magpies. He had discussed his predicament with Mains during the UK tour, and been advised to stay. A development team would tour Argentina in March/April, and that squad would include fringe All Blacks such as himself. There were also New Zealand 'A' and Maori games scheduled against international competition, so he would have plenty of opportunities to keep a high rugby profile. But sacrifices would be required.

'It was getting to the stage where I couldn't continue to work for the community trust and still play this level of rugby as well. I mean, I wasn't even a real All Black and my 1994 year was already riddled with a month away here, a couple of weeks there. And that's what made it so hard for the other players to keep jobs — there were always rugby demands on you and you couldn't do justice to both your employer and your team.'

However, the All Black Supporters Club was in the process of being established, and this allowed players to receive payment for taking part in promotional activities, which eased most of Norm's financial concerns. It was further confirmation that premier rugby was amateur in name only, providing a multiplicity of ways to evade IRB regulations.

'I had a pretty hardened attitude by this time. My view was that I deserved to be paid — that all players at that level did. We were the ones who brought in the crowds, made millions for our national bodies, provided the entertainment, and had no comeback if we got injured or didn't get selected.'

Although the attitude of the new Hawke's Bay CEO was indicative of the view of even the most modern of rugby administrators. In discussions with both Norm and with me, Wayne Smith stressed his abhorrence of player payments. By the end of the '94 season he had decided to void Hewitt's unofficial arrangement with the HBRU — a decision that would have significant repercussions for both the union and the hooker.

But those clouds were still months away. Of more immediate significance was Norm's calculated decision to get off the wagon. He had been off the booze for over a year, and he well understood the benefits that had followed that decision. He had also made a private agreement with Laurie Mains that he would not drink during the UK tour, but as the tour came to an end, so too did that commitment. And if he had no chance of supplanting Fitzpatrick as the All Black hooker, then what was the point in staying dry?

'I reasoned that I was a big boy now. I could handle the occasional drink. Everyone was getting pissed, so why not me?'

Come the Development Team's tour of Argentina, and Norm was well and truly back into his boozing ways. And he was not alone.

'It was the shittiest tour I've ever been on, and I think everyone agreed. Lin Colling had replaced Peter Thorburn on the All Black selection panel, so they gave him this tour as a reward. Whatever the reason, I didn't want to go because the New Zealand Maori team was playing in the M-Net tournament in South Africa and I preferred to be with Boom, Gordie and my Hawke's Bay mates. But I had no choice — the Maoris weren't the NZRFU's priority — Argentina was.'

The tour quickly deteriorated into a hellish grind, with the games being played on rock-hard grounds against often brutal opponents, presided over by inept home-town referees. The culture shock of midday siestas, late-night dinners and early-hours parties scrambled the players' remaining sensibilities. A firm disciplinary hand was required by the team's management, but even that was missing, and Norm's decision to drink soon found him in all the wrong places at all the wrong times.

'Colling was known as "the rugby nerd" by the players — he had all the theories but couldn't translate them — while the manager, Richard Crawshaw, was a helluva nice guy but gave us a fair bit of freedom because he got so pissed off with the Argie authorities. Their officials basically didn't give a stuff: the accommodation was dreadful, the food was bad, and the training facilities were either locked or just substandard and scungy. And when we did play it was like we were up against a team who'd just come out of some crackhouse somewhere, with blind refs and spectators egging them all on and spitting at you.'

The players soon retreated into themselves, and the court sessions under captain John Mitchell took on a riotous purpose.

'We would just get hammered. After one session we went to the official post-match function — which were always late. This one was in Buenos Aires, after the last game I think, which we'd lost. I mean we were messed up to start with, but then we did a haka to impress them during the formal part before dunking the bread rolls in red wine and biffing them around the show. Then the Argies joined in and it went from bad to worse to disaster.'

By the time he arrived back in Hawke's Bay Norm's social drinking had returned to its former levels, although it didn't noticeably affect his strength work at the gym or his general level of fitness. Similarly, it didn't encroach on his few remaining duties with the trust. But it did dull his physical and mental edge compared with the previous year, even if this was not immediately apparent on the playing field.

There were still a series of rugby priorities to motivate him — leading Hawke's Bay back into the first division was one; maintaining his place in the All Black squad another. He might not be able to supplant Fitzpatrick in the selectors' eyes but he could at least keep the skipper honest. But mostly it was about pride. He wasn't going to lie down for Fitzpatrick: the All Black captain would have to earn his status.

The two clashed early on in the 1994 season at the All Black trials in Gisborne. That Fitzpatrick still regarded Hewitt as a threat was obvious in the first few minutes of the game. After an early clash Hewitt reeled away from the melee, his nose bleeding and broken.

'Fitzy lined me and — wham. Broke my nose. It was deliberate, un-provoked and a bloody good hit. I knew the damage as soon as he hit me, and I thought what a stupid bugger I'd been for not getting my retaliation in first. I was too polite — although dishing it out to the AB captain in front of Laurie and the others wouldn't have been the smartest thing to do. I couldn't stop the nose bleeding but I refused to come off. I wasn't going to let the bastard think he'd got the better of me . . . even though he had.'

After the game Fitzpatrick mumbled something vaguely apologetic in Norm's direction, but the Hawke's Bay hooker wasn't interested.

'I just thought . . . mate, if we ever get into that situation again then next time I won't hold back. I was so pissed off. But that was Fitzy — he'd do anything to win. So I didn't have much sympathy for him when he screamed blue murder over the ear-biting incident with [Springbok prop] Johan le Roux later that year. My nose was a lot worse off than his ear.'

Ten days later and Norm was again on the wrong end of more foul play — this time while playing for New Zealand Maori in their 34-3 win over the visiting Fijians.

'I was at the bottom of a ruck and big Joe Veitayaki came flying in, boots everywhere, and almost ripped my ear off. I could feel the tear . . . this horrible slice as he rucked my head. It was the first time I ever had to be replaced in a game for an injury and I was screaming at the Zambucks to tape me up . . . let me get back on the field. But my ear was only hanging on by a piece of cartilage at the earlobe. I had to go into Christchurch hospital to have the wound cauterised and sewn up — the smell was horrible. Like pork rind crackling under a grill.'

Thirty stitches later, Norm was advised that his recovery could take months. But in a fortnight's time the New Zealand 'A' team were scheduled to play the visiting French, and he needed to prove his match fitness if he wanted to retain his reserve's spot in the All Blacks. Fortunately the doctors proved sympathetic, and they devised a specially moulded plastic cover to protect the ear.

The irony was that far from confirming Norm in the All Black squad, the earguard almost cost him his place. In the France game, played at Wanganui, he misheard two vital lineout calls, with the result that the ball was overthrown, seized by the French loosies and tries fashioned. It allowed the French to escape with the most fortuitous of wins.

'I didn't catch [captain] John Mitchell's instructions properly. My lineout throwing had always been good — it was something I practised over and over because so much of the modern game is getting set-piece possession. But I stuffed it up totally.'

After the game an incensed Mitchell bagged his hooker's performance on nationwide TV, and *Rugby News* headlined their match report 'Hewitt blew it'.

'I just wanted to find a hole to hide in. When the All Black team was later read out with "N.J. Hewitt — Hawke's Bay" in the reserves, I was so relieved. I thought I'd blown it big time. But that's what I meant before — sometimes it's harder to get out of the All Blacks than get in. This time the rule worked for me.'

CHAPTER NINE

The bench

For the entire All Black schedule of 1994 — two tests against France, a home series against the Springboks, and a Bledisloe Cup clash in Sydney — Norm was the unwilling spectator, a grim and increasingly forlorn figure on the sideline, watching each game as it was played without him. His experience of international rugby remained a frustrating sequence of practice ground, hotel room and reserves bench.

As an All Black reserve he was required to play a designated if soul-destroying role — take part in all the gut-busting practice sessions (although mostly as a surrogate opponent), mentally prepare as if he was required to play, learn the drills and lineout calls, kit up on test day, sit on the sideline, follow the game, watch the rock Fitzpatrick survive all that was thrown at him, head back to the dressing room, shower, get back into his number ones, and then trail the team to the official reception. He had become a phantom All Black — the spare part turning to rust in its blister pack.

While he might be treated as the conquering hero back in the Bay, once he was in camp he was the water boy, the training opponent, the silent and unsmiling junior.

'I hated it. You were an AB but you weren't, and even within the team you were treated as a hanger-on. And no matter if we won or we lost, you never felt a part of whatever had happened on the field. Jeff Wilson reckoned that he started to drink a bit because he was always on the reserve bench but, with due respect to Jeff, his idea of drinking was a couple of light ales. I really got stuck into the grog during that time — I was just so frustrated at doing nothing.'

For eight weeks he remained in this holding pattern, growing increasingly stale and grumpy as the team went through its international itinerary. But if his concerns were recognised by the All Black management, they were dismissed as inconsequential. Reserves were lucky to be in the squad — that was the conventional currency. Besides, there were more immediate problems to contend with, not least the noisy campaign to unseat coach Mains and replace him with John Hart before the next year's World Cup. There were also problems on the field. The team remained strangely unsettled, unable to find a playing rhythm and missing the maturity and influence of Grant Fox.

For Norm, though, things kept turning a nastier shade of brown. His relationship with Keri ended — after five years, their worlds had grown apart under both the strain of separation and their differing expectations for the future. They had been together since high school, and when Keri eventually moved out of their Greenmeadows home her absence only increased Norm's sense of isolation. She had been a reference point, a source of security that had seemingly always been there. But in typical macho style he shrugged off the effects of the break-up. Rugby was the number one priority. Everything else was a distraction.

Ironically, the only game of first-class rugby Norm was to play during that two months was when the All Black camp released him to play for Hawke's Bay against France. The tourists had grabbed a startling 22-8 first-test win at Lancaster Park and the manner of that win — and their victory in the deciding test a week later — made an indelible impression on the Bay hooker.

'Only four teams in the history of the game have taken a home series off the ABs. So you've got to be pretty special. And our '94 team wasn't as bad as the '71 All Blacks [who lost to the Lions] or as divided as the '86 Blacks [who lost to the Wallabies]. The French were seriously good — I don't think they've ever been given the credit they deserve.'

Nevertheless, with the Hawke's Bay game sandwiched in between the two internationals Norm fancied the chances of an upset, which would provide him with a measure of revenge for his humiliation at their hands in the New Zealand 'A' game.

'They put a good team on McLean Park that day — full of seasoned internationals —but it wasn't their test team and I reckoned they'd still be a bit hung over from their celebrations the previous Sunday. It was another hot, sunny afternoon — same weather as we had for the Lions — and although we started slow, we blitzed them in the second half. Gordie [Falcon] played out of his skin — all snarl and aggro — and their inside backs soon got shy. We were really buzzed up coming off the field because that meant that little old Hawke's Bay had two wins in two years over the top teams Europe could muster. No Bay Shield team could boast a record like that. And, as it turned out, neither could the All Blacks!'

But he was not allowed to enjoy the company of his team, even on that most special of nights. He was required back in Auckland — a management call that rankles to this day. When he arrived at Eden Park for training the next morning it was to find that the New Zealand selectors had dropped first-five Simon Mannix for Steve Bachop, and replaced Arran Pene with Zinzan Brooke. At least he was still in the camp, he consoled himself. Simon Mannix would never play for the All Blacks again.

'I wasn't confident about the boys winning that second test, even though everyone said we'd bolt in. The excuse was that last Sunday's test had been the traditional shocker the All Blacks always play at the start of a season. Without Michael Jones [who declared himself unavailable on religious grounds] we were always vulnerable in broken play and especially against a quick break. Laurie played Brewer on the openside and Larsen on the blind but they were no match for Cabannes and Benazzi. I don't know what dork in the NZRFU scheduled those tests for a Sunday but he lost us the series in the end.'

For much of the second test it looked as if the pre-match optimism would prove to be justified. France were barely hanging on, surviving on scraps of possession and territory. With a minute to go and at 20-16 the series looked to be levelled. And then the impossible.

'You could see that Sadourny try happening from the moment their winger [Saint-Andre] fielded Bash's [Steve Bachop's] kick in his own 22 and started running crossfield. I stood up from the bench and gawped because, I don't know, I just *sensed* something was on. The strange thing is that I reckon the guys on the field knew it too.

'Sometimes the French tap into this irresistible force, like it's an electric current or something, and it just flows through them . . . zap, zap, zap! The try that followed was just stunning . . . a genuine work of art. Every bit as good as anything you'll see at the ballet or the movies. Afterwards, we just sat around the changing shed, totally gutted, but knowing there was nothing we could have done to stop it. Well, except Bash. Now he could have found touch!'

Neither players nor public were allowed to wallow, as is the usual custom when the All Blacks suffer a defeat. The Springboks were in town and there was a test to be won at Carisbrook in six days' time. The national focus switched immediately to the 'old enemy', thereby diminishing the scale of the French feat.

'They were the best team in the world that year. Better than us, the Boks or the Wallabies . . . and I saw them all play, if only from the sideline. The Frogs had no real weakness — a huge pack with Benazzi outstanding, a rock-solid midfield in LaCroix and Sella, and gas to burn in their back three of Sadourny, N'tamack and Saint-Andre. We not only underestimated them, but Laurie made it harder by experimenting to the point of putting a very green Jonah Lomu up against them. No matter how big Jonah was, he was still a kid — just out of school — and he looked lost every time N'tamack ran at him. It wasn't his fault that he wasn't ready. And then the media mercilessly bagged him afterwards. It was bloody cruel.

'I was talking to a couple of the Frogs at the post-match, or at least doing my best to talk to them, given the language problem. They told me that the All Blacks are the ultimate test for them . . . a sort of Mt Everest, or if it was soccer then we'd be Brazil. We represent a challenge to them not just as a team but as individuals. Like they have to beat us to assert their manhood or something. Sometimes I think the black jersey means more to them than it does to some of us.'

In contrast the Springbok series turned into a dour contest, with the All Blacks narrow winners in the first two games and reliant on Shane Howarth's uncrring boot to draw the third. It was grim stuff, with both teams more desperate not to lose than determined to win. The Johan Le Roux biting incident during the second test at Athletic Park seemed to summarise the Springboks' attitude — their only tactic was to physically dominate and they would try and do so through fair means or foul.

'No-one had any sympathy for Le Roux, but then I wasn't all that choked up for Fitzy either. Fitzpatrick could put in the dirt himself when he wanted. But the Boks are gorillas — all Afrikaner aggression. Our guys had a higher skill level but sometimes that's not enough, so Zinzan Brooke's combination of cunning and mongrel was really needed. He was the major difference in my book — as tough or as subtle as the occasion demanded. I thought he took No. 8 play to a new level in that series.'

However, it was obvious to most rugby observers that the All Blacks were still in stuttering mode. The backline missed the kicking talents and general leadership of Fox, the midfield seemed slow and hesitant, and the loosies were not linking as effectively as their potential promised. In particular, the team lacked a loose forward who could get to the breakdown quickly and secure possession.

While all these deficiencies, real or imagined, dominated the sports media and the talkback shows for months, the Mains/Hart divide continued to run down the middle of the country like a mountain chain. With the World Cup less than a year away, Mains was accused of a pathological dislike of all things Auckland and a lack of tactical flexibility, while his relationship with some journalists plunged from terrible to toxic. When John Kirwan was dropped for the final international of the year against Australia, to be replaced by Otago *wunderkind* Jeff Wilson, the veteran winger lashed out. Mains, he declared, had lost the plot. A good measure of the country agreed.

However, Norm had reached a wholly different judgement.

'The thing about Laurie was that he was honest. Honest with the players, honest with the team. And the reason players appreciate a coach who's straight up is because so few of them actually are. Too many coaches criticise players indirectly, either ignoring them or talking behind their back. Or they'll drop a player without ever telling him why. Mains might have been a piss poor media communicator but the team and the players always knew where they were with him.

'In addition, he was a brilliant technical coach — the best I've played under in fourteen seasons of first-class rugby. When it came to getting something right in the scrum, or getting the lineout spot-on, or explaining the defensive lines . . . the guy was always thinking, always talking things over with the players. That was the main point of difference between him and Hart. Mains actually wanted to improve your game as much as you did.'

But by half-time at Sydney, with the All Blacks down 6-17 in the last test of the year and playing poorly, it appeared Mains would soon be out of a job. The atmosphere in the changing room at half-time was grim.

'The thing is that no-one panicked. Sure, Laurie was animated, and he made a point of listing what was required. Fitzy gave everyone a bit of a rark-up and the tactics were spelled out — "Let's cut loose. There's nothing to be gained from playing defensively." So it wasn't the big change in playing style that the media would later claim. It had always been Laurie's strategy to play a fast game — it was just that it took until the second half for the players to relax a bit, I guess because we were so far behind. Sometimes you play better when there's nothing to lose. And so, that second half, it just clicked. And gave everyone the confidence to know that the team was on the right track. These were the tactics and this was the style of game to take to Africa.'

The forwards laid a platform, the backs ran freely, and the loosies, with a recalled Michael Jones prominent, were the hyperactive link. The pace of the game quickened appreciably and with twenty minutes to go the All

Blacks had reduced the gap to one point. Better still, the Australian forwards were getting slower with every breath, and their cover defence thinner. It was just a matter of time. After a couple of near misses, the opportunity to seal the match finally came. Jeff Wilson found himself in the open, threaded his way through tiring defenders and dived for the winning score. And then out of nowhere, a bolt of gold under the floodlights, Wallaby halfback George Gregan. The resultant tackle jolted the ball from Wilson's grasp, as despair and euphoria flooded the rival camps in roughly equal proportions.

'In the dressing rooms afterwards, Jeff started bawling again and I was sitting there, all staunch and embarrassed-like, thinking, "Get a bloody grip." That's what I thought at the time — "Jeff Wilson: cry baby." Jeez, I'd never do anything like that. Never. Couldn't believe the fuss he was making.'

Despite the loss, the All Blacks' second-half heroics choked off the worst of the critics' vitriol. There would be further moves to unseat Mains — official and unofficial — but the players were having none of it. They had come to enjoy Mains' honesty, and they appreciated the strategy required for the next year's World Cup. From Sean Fitzpatrick down the message from the All Black team was consistent and clear. Leave Mains where he is.

'BYE TO THE BAY

A couple of days after the Bledisloe Cup test Norm was back playing for Hawke's Bay in a second division match against Manawatu at a gusty and overcast Palmerston North Showgrounds. He didn't care that the grandstand was near deserted, or that the game would be ignored by nearly everyone except a few earnest scribes. He was back on the field playing the game he loved. Enjoying the contest in the front row, the battle in the lineout, the scramble for possession at maul time. Getting his hands on the ball. Running with purpose against a real team and with another real team in support. By the end of eighty minutes he was blowing hard from the exertion but it didn't matter a damn. He felt good. This was rugby.

'We had a good team in '94 — one of the best I think Hawke's Bay's ever had. John Phillips wasn't much of a coach — a rip-shit-and-bust type — but it didn't matter. Jarrod Cunningham was at his peak at fullback — Orcades [Crawford], Gordie, John Bradbrook, Aaron Hamilton, George Konia — they were fit and hard and playing well. It was a bloody good unit and we played open, winning rugby and we enjoyed each other's company off the field too.'

The wins came easily — a record 65-18 semi-final victory over Bay of Plenty indicating the gulf between the Magpies and the rest of the NPC second division. There was no doubt that they would win the divisional final and gain reinstatement to the big time, and the Hawke's Bay Rugby Union were rumoured to be in the process of recruiting All Black Robin Brooke and other leading players for the next year's season. Their last opponents would be Southland at Invercargill — thrashed 43-10 the previous month and barely rated by their own locals, let alone the Bay's supporters.

'Right from the first day down there, the attitude of our guys was bad. Everyone expected us to win and that feeling affected the whole team. We believed our own publicity — classic pride-before-the-fall stuff. And their locals were amazingly good to us. Too bloody good. There was a helluva lot of free booze dished out and some ultra-friendly girls kept hanging around until someone bedded them. Kept a couple of our boys at it the whole night — the night before the game, I might add.'

The team woke to a bleak winter's day, icy showers racing horizontal down the middle of Rugby Park, and a partisan crowd screaming for their balls. Led by the outstanding Henderson brothers, the Southland pack ripped into their much-vaunted opponents from the first moment, while the Bay team were still working out if they would survive the inevitable hypothermia. Southland's tiny first-five Simon Culhane began kicking penalty goals with metronomic efficiency and the score began to mount. With growing frustration Norm realised there was nothing he could do to get his team out of first gear — at times it seemed as if only he and a couple of others were hitting the rucks and mauls with any regularity.

'We hadn't had a hard game all season, and if we were ever under pressure then there'd always be someone to do something brilliant and restore the momentum. Over the past couple of seasons we'd beaten the Lions, the French, scored a record five tries against Auckland, smashed all the other teams in the second division . . . but we just didn't have it that day. Mentally we couldn't beat underdogs who kept fighting. We choked real bad.'

In the end the gap was just two points, but the 18-20 loss plunged the whole Hawke's Bay rugby fraternity into shock.

Worse was to follow on Norm's return to the Bay. Chief executive Wayne Smith announced that he was suspending all player payments for the next season. Hawke's Bay players would have to play for the love of the game — all other arrangements were void. Norm asked his lawyer Steve Lunn to intercede but Smith was adamant.

'According to a couple of the Hawke's Bay board, I was the greedy Maori boy, always with his hand out. When Steve reported back what had been said, that confirmed the vibes I'd been picking up all year. I could have stayed in Hawke's Bay — the '95 World Cup was going to be played in May and June of the next year and there would be no first division rugby before then. But my reaction was instinctive. OK, sport — you don't want me? You want to break our contract? Fine: I'll never play for you bastards again.'

Not only was Norm incensed at the breaking of his agreement with the Hawke's Bay union, but he was annoyed at the administrators' attitude that players were not entitled to any financial return for their efforts. They were required to train and play as professional sportsmen, sacrifice career opportunities, and fulfil any number of union sponsor commitments. But be paid for their efforts?

'When the Murdoch deal finally came I welcomed it because it brought all those administrators kicking and screaming into the real world. They hated it but they had no option. The fish-heads were still living in this old-fashioned belief that they could use the players as chattels, ride on our backs all around the country and around the world, make money out of us and our efforts, but not return a dividend to the players who created that entertainment.

'There was this attitude — "We own you: you do what we say." That was the line Smith and the others took with me in Hawke's Bay, this bullshit appeal to loyalty, while Smith gets the nice CEO salary package and the others had walked away from me when I needed them. There was no way I was going to take that kind of bullshit any more.'

Norm called the newly promoted Southland Rugby Union and asked if some of the booze talk he'd heard the night of the final was true. Were they really interested in him playing for them? Their answer was an offer of $30,000 cash and a promotional job with the Gore Licensing Trust if he played eight NPC games for them the next season.

'I started rolling my "r"s.'

CHAPTER TEN

World Cup

Reaction within the Bay to their star player's defection was sharp and negative. Norm was a turncoat and a traitor — words that he would hear almost every time he walked into a hotel bar or down Napier's main street. If he turned, ready to confront the accuser, the name-caller would scuttle away, leaving the sting to linger. Even in the rugby circles where previously he had been lionised, he was now portrayed exactly as his lawyer had reported — as the greedy Maori boy who ratted on his mates.

Half-hearted efforts were made to persuade him to stay. Coach John Phillips approached me as the local MP and asked me to intercede on behalf of the union. Employment had been found for Norm, he said, at the same dollar sum as the previous year's unofficial arrangement. When pressed for further details, Phillips revealed that the job was selling advertising for Radio Pacific. On commission. He was shown the door.

Over the off-season Norm worked out the remaining weeks of his contract with the community work trust, trained hard, and trusted in Laurie Mains' advice that if he stayed off the booze he would be in the World Cup squad to go to South Africa. His fondness for a drink — for drinking to excess — was still recognised as an issue that required attention. There was no question about his ability on the practice ground or the playing field, but uncomplimentary reports about the hooker's behaviour continued to percolate through to the game's administrators — now given an extra twist by those in the Bay who had previously turned a blind eye.

'I started to resent all the attention that was paid to my drinking, so I'd get into the occasional sly grog. Well, I thought it was sly, but then I'd get written off and someone would spot me and pot me to Laurie or Earle [Kirton] or someone. My problem was that once I started drinking, I didn't have an "off" button. I didn't think of myself as an alcoholic because I didn't wake up each day with the thirst and need another fix. But if I was in a social situation with the boys — getting on the turps —there was no stopping me until I got completely wasted. I was the classic binge drinker.'

And then, unexpectedly, Norm found himself distracted from both rugby and the booze. For the first time in his life, he fell in love.

Despite his All Black status and a past that had at times hovered on the border of criminal, Norm still lacked confidence in many social situations. His relationship with the opposite sex had been characterised by an overwhelming shyness. He might have travelled the world, played in the famous black jersey, been feted by politicians and the media, recovered and resolved any number of employee situations at the trust, but in the company of a pretty girl he remained as tongue-tied and nervous as a schoolboy. He may well be a 110-kg, fire-breathing monster on the rugby field — and at any number of late-night parties — but beyond rugby his emotions remained stunted and immature.

'My priorities had always been rugby, training and drinking, and if you'd asked me what an emotion was I would have told you that it was a weakness. I could do anger, and maybe I could do pride, but that was about it. It might have been that I was insecure because I wasn't one of the pretty boys, but I wasn't brilliant at one-to-one communication either. And then there was the usual young male fear of rejection . . . sometimes I think I'm still like that. Still unsure of myself and how I should be handling a certain situation in public or in private.'

But his insecurities were shunted to one side when Norm met Katherine at the Napier physiotherapy practice run by All Black physio Gary Sye. She was the part-time receptionist — attractive, friendly, the daughter of a TV journalist, and not in the least awed by their client's reputation. As an almost habitual attender of the practice, Norm began to time his appointments for when Kat, as she was known, would be working, never stopping to think why she might work only in the late afternoons or at weekends.

'Eventually I asked her out to some rugby club function. Got all sweaty-palmed about it and had to run through all the words in my mind. It must have worked out OK because she said "yes" — I almost melted to the floor in relief.'

It was then he learned that she was still a senior student at Colenso High School, a couple of months off her seventeenth birthday. He shrugged his shoulders. It was one date: who could it hurt? But they hit it off immediately, and soon there was a second, and then a third. Before long they were a much-discussed gossip item in Hawke's Bay — the All Black and the schoolgirl. Those who had met Kat generally agreed that, emotionally at least, the two seemed of the same age — Kat far more mature than her years, Norm the reverse.

Graeme Taylor and his wife Wendy had stayed in touch with Norm despite Taylor's sacking from the Hawke's Bay job, the earlier coolness between the two men easing over time. Certainly they were interested to meet the lady in question.

'It was a bit of a mini-scandal,' recalls Wendy. 'Especially when Kat would arrive at school driving the V8 Falcon that Norm had been allocated by the All Black sponsors. That put a few noses out of joint. But then as soon as you met them both, saw them together, you relaxed. They were obviously a couple, and Kat was a smart, assertive young lady. It wasn't an issue for most people, although the big black Ford in the Colenso student parking lot drew a few tut-tuts.'

For some, though, the affair with the schoolgirl provided further support for the view that the Bay was well shot of its All Black hooker. The feeling was mutual. The only regret Norm now harboured about transferring to Southland was that Kat would not be with him.

But rugby remained his premier mistress. The game was more than just a priority — despite Kat, it was his life, and he was soon off on another overseas tour, this time with the New Zealand Divisional Team to Canada and Fiji. The team had been selected from the previous season's second and third division sides and included his good mate Gordon Falcon, although the two fell out on the return leg.

One night Norm confessed that he had been unofficially paid by the Hawke's Bay Rugby Union for his services, despite earlier telling Falcon that he had not. The flanker had considered approaching the union for a playing fee but had checked with his mate first. In the contest between confidentiality and friendship, the union had unaccountably won. Falcon took this revelation poorly.

'There was a bit of truth to the rumours — I was a bit of a "user", and when it came to money I wanted my fair share. But lying to Gordy over it was a low act and I wasn't proud of myself. We didn't talk for quite a while after that. I went down to Southland and Gordy went over to Australia for an NRL league contract. It wasn't until much later that we resumed our friendship and he forgave me for misleading him. To lie to one of my best mates was pretty gutless.'

The divisional team played games in both Canada and Fiji before returning home to play a couple of trials against potential World Cup hopefuls. The latter games were crucial if Norm was to stake his claim to one of the hooking slots now that young hookers Slade McFarland and Matt Sexton had caught the public eye.

'I was desperate to get to South Africa, but I'd trod water for much of 1994 and then played second division rugby when the other two had good profiles with North Harbour and Canterbury. So there was this niggle in the back of my brain whether I'd make it. The trial against the President's XV was a couple of days after we got back from Fiji and most of the President's team were first division players so we weren't expected to win. But we'd built up a good combination on tour and we had a real underdog or mongrel mentality. That gave us an added incentive.'

The resultant 71-22 massacre destroyed some of their opponents' reputations, but it relieved any doubts about Norm's fitness and form. A few weeks later, though, and it was his turn to be on the end of a hiding — this time from the shadow All Black team in the only official trial of the year, held at Whangarei. The Probables team was essentially composed of the same All Blacks who had thrashed Canada 73-7 a week earlier.

'We were set up to lose. They kept changing our combinations right up until the game, and then during the game itself. It was frustrating because the selectors had obviously already decided on their top combination and weren't prepared to give the fringe players a real crack. It wasn't so much a trial as an exhibition — a bit like the Harlem Globetrotters playing their donkey team. The donkeys have to lose. That's the deal.'

The reverse deal seemed to be that most of the defeated Possibles would make up the balance of the World Cup touring party, and any disappointment was quickly erased as the squad was publicly confirmed. Better still, Laurie Mains had assured all the players that they would get at least one World Cup game — for reasons of both fitness and morale every player would have their chance to take the field in a true international match. If they survived the training.

Mains was determined that the All Black squad would be the fittest at the World Cup and that every player on the field would still be running at the 80-minute mark. The high-energy, high-skill game plan required superior levels of aerobic fitness plus a level of concentration that would not flag as fatigue set in. For that reason Mains determined on a new series of tortuous training exercises, including the feared 150-metre sprints and brutal drills which saw forwards and backs running at each other at full speed. Norm would often find himself kitted up in a tackle bag as the shadow All Black pack charged into him and the other defenders. Mains wanted the ferocity of these drills to match the likely physicality of the coming internationals, and Norm soon discovered that he needed to give as good as he got if he was to survive the sessions.

He remained determined not to be broken by the training regime. Between weight drills, the 150 sprints, the three-kilometre runs and the various drills at practice Norm feared that he must eventually falter. But each time he fleetingly considered quitting or feigning an injury he reminded himself that Mains was looking for mental toughness as well as physical ability. If he showed any weakness he could kiss South Africa goodbye. And there was no way he would concede his World Cup dream, no matter how sadistic he considered the coach's motivations.

'We'd have all the aerobic and anaerobic drills, but the thing I hated most — apart from the sprint 150s — everybody hated them — was the "ruck-and-runs". You'd have a ruck machine on either side of the paddock and you'd rush over to one, crunch it, free the ball and then sprint over to the other one with Laurie barking at you all the time. And he'd never let up until you either spewed or were that close you wanted to. Some of the guys didn't make it — Mark Cooksley was one, Jonah Lomu another. And no bloody wonder. It was murder.'

SOUTH AFRICA

The World Cup was Norm's first time in the Republic, and despite the previous year's home series against the Springboks, nothing had prepared him for South Africa itself. The New Zealanders were met at Johannesburg airport by an array of armed, uniformed men who escorted them to their luxury coach and then accompanied them in an armed convoy to their upmarket hotel. There was an edge to the place, Norm observed, as if something nasty was seething behind the welcoming smiles. He was well aware that this was a nation in transition, taking its first tentative steps from apartheid to democracy under the inspirational Nelson Mandela, but there was something more — a palpable unease, a wariness that stretched the nerves. Maybe it was his conversation with Bull Allen and a few of the others about Jo'burg being the murder capital of Africa, or maybe it was the tales of violence and crime he'd heard from rugby folk who had toured three years earlier with the All Blacks — but there was definitely something.

'I told myself that I was being silly — that I was in a foreign country so I was bound to feel a bit funny. But the guns and the uniforms and the beggars on the streets . . . it sure didn't look like any country that I knew. And then there were the white Bok supporters . . . they were something else again. When you meet some of them you just know how apartheid got started.'

All Blacks — indeed, any rugby team from New Zealand — develop a special loathing for the white South African rugby supporter. In Johannesburg and Pretoria, rugby is a symbol of the Afrikaner's identity, a reference point as to their culture and identity. It's a game that allows them to assert their strength, their courage and their defiance to an often querulous outside world — a game that encapsulates their belligerence and their fierce pride.

'If you think Canterbury supporters are one-eyed or the Otago scarfies are fanatics, then you've seen nothing until you've seen the Afrikaner rugby crowd. They're fanatical to the point of irrationality. You look up at their faces and they're all screwed up with hatred, screaming at you like you've had it off with their sisters or something. They can be an ugly people, and despite the amazing hospitality you get from some of them, you always breathe a sigh of relief when you fly out of there.'

Fortunately, the diverse structure of the World Cup, and the fact that the Springboks were on the other side of the draw, tended to draw some of the fire away from the All Blacks. That would be reserved for the following year when the All Blacks would do the unthinkable and win a home series against the World Cup champions. For now, South African expectations were reasonably low — they had lost a series to the Wallabies the previous year and now the Australians were the more immediate foe, with the two teams drawn to meet in the Cup's opening match.

'We were actually a bit lucky really because we had a great draw — Ireland, Wales and Japan in our pool, and then Scotland and England in the quarters and semis. South Africa had to play Australia and beat France in their semi to get into the final, so that was the harder route. None of the Brit teams were particularly tough. Sure they'd go mad for fifty minutes, but our superior fitness always found them out. All Laurie's preparation really paid off. Although England had a pretty useful team — bloody good forwards, but their back division were dreary and the Underwood brothers and Mike Catt were their back three, so they were defensively vulnerable.'

In the meantime the All Blacks needed to concentrate on building their own combinations and ensuring that their key No. 8, Zinzan Brooke, was nursed back to full fitness. Unfortunately, he was not able to achieve the

Left: *Stormin' Norman.*
Turbo-charged teetotaller
Norm veers inwards to do some
damage to Lions winger Tony
Underwood. Critics described his
game against the Lions as the
most complete performance by a
hooker in the 1993 season.
Hawke's Bay won 29-17 after
trailing 5-17 at half time.

Below: *And the reward . . .*
Norm on his All Black debut
against Midlands during the
1993 All Blacks tour of the UK.

A study in contrast: dejection as Hawke's Bay succumb to Southland in the 1994 NPC Division 2 final; and delight at securing the division's 'player of the year' award in 1996 playing for . . . Southland.

Dirt-trackers' day out. The All Blacks have just thrashed Japan 145-17 at the 1995 World Cup in the mismatch of the century. Marc Ellis celebrates scoring six tries and Norm his starting international debut for the All Blacks . . .

Relaxing in the South African sunshine ahead of the World Cup final. Kevin Schuler, Norm, Josh Kronfeld and manager Colin Meads.

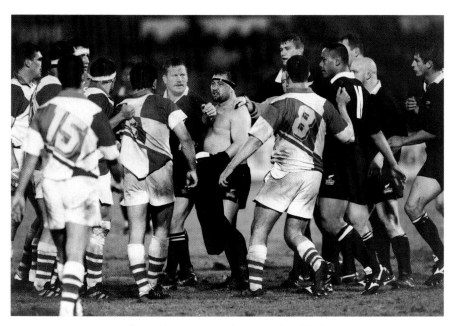

*Dirty bastards. Norm confronts the head kickers —
All Blacks v Côte de Basque at Bayonne.*

*The brown brothers — Eric Rush, Frank Bunce, Jonah Lomu and Norm in France 1995.
Acutely aware that this was their last amateur tour.*

Above: *Laurie Mains. In Norm's opinion, not only the best but the toughest coach he played under. Ian Jones, Sean Fitzpatrick and Robin Brooke trudge back after one of Mains' dreaded '150s'.*

Below: *Norm leading the midweekers' haka against the French Barbarians at Toulon. Note the numbers of non-paying spectators in the apartment blocks surrounding the ground. Note also the Steinlager labels that have been covered over on all but Norm's jersey — courtesy of a sponsors' scrap. Norm refused to defile the jersey.*

standards he'd set the previous year, and the general fragility of the All Black loose forwards was masked by the outstanding play of the young Otago flier Josh Kronfeld.

But the talk of the All Blacks — of the entire World Cup for that matter — was the return of Jonah Lomu, no longer a bewildered schoolboy watching French jerseys fly by, but a young behemoth of staggering strength and speed. His size would have commanded awe anyway — the heaviest All Black ever to take the rugby field. But it was his speed off the mark and his sizzling pace that confused the critics. A genuine freak of nature and, thank God, wearing a black jersey.

'When Jonah's switched on he's awesome, and even us cynical types just stood and gawped whenever he took off on one of his runs at the Cup. It wasn't just his power and his ability to bump off tacklers, but his speed. I mean you're not used to seeing guys that huge run that fast and have such great balance. And at no time did he get big-headed about it. He knew how to handle himself from a team perspective. I mean if he'd had Mike Brewer or Jeff Wilson's personality the guy would have been unbearable. But he seemed confused and shy of all the fuss, and it's that humility I've always liked about him. He's a real humble guy to this day.'

In the opening two pool games, against Ireland and Wales, Lomu's spectacular running tended to distract attention from some of the problems the All Blacks were having during the forward encounters. The Irish in particular were a real contest, the 43-19 scoreline not doing their efforts justice. From the sideline Norm watched as Lomu almost single-handedly ended the Irish challenge.

And then another miracle occurred.

'I saw Fitzy with blood pissing out of his head and I almost didn't take it in. It wasn't until [Martin Toomey] shouted to me that I lost the tracksuit top and raced on. I couldn't believe it . . . I was suddenly in the middle of a test and packing down in a scrum with Olo Brown on one side, Craig Dowd on the other and getting twisted from the pressure. And then the ref pointed to me and I was wandering off again. Fitzy had had the wound bandaged and I was back on the sideline with barely a sweat raised. Instead of going "Yahoo — I'm a real All Black," I just felt bloody stupid. Go on, run around for a couple of minutes, go off. Jeez, it felt weird.'

But the promised game was just around the corner — the Japan match was to be the dirt-trackers' day out. In retrospect, the poor Japanese never had a chance; they could not possibly have faced a more motivated All Black team. As the scoreline proved — a record 145-17 thrashing that is unlikely ever to be matched at World Cup level.

'The boys were just so keyed up — the whole lot of us. This was it. This was probably going to be our only game of the tournament and we knew it. We hadn't played a game in six weeks so there was a bit of nervousness about whether we'd have the combinations or the finesse.'

In total the All Blacks scored 21 tries in a massacre that displayed the vast chasm between a top class team and the also-rans at the Cup. Marc Ellis scored six to set a World Cup record, but then almost every minute of the game produced a new one — the highest half-time score (84-3), the greatest number of team tries, a record individual points total to Simon Culhane of a try and twenty conversions. And at no stage did the All Blacks let up — their brutal efficiency sending a cringe through even the usually one-eyed Kiwi supporters.

But Norm didn't care and neither did his team-mates. This was their one moment and they were determined to wring everything they could from it. For players like Eric Rush, Alama Ieremia, Simon Culhane, Ant Strachan, Paul Henderson, Kevin Schuler and Richard Loe, this was their one international of the Cup. For the Brooke brothers, Zinzan and Robin, it was a chance to prove their fitness ahead of the play-offs.

'Looking back you realise that a game like that is no good for rugby. The World Cup should be a bit like the NPC — divided into, say, two divisions of ten teams where like plays like. Maybe it's me, but I fail to see the pleasure in pasting teams like Japan or Portugal or Spain at World Cups. Although that night I didn't care and neither did anyone else. I was now a bona fide All Black and that was all I cared about. And did we get pissed that night. The boys really let their hair down.'

But, again, Norm drank to excess — to the point where he couldn't remember much past midnight. The next morning he was shaken awake by team boss Brian Lochore and told he was holding up the team bus. A trip to a safari park had been scheduled, the All Blacks' military escort shadowing their every step. Norm enjoyed the experience, even if he was still a little groggy from the night before, but when he got back to the hotel Lochore and manager Colin Meads bailed him up. He was accused of breaking his non-drinking arrangement with Laurie Mains, and of trying to break into the team room in the middle of the night.

'I denied doing the damage to the team room, but in the back of my mind I vaguely remembered something. But Brian and Colin were more concerned about me dishonouring my deal with them and Laurie. I put up the lame defence that it was traditional for a new All Black to get pissed after playing their first test but they weren't having any of it. I was made to feel pretty stink about it all and I didn't drink again until the night of the World Cup final. And on that night everyone got wasted.'

Nevertheless, a justification for his behaviour wormed its way into the hooker's thinking. He'd seen other All Blacks get considerably drunker and do considerably more damage in his time as a tourist. He particularly remembered an incident involving Zinzan Brooke, where the No. 8 had been excused a drunken act of vandalism. And so his resentment at being singled out grew. It became an inner core of bitterness, and his later drinking would take on an ugly defiance. Stuff Meads and Mains. Stuff the All Black management. Stuff them all. If he was going to drink, then he was going to drink. Fuck them.

Meanwhile, the rest of the World Cup was running to plan. After a comfortable victory over Scotland in the quarters, the much-anticipated clash with England raised the temperature. The hated Poms and their baying press considered they had a real chance after their last-minute win against the reigning champions Australia in the quarters. But by half-time it was all over. 25-3 to the All Blacks, two Jonah Lomu tries and Andrew Mehrtens kicking like a dream. The second half began much as the first half had ended — Lomu in space, Lomu scores. Then the underrated Graeme Bachop went over before England replied with a brace of their own. Final score 45-29, and all anyone could talk about was Jonah Lomu, his four tries, and his literal steamrolling of English fullback Mike Catt.

'There was an even more phenomenal response to Jonah after that. I mean it had been huge beforehand but now it was like . . . bigger than the World Cup itself. I don't think New Zealanders really appreciate just how the rest of the world sees the guy. And after we'd dished it out to the Poms it was as if they had to find an excuse, any excuse, to say why they'd got so badly beaten. So they settled on Jonah. He was the only reason. And maybe there was a bit of truth in that. Maybe we all came to rely, even if subconsciously, on thinking that if we got the ball to Jonah then he could finish it off.

'And yet we were also the best team there. Everyone knew and acknowledged that — apart from idiots like [South African rugby head] Louis Luyt at the awards ceremony later. I mean the guy was just your typical ignorant Afrikaner boofhead. Some people accuse the ABs of hating to lose — of taking a loss badly — and they're right. We do. But the South Africans don't know how to win. They rub it in. They want it to hurt, they want to grind their heel into your face. And Luyt was their man all right. He twisted the knife big time.'

But the humiliation and the All Black walk-out at the awards ceremony were yet to come. The final was in prospect and the All Blacks were supremely confident that they had the measure of the home team. The Boks were lucky to be in the final, helped by some dubious refereeing against France in the semis, and having little to offer except a fanatical defence and the boot of their first-five Joel Stransky.

'They were ours — we knew they were ours.'

And then the infamous food poisoning.

'It was all getting very tense and Laurie and the management were all getting a bit paranoid in my view. Over the top stuff like sweeping the team room for bugs — that sort of thing. Meanwhile the armed guards, who'd been with us throughout the Cup, seemed to get extra edgy as if they were expecting trouble or something. It was a weird atmosphere. Here we were ready to play the biggest game of our lives and there's all this weird shit happening all around us. It got real tight, real tense.

'Anyway, we go off to training — on the Thursday morning — and Laurie concentrates on the calls, on getting the drills right, on making sure everyone knows where they've got to be on the field and when. Perfection stuff. There was a lunch after the training, I remember it as being right after the training, and there were burgers on offer — chicken, I think, and beef. I looked at the chicken and ate one, didn't like the taste, had the beef. In the end I ate four of the burgers and had everything else the others had, including the tea.

'I remember Ian Jones spewing up in the car that afternoon but I didn't think much of it until I got back to the hotel and had a few stomach cramps and then the screaming shits. I thought it was a touch of food poisoning then and there, but I was a hostel boy and I reckon our constitutions were a bit tougher than some of the other delicate flowers. Anyway, when I woke up the next morning half the team seemed to be affected, including Colin Meads and Doc Mayhew. It definitely affected the team, and some of them played and shouldn't have. Jeff Wilson, for a start. I mean he was a key player, sure, but you don't put players on the field who aren't a hundred percent. So, in some ways, the selections made it worse. The ill guys should have been spelled — the reserves and the dirt-trackers could easily have taken their places. It was really a vote of no confidence in the guys outside Laurie's playing XV. Maybe we actually made the effects [of the food poisoning] worse than they were.'

Norm doesn't buy the deliberate sabotage argument since proffered by Mains and others. Yes, there were desperate bookmakers, and even more desperate nationalists, who would have suffered financial and personal embarrassment had the All Blacks won the World Cup. But the random nature of the poisoning wouldn't have guaranteed a loss. Especially if the

All Black management had been prepared to think laterally and, say, put Marc Ellis on for Wilson, Kevin Schuler for Zinzan Brooke.

'It was the chicken, I'm sure of it. It could have been campylobacter or something — I've had that and it can sure knock you around. But it didn't affect the whole team — it didn't affect Jonah, and he was the main man — and it affected each person differently or not at all. It was just one of those things. And the selectors made it worse by not adapting quick enough — by not fielding, literally, our strongest fifteen of the moment.'

Norm also believes some of the players allowed themselves to be overawed by the occasion.

'The Boks are great psych boys. They use every advantage they can, and Mandela arriving in Francois Pienaar's jersey sent them into a real frenzy. So they kept knocking us down while their blood was up and we didn't vary our tactics enough. By midway through the second half we were in a lottery because we weren't smart enough on the field to try something new. Fitzy may have been a great hooker but there were times when you could rattle him. And his captaincy that day was not all it could've been.'

Otago loosie Jamie Joseph replaced Mike Brewer on the blindside just before half-time, and he found the on-field attitude of some of his team-mates equally perplexing.

'Everyone looked so lethargic, especially the forwards. We weren't hitting the rucks with our usual zing and it was as if the guys had just switched off. I hadn't been affected by the food poisoning so I didn't really appreciate what effect it might have had. But the boys seemed really flat. It was such a frustrating game to play in because I knew we were better than that.'

On the sideline, Norm was watching the game revert to a duel between the rival kickers Joel Stransky and Andrew Mehrtens, with the momentum gradually swinging towards the Boks. Although it's the conventional wisdom that the game was lost through a combination of food poisoning and some wayward Mehrtens drop-kicking in the final minutes, Norm concedes that the better team on the day won. The Bok forwards created the opportunities for Stransky to complete the hosts' fairytale.

Nevertheless, the overtime loss, by 15 points to 12, devastated the entire All Black squad. Whether they were players or reserves, dirt-trackers or officials, it was an intensely personal disaster for each of them. The euphoria of their hosts, and Luyt's boasting at the dinner that evening, only amplified their despair.

'At the time I thought nothing could ever be this bad. That whatever came after this, this would always be the lowest point in my life. It felt that bad for me and I didn't even play. I know for some of the others — Fitzy and Zinzan in particular — it gave them the spur all through the off-season to go back to South Africa the next year and beat the Boks. For others like Josh Kronfeld it was a shrug of the shoulders and on to the next thing. But for me, it was like . . . shit, we've lost . . . where do I go from here? And I wasn't even on the field.

'It was like a double frustration because I was part of the general disappointment but I hadn't had the chance to do anything myself. So I went out and got totally written off. Although this time so did most of the other boys. I sure had company that night. And the next day.'

There were three days before the All Black squad left South Africa, and for a good part of that time Norm wallowed within a blur of booze. Most of the World Cup squad unwound in a succession of team parties that dulled the pain of their finals loss and, despite their depression, bound them closer together. Outside their Johannesburg hotel South Africa was still in a mood of celebration, and the William Webb Ellis trophy was paraded as a talisman of the rainbow nation's future under Nelson Mandela. Even in New Zealand there were those who were prepared to concede that the Boks' win may unite a country previously divided by the code and was therefore in rugby's best interests.

But within the All Black camp no such rationalisation was possible. They had been the form team and they had somehow conspired to lose a contest that had been theirs for the taking. Forget the expectations of the All Black supporters who had travelled with them or the disappointed fans at home — the team had let itself down. And regardless of the nature of their defeat — in extra time and against a background of food poisoning — the players were shattered that all their previous sacrifice had been for nothing. They retreated into themselves, seeking solace with the only others who might understand.

'The party began on the night of the [finals] dinner and didn't let up from there. Luyt's gloating gave us the perfect excuse to vamoose and the court session the next morning was a giant piss-up. Everyone attended and I think just about everyone got hammered — Laurie, Colin, the med team — everyone. We played a whole variety of drinking games and at one stage I thought I'd killed Ant Strachan. We were playing a game where you basically hit the guy next to you once you've finished sculling . . . and I mean "hit". It wasn't a gentle game. Anyway, I finished my beer and slammed Ant in the chest — right over the heart. He just collapsed and his head hit one of the tables on the way down. As he lay there groaning I thought, "Oh, no . . . what have I done?" That sure sobered me up in a hurry.'

As the team prepared to pack up and head for home Norm's brain was still active enough to see a market opportunity when it strayed across his path. The players were chucking out most of their training gear in preparation for the flight home. Their bags were already overweight with rugby mementoes and gifts for families and friends, and the training kit and other rugby gear was being jettisoned to make room. An entrepreneurial light went off in Norm's brain.

'In the wake of the Cup win — and all during the Cup actually — the Bok supporters were going crazy for anything that had "All Black" on it. They kept hanging around the hotel begging for the slightest thing — a singlet or a sock — anything remotely associated with the ABs. So I just did the simple correlation — supply . . . demand: rugby gear . . . fanatic collectors.'

He made a financial killing from procuring the surplus All Black kit and on-selling it to South Africans. Mostly he worked on commission for other players, but when he arrived home at Auckland International Airport he wasn't sure if he should declare the excess South African rand in his luggage or simply keep walking. He took the latter option.

'I thought, "Norm, mate, you're still the shop boy," and I was pretty damned pleased with myself. But then the whole rugby rebel stuff really took off, and my rand seemed pretty pathetic against the big American bucks being talked. But at least it did allow me to buy a better class of Christmas present that year!'

MONEY

While the All Blacks were coming to terms with the loss of the World Cup, outside a fight to the death was going on for control of the game itself. In one quarter, the arthritic establishment sought to retain its hold over the game's fabled amateurism, while against them an unusual alliance of rugby revolutionaries and businessmen was equally determined to drag the game, kicking and screaming, into the commercial world.

The history of this battle has been well chronicled. Under threat from the Kerry Packer-financed World Rugby Corporation (WRC), the South African, New Zealand and Australian unions (SANZAR) signed a deal with rival media tycoon Rupert Murdoch. In return for a decade of television rights, Murdoch's News Corporation would inject US$520 million into the game — an astonishing amount of money that took the breath from officials and commentators alike. It was the deal that made rugby professional, although many of the game's administrators still had difficulty reconciling that fact.

But the contest for the code's top players continued, with the WRC beginning the wooing with talk of $750,000 base salaries and a $100,000 signing-on fee.

'It was huge money, and I think the gut reaction of most of us was, like . . . "Where do we sign?" Although the first decision we made was that whichever way we jumped, we'd all go together.'

Norm was still very much a junior in the All Black set-up and was content to leave the negotiations to senior players like Sean Fitzpatrick, Mike Brewer and Zinzan Brooke. He also saw coach Laurie Mains as a fan of the new venture, while Colin Meads' silence was interpreted as assent. Had Mains and Meads been hostile to the WRC, then Norm believes the team may have reconsidered its welcome of the rebels' representatives.

'Laurie and Colin understood where we were coming from — that if we were going to train and play as professionals, then we deserved to be paid as such. They both got some stick later from the NZRFU, but their loyalty was to the boys and that probably brought us even closer as a unit.'

However, Norm was also aware that signing with the WRC might end his All Black career. On the other hand, if he stayed with the NZRFU — and Fitzpatrick went — he would then be the number one hooker and automatically succeed to the new All Black front row.

'I knew I could get real cunning if I wanted to. But my first loyalty was to the guys and not to the All Blacks or the NZRFU. I had no time for the fish-heads. They were a bunch of boofheads as far as I was concerned. They treated us like horses. Just meat that they could move from one place to another and then discard as they wanted. And I guess I realised that it was the other players — the boys — who made the All Black jersey what it was for me. Without them it wouldn't mean the same — I'd just be a substitute, a sort of pretend AB if I stayed and the others signed up.'

Although he took part in various clandestine meetings, Norm missed the crucial gathering that was held in Sydney after the Bledisloe Cup clash.

'I came back from the World Cup with my knee needing surgery. I didn't want to have the op because I knew Anton Oliver would take my reserves place. And, like, I didn't want to give anyone else an opportunity. Just like Fitzy didn't want to give me one, I guess. Anyway, I took a gamble on the WRC thing sorting itself out and the French tour still going ahead. Plus I had the NPC still to play for Southland.'

His instincts proved correct. While recovering from the surgery, he attended an NZRFU presentation to various South Island provincial players.

'Rushy [Eric Rush] kept me informed of what was going on from the

WRC end and both he and Andy Haden acted as their reps with us. So I knew that the Boks, the Wallabies, the Poms and quite a few of our top provincial players had signed to the WRC and so it was starting to look real big. But then you'd hear things — like [Francois] Pienaar backtracking and signing with SARFU, or the Poms getting cold feet.

'It was rumour after rumour, but in the believability stakes a player will trust a player over a fish-head any day of the week. So Rushy always had the inside running with me.'

Instead of making him rethink his earlier decision to join the WRC ranks, the NZRFU presentation had quite the opposite effect. Vice-chairman Rob Fisher and former All Black captains Brian Lochore and Jock Hobbs made an amateurish presentation, and Norm was startled by their lack of a counter-proposal.

'Lochore gave the "ra ra" speech but seemed out of touch with where the game should be heading. I mean I know the guy was a great AB and a legend and all that but we needed a bit more than a call to tradition. If you live in the past then you get buried there. Rob Fisher promised that the union would pay players from now on — openly, and from the News Corp money — so that was good news. But it was Jock Hobbs I found really off-putting. He begged the players to stay. It seemed really weak to me — not what I was expecting at all. It was all "the game will die without you" crap instead of "look, we've got something better for everybody". I came away thinking that the NZRFU didn't have its shit together — that the other lot seemed a lot more professional and competent.'

Colin Meads has a different impression. He credits Hobbs with saving the inept NZRFU from itself, and for at least understanding that the initial pleas for loyalty were not having the desired effect. As a consequence, he says, Hobbs set up a 'war room' to conduct and monitor negotiations with various All Blacks, receive intelligence on WRC actions, and generally liaise with the shell-shocked NZRFU executive.

'I was desperately trying to stay out of it,' says Meads. 'My problem was that I could see where the union were coming from but I could understand the players' viewpoint too. It was bloody tough, and I think the players appreciated my divided loyalties.'

As a consequence the leading All Blacks sought to manoeuvre around their respected manager, even to the point where Mike Brewer misled Meads about the vital meeting with WRC officials after the Bledisloe Cup test in Sydney.

'The bugger said that they wanted the team to get together after the test in a private room at some local pub because it was the last chance all the

World Cup boys would have together. A sort of private celebration. Anyway, I agree and the bus turns up after the game for Laurie and the boys, with me on it. But it starts heading well beyond the Sydney Football Stadium and I turn to Laurie and say "What the bloody hell is going on?" So, Laurie tells me — that they're all off to some WRC official's home to discuss their contracts. Jeez, I was wild. Anyway, the reason Laurie stayed on the bus and didn't go to that meeting was because he knew I was upset about being misled. But other than that, Laurie was very much on the players' side.'

For the first time in the history of the game, the premier players now held the whip hand. From being the playthings of grey old men with grey old minds, the players appreciated that their sport was destined for professionalism and that those who embraced the new reality would be better placed to negotiate the new boundaries. And they were also in the unique position of dictating their demands rather than simply accepting the NZRFU's offers. Norm reasoned that if they just sat back and waited, the bidding war between SANZAR and the WRC must work to the players' benefit. They would never again get such an opportunity to substantially improve their pay and conditions.

Others were less sure. The 'defection' from the players' camp of the young Otago stars Josh Kronfeld and Jeff Wilson came as a shock to Norm and most of the other World Cup All Blacks. Not only did it seem a premature decision, but it also breached the squad's 'one for all and all for one' philosophy.

'My first reaction was, "You Judas bastards." Honestly, that was my first reaction. And all that crap about loyalty to the game was just so much bullshit. They signed with the NZRFU because that was the best option for them, personally. And when I thought about it I thought, "Well, fair enough. I guess we're all doing the same. Doing what's best for us."

'I mean, that was the thing about that whole WRC scrap. There were no good guys. There were just different agendas, different players at different stages of their careers, different objectives. The interesting thing was that Jeff and Josh later stated in their books that their loyalty to their Otago mates was a factor — and a lot more important than their loyalty to the AB squad. Maybe that was true, but they were also young men at the start of their careers and they wanted that All Black career more than anything else. That wasn't the case for the Fitzys or the Brewers or the Zinzan Brookes. So there were rival agendas within the team that, in hindsight, were easy to exploit.

'And Brewer and Fitzy could put anyone's back up. Looking back, I can see where the two J's were coming from. The All Blacks were a brotherhood with a pecking order and they didn't necessarily fit in. Certainly Josh never did. And he was right — there was a kind of bullying within the team. And why would they throw their lot in with people who they felt no close relationship to?'

But by now the contest for players' signatures had broadened well beyond the NZRFU and the WRC. Both the new Super League franchises and a number of Japanese companies were trawling through New Zealand looking for superior players. World Cup All Blacks Jamie Joseph and Graeme Bachop signed up with company teams in Japan, thankful that the WRC's entry had raised the whole bidding environment.

'It was just great for us,' Jamie Joseph recalls. 'The WRC were a negotiating tool and we really needed them, because the NZRFU's first offer to the players was just pathetic. They had all that Murdoch money and were basically offering us nothing. We would get NZ$100,000 a year and have to sign for three years. But we only got paid if we actually played for the All Blacks. And yet the three-year restriction stayed, meaning you couldn't go offshore or sign a league contract. It was a very one-sided arrangement.

'And the way the NZRFU approached us really got our backs up. They knew what the WRC was offering — they'd seen the draft contracts. Their counter-offer was only a fraction of the WRC's but they still wanted to bind us for the three years irrespective of whether they paid us or not. And they gave you the feeling that it was them doing you the favour.'

Ultimately, though, the WRC foundered on its own ambition, and a doubt that seeped into players' minds as to whether something so new and radical could really succeed. Rugby players are conservative beasts by nature. And when first the Springboks and then New Zealand provincial players signed en masse with their national unions, the earlier cohesion fell apart — although not before Norm and other All Blacks had wrung a better deal out of the NZRFU.

'The final offer was $250,000 a year for three years, and we didn't necessarily have to get selected for the All Blacks to qualify. So it was a good deal, although not as good as the WRC's. In the end, though, I think everyone — well, except maybe the WRC and the diehard traditionalists — got what they wanted. The game was now professional and ready to lift to another level. As a sport and as an entertainment rugby could now join the big time. And we players would finally get a fair percentage for our work.'

Fair?

'The moment SANZAR signed with Murdoch they made the game

professional. The players deserve a slice of that action. Rugby should have gone professional long before 1995. Instead we had boot money, backhand deals, shamateurism at its worst . . . all the lies and the deceit. All the other top sports like soccer, league, cricket, basketball, athletics were paying their players, so why not us? I mean I was expected to be a professional. I was expected to train like one, play like one, put myself at risk of permanent injury, give up all work opportunities, face long separations from family and friends . . . but still remain an amateur. Yeah, right. This was 1995, not 1935.'

In many ways, the WRC controversy was a clash of rugby generations. Most rugby officials, including the leadership of the NZRFU, had grown up regarding rugby union as a kind of moral code. Rugby was seen as character building and, at its elite level, the truest test of a man's character and courage. The self-sacrifice and the mateship went hand in hand — in return for giving all for country and team-mates, one was rewarded with respect and the camaraderie of one's peers.

Norm Hewitt's generation possessed no such perception. Yes, they loved the game, but they also understood that it was as much a part of the entertainment industry as Hollywood or Lotto. That made the modern player a machine to put bums on seats, attract sponsors and generate revenue for their union or franchise.

'At no stage did I, or any of the other AB's for that matter, feel any particular loyalty to the NZRFU. If anything, the opposite. There was a real rift between us and the fish-heads because their initial approaches were unreal. I mean, people say Jock Hobbs saved the NZRFU, but that's bullshit. Jock had no real people skills to speak of, and his idea of convincing us to sign up with them was pretty ordinary — the old "Think of the silver fern", "Think what the game's done for you" . . . I mean, that wasn't going to work with us. I mean here he was saying we should play for the love of the game, but I kept wondering, "Yeah, and who's paying your bills, eh?"'

Norm remains adamant that without the WRC challenge nothing would have changed. 'The players would have continued to be the peasants of the game. From now on we were partners. Junior partners maybe, but they couldn't brush us off any more.'

FAREWELL TO LAURIE

The knee injury that caused Norm to miss that crucial meeting in Sydney was his first concern on his return from the World Cup. He had gone to South Africa with a tear in the medial ligament in his left knee, an injury the medical staff thought was connected to an earlier dislocation of his kneecap. Although he could still play on the knee, he required constant pain-killing injections, even before practices, and the hard South African games had only exacerbated the original tear.

'We were like a drug assembly before training. There wasn't just me, but a good number of the senior forwards getting injections before a practice or a game. Jamie Joseph had a really painful one — a tear across his pubic bone — but "jab, jab" and we were pretty right. At this level, nearly all players are carrying an injury. It's a tough contact sport and you can't have 110-kg forwards running into each other without something giving way. So, the odd injection just goes with the territory.'

But by the time he returned to New Zealand he knew that if he didn't get the knee attended to then he might miss both his first season with Southland and the end-of-year tour to France. But it would mean pulling out of the Bledisloe Cup tests and that was not a choice he wished to make.

'Once you're an All Black you're always looking over your shoulder at who's challenging you for your spot. I might only have been the reserve hooker but Slade McFarland and Anton Oliver had been playing well while I was in South Africa and you never really know what's in the mind of a selector. I mean, at that time I considered myself a better player than both of them — a better scrummager, a better thrower into the lineout, better in the tight stuff. But that's only your opinion. Politics is as much a factor in rugby selection as anything else — I'd seen that already. So I was balancing getting the surgery against giving someone else the chance to take my place. In the end, I had no choice. The knee just got too bad.'

While he recovered from the surgery, Norm watched the Wallaby tests with both eyes firmly fixed on Fitzpatrick. For the first time in his career he had a vested interest in the All Black hooker staying on the field — afraid that Oliver might indeed get game time and perform well enough to shut him out of the French tour.

Although ultimately the solution would be within Norm's control. His form for the NPC Southland team was dynamic — relishing the tight exchanges, and particularly relishing meeting his rival hookers head-on. In each game, with the possible exception of his head-on-head with Slade McFarland, Norm more than had the measure of his opponent. And so generally did the Southland forwards. But once the ball strayed beyond the trusty boot of first-five Simon Culhane, the greater class of their first division opponents became apparent.

For game after game, Southland would seize the initiative against their more illustrious opposition only to surrender it in the last quarter of the match. A four-point loss to Otago at Carisbrook was followed by an achingly close Ranfurly Shield challenge against Canterbury. The 22-27 scoreline cannot truly reflect the severe fright the holders were given, with Norm outstanding in both the tight and the loose. A week later there was another five-point loss, this time to Wellington. It was like Groundhog Day, with the end result always the same — a brave Southland scaring the bejesus out of the big boys only to narrowly succumb. Then, in a weird parallel with Hawke's Bay two years earlier, it all came down to the last match — a home game against King Country. And with no better outcome — a one-point 12-13 loss that plunged Southland back into the second division.

'I couldn't believe it. We were the better team and had much the better of the game. But there I was — back in the second division — and I could hear the mocking laughter coming all the way down from Hawke's Bay. It was so bizarre because it wasn't just King Country at home and losing a game that we should've won — but also because for me losing was compensated for by selection in an end-of-year All Black tour to Europe.'

Norm remembers that French tour as a particularly happy one, despite the first-test defeat at Toulouse. If anything the tourists were too relaxed, winding down after the World Cup and still enjoying their two-nil triumph over the Wallabies. But after the three tries to nil defeat by the French, manager Colin Meads pulled the team together and delivered a scathing address. They were not worthy, the great one intoned. Not worthy to wear the black jersey, not worthy to share the company of those who had worn the silver fern. They were a bunch of soft cocks and he was ashamed to be sharing their company.

'We all respected Colin — both as a rugby legend and as a manager. So when he said anything, and it wasn't that often, you had no choice but to listen. I mean it wasn't just that he was the All Black of the Century — it was also because he was so tough, so adamant. He was like the father you respect but secretly fear. And he sure gave us the message.'

The whole touring party snapped into action. The midweekers thrashed their French opposition 55-17 and the All Blacks easily won the second test 37 points to 12, with Jonah Lomu gaining revenge for the previous year's humiliation by charging into the French backline and allowing his supports to feed off his energy.

At the traditional post-match dinner, Meads was required to present a Maori carving to the French rugby union as a fraternal gesture from their New Zealand counterparts. Feeling awkward that a Pakeha should present such an important carving, he instead called on the team's reserve hooker to make the presentation.

'Fitzy and Zinny gave me a few funny looks over that one,' Meads recalls. 'But it was my call, and Norm had given his guts during that year and, because of his Maori background, it also seemed the right thing to do. And it was. He gave an excellent speech in Maori and then in English, and brought a real dignity to the occasion. He turned something routine into something special.'

It was also an important gesture for Norm. Colin Meads' decision confirmed a sense of attachment to the All Blacks that some of the senior players had continually denied him. And he was also genuinely thrilled at having been involved in Laurie Mains' last moments as an All Black coach, even if only on the periphery.

'Laurie deserved that [French test] result. We respected him absolutely — as a coach he was always looking to make you better, get you to play to your limit. And as a man, I always found him upfront and honest. If you'd pissed him off, he told you and why. I mean I'd suffered a few lashings of Laurie's tongue but you could always see where he was coming from.

'He was the best coach I've ever played under, and not necessarily because he was the greatest thinker the game's ever seen or the best motivator. But because he was honest. And that counts for a lot in most players' books. There aren't all that many really honest coaches around — most of them have got a touch of politician in them.'

CHAPTER ELEVEN

Revenge

After that end-of-season tour of Italy and France, Norm was glad to return home to sunny Hawke's Bay and spend a restful summer with Kat. He had played well on the tour, refusing to bow to the intimidatory tactics employed by opposition teams, and cementing his reputation as one of the hard men of the All Black squad. In one memorable dust-up, against a Cote Basque selection, he had taken on a couple of French forwards who had attempted to kick Richard Loe's head as he lay helpless on the ground. His jersey was ripped from his back during the ensuing fracas and sensational photographs and headlines appeared in the press. But not a word of censure from the All Black management. *Take no shit* became the *sotto voce* motto of the tour.

Yet despite both his playing form and his new-found status within the team, the All Black test jersey remained as elusive as ever. After the loss at Toulouse and Meads' fiery call to arms, Norm had played his heart out against the French Barbarians in the mid-week game, but to no avail. While there were changes made to the second test team, Mains had no intention of dropping his captain. Norm's frustration only increased in response. No matter how well he performed or, conversely, no matter how poorly Fitzpatrick played, it was obvious that his lot would always be to observe, never to serve.

His mood was not helped when the Otago Highlanders franchise rejected him for the new Super 12 competition, set to kick off the following year. The Super 12 was based on the previous season's Super 10, but it now possessed all the trappings of professionalism, including a huge marketing budget, saturation media coverage and a player draft system. Despite Norm's national ranking, the Otago hierarchy insisted on the younger Anton Oliver as their first-choice hooker. They then salted the wound by choosing another Otago player, David Latta, as Oliver's back-up. The Highlanders might have been designed to represent both Otago and Southland interests, and Norm qualified as a Southlander, but the wrecking incident of four years earlier had not been forgotten by the dominant union.

'It was a political decision. Nobody discussed it with me . . . it was just, "Oh yeah, Norm — you'll be playing for the Wellington Hurricanes." Typical NZRFU. Once those contracts were signed and the WRC were out of the way, their communication skills disappeared real quick.'

Ironically, Norm's reluctant assignment to the capital-based Hurricanes would give his rugby career fresh impetus and provide him with a welter of new opportunities, both on and off the field. Although it took a bit of getting used to. Here he was living in Napier, playing NPC for Southland, and now playing the Super 12 for a Wellington franchise.

There were compensations. Kat had decided to study tourism at Victoria University, so at least the Super 12 selection meant they could set up house together. From his new contract monies Norm put a deposit on a two-bedroom bungalow in Highbury, then he began to introduce himself to his new team-mates. But Kat's presence was vital to the transition — she had become his most intimate confidant, easily assimilating the pressures and privileges that go with being an All Black's partner, and helping him to unwind and relax. The capital itself, he found a pleasant surprise.

'I'd always hated Wellington. Some of Mum's family lived out at Strathmore, down by the airport, and all I remembered from staying with them was howling southerlies, rain and the noise of the planes as they took off at all hours. Then there were all those drab, rusting warehouses down by the waterfront and grey civil-servant types trudging everywhere in their cardies. So no way did I ever want to live there — it made Invercargill seem like the Riviera.'

But his childhood memory had let him down. When he returned to Wellington at the start of 1996, it was to a vibrant, sunny city that had rejuvenated itself beyond belief. There were stylish shops, an overflow of cafes and restaurants, and the waterfront was getting a facelift, including the siting of the new national museum, Te Papa.

As well, Norm was able to team up with his good mate 'Bull' Allen, the

Hurricanes' inaugural captain. And his old Hawke's Bay coach Graeme Taylor was also part of the new structure — assistant to head coach Frank Oliver. But most of all Norm enjoyed the idea of being part of a 'mongrel' franchise — a team thrown together from nine nondescript unions, with few real stars and fewer expectations. Every other New Zealand franchise — the Auckland Blues, Waikato Chiefs, Canterbury Crusaders and Otago Highlanders — possessed a solid core of players and an experienced administration. The Chiefs had been further strengthened by joining Waikato with first division unions North Harbour and King Country; the Blues were virtually a shadow All Black line-up, with NPC runners-up Counties thrown in for good measure; the Highlanders had finished third in the previous year's NPC and added Southland to their young talent base, while the Crusaders had recruited well during the off-season and were based on the strong Canterbury union.

'Nobody expected anything of us. We were the dregs. Wellington's NPC team was a joke and had finished second or third to last, while both Taranaki and Hawke's Bay were second division unions. Then you added Wanganui, Horowhenua, Wairarapa-Bush, Poverty Bay, East Coast . . . not exactly the cream of provincial talent. So we required heaps of draft players, and they all knew they were a second choice. Like me, they'd been rejected by their home franchises. We were the Kiwi equivalent of the ACT Brumbies, although we didn't have their international players . . .'

Norm may have relished the team's underdog status, but the coaching staff were less sure. Graeme Taylor openly wondered if the team had been set up to fail. Only two All Blacks were included in the Hurricanes squad — Norm and centre Alama Ieremia — and neither were first-choice picks. Indeed, their only test appearances had been in the dirt-trackers' benefit against Japan at the World Cup. It was also rumoured that should the Hurricanes under-perform to expectations their place in the Super 12 would be taken by another franchise. South Africa was unhappy that no place could be found for the powerful Orange Free State, while many Aucklanders considered that the Queen City's playing depth deserved a second outfit centred on the North Shore.

Off the field, the Hurricanes' administration had the more immediate problem of how to break even financially. Franchises needed to be economically viable, and the chief sources of revenue were gate-takings and sponsorship. How to attract punters to a team with no stars, no chance, and drawn from such disparate unions? Worse, the team had no home venue as such. Two games would be played at the ageing Athletic Park, while the other three were allocated to Palmerston North, New

Plymouth and Napier. Although this roster might have the advantage of taking the team to the provinces, it had the more obvious downside of smaller population bases from which to draw revenue and the negating of any home-ground familiarity.

Which all made the Hurricanes' successes of 1996 and 1997 even more remarkable. From their first match against the powerful Auckland Blues at the Palmerston North Showgrounds — the first game of professional rugby union ever staged — the Hurricanes stormed into the public's affections with their open, adventurous play and an apparent on-field disregard for reputations and results.

Led by their charismatic captain, the shaven-headed 'Bull' Allen, the forwards adopted a frenetic style based on hitting the ruck or maul in numbers and charging directly at their often larger and more experienced opposition. This ferocity had been instilled into them by their no-nonsense, take-no-prisoners head coach Frank Oliver — a man with a thoroughly deserved reputation as a 70s hard man and a playing nickname of 'Filth'.

The Hurricanes backline included the young and exciting back three of Christian Cullen, Tana Umaga and Roger Randle, while Ieremia and Wellington's Jason O'Halloran were a combination of strength and finesse in the midfield. But despite the ever-reliable Jon Preston at halfback, the backline could be a brittle affair and was hampered by the lack of a reliable first-five and frequent injuries.

But on that first night under the lights at the Palmerston North Showgrounds, a strange magic went to work. A magic that survived the medium of television, exciting every true sports follower and kicking off the Super 12 with a bang that could be heard right around the rugby world.

'Only a few of us had played a top-level game under lights before, and certainly not that early in the season. It was a real summer's evening, sunny and still, and we were inside the dressing room listening to the crowd getting revved up and the rock music thumping through the loudspeakers while we were trying to concentrate on what Frank and GK were saying. I think they were as blown away as us that night, because they had somehow fitted 17,000 people into the showgrounds and the place was going off.

'We were also keyed up because this was basically the All Blacks we were going to be playing and all their stars were there — Zinzan Brooke, Michael Jones, Olo Brown, Robin Brooke, Jonah Lomu — I was going to be up against Fitzpatrick and I had a hell of a lot of frustration to take out on that bastard! I was thinking, "Fitzy, I'm coming after you." And then we ran out on the field and the crowd noise was deafening — they were chanting "Hur-ri-canes . . . Hur-ri-canes". It was such a rush, such an amazing atmosphere. I've played in bigger matches since, including tests at bigger stadiums and with bigger audiences. But that night was special. We all knew — players, coaches, the ref, the crowd — that we were creating history.'

Despite the enthusiasm, no-one expected the Blues to be troubled by the Hurricanes. People had come to watch the All Blacks as much as to be part of the occasion. And to reinforce their expectations the Australian gambling agency Centrebet had Auckland at 7:4 favourites to win the first Super 12, while Wellington were at 33:1 and their favourite to take the wooden spoon.

Then, within minutes of the game kicking off, the Hurricanes attacked in the helter-skelter fashion that was to become their trademark. Alama Ieremia was freed on the left and dashed to the line to score. The crowd went nuts.

Eventually the game would be lost 28-36, with a last-minute try robbing the hosts of a deserved bonus point, but it mattered not. The openness and quality of the game provoked global interest, and the Super 12 went on to its climactic conclusion at Eden Park with the Blues seeing off a brave Natal.

The Hurricanes won only three games that first season but two of their wins were against New Zealand franchises, and the Canterbury Crusaders finished below them on the final points table. At Dunedin they had thrashed the Otago Highlanders 44-15 (with the Hurricanes' front row of 'Bull' Allen, Norm and Phil Coffin wholly outplaying their opposites) and they'd also beaten the Waikato Chiefs 23-15 — a double surprise given that the Hurricanes had just returned from South Africa.

Any talk of the Hurricanes franchise being transferred elsewhere withered and then died. Somehow this team of mongrels, brilliantly led on the field by Bull Allen and expertly marketed off the field by PR man Peter Parussini, had captured the public imagination.

'There were three reasons we did so well. First, we were always the underdog in every game we played and Kiwis love underdogs. Second, we played with a real intensity in every game and played above our weight. That was all down to Frank [Oliver]. He was a "rip-their-heads-off" sort of coach — "intimidate them, get in their face, don't back down" — and that style suited me and the rest of the Hurricanes forwards. I mean that's how I played my rugby, and there were others like Dion Waller, Chresten Davis, Inoke Afeaki and Filo Tiatia who just loved running at guys.

'And third, I think Bull deserves a lot of the credit. He was a cult figure — every time he got the ball in a game there was that "Bull, Bull, Bull" roar from the crowd. Off the field, he was always smiling, happy and talkative, and I learned a lot from just watching him. How he got people on side with a "Gidday, mate" or rubbing a kid's hair as he walked past. The rugby public loved him even though he wasn't a top All Black. He had charisma. And rugby players with charisma are bloody rare.'

THE HART-MAN RETURNS

With the retirement of Laurie Mains, John Hart was able to realise his ambition of again coaching the All Blacks, and this time without the distraction of a co-coach or a campaign to unseat him. Mains might have been tempted to stand again, but his role during the WRC insurrection had torched any NZRFU sympathy for him, and there was a general feeling, both around the union's executive table and in the country at large, that Hart's time had finally come. In addition, the Aucklander was seen as being more in tune with the new professionalism — the Murdoch money demanded a new standard of management throughout the rugby world, and that included the All Black coach. After all, it was reasoned, Hart was a product of the corporate world and rugby was now just another big business.

It was the nature of the man that he would seek to impose his regime and his personality upon the All Blacks as swiftly as possible. That included a belief that the All Blacks were no longer just his players, but his personal charges — that they required a level of man management far beyond that provided under the old amateur regime. To that end, Hart organised a seminar at the Waipuna Hotel in Auckland and invited forty of the country's leading players, including Norm.

'I was a bit bemused actually,' Norm says, 'because our first Super 12 game was only a couple of days away and here we were going back to school. But I understood where he was coming from . . . he wanted to point out that the new professional world had its dangers as well as its opportunities.'

Hart ensured that the invited line-up of speakers — who included lawyers Tim Castle and David Jones, broadcaster Paul Holmes, US gridiron star Ricki Ellison and PR director Paul Norris — all emphasised the new standards of conduct that professionalism demanded. Well, all except Ellison. The Super Bowl winner stood up, took one look at the assembled rugby talent in front of him, and sat down again.

'He reckoned he was overawed,' says Norm. 'I thought, "Jeez, if that's professionalism, let me outta here!"'

But Hart's message was deadly serious.

'There were huge potential problems with professionalism and its impact on players' lives. All that quick money. Gridiron in the States, for example, was littered with stories of alcoholism, marital break-ups, burn-outs, bankruptcies . . . that sort of thing. My aim was to point out how the new process needed to be managed, but also to assist players to become more rounded . . . to grow as people.'

But despite Hart's ostensibly altruistic aims, Norm felt uncomfortable with the new coach, and with the sudden trappings of corporate rugby.

'I guess I was a bit overwhelmed and a lot of what they said went over my head. That was true of a lot of the other players as well. At that time professionalism was just a word. And a bucket load of money. But I was pleased just to be included in the seminar because it meant I was still in the All Black frame.'

So too was Anton Oliver, a young man marked out by Hart for greater things.

'There were three hookers who were of the top standard when I took over — Sean, of course, Norm, and Anton. I saw Anton as a potential All Black captain because to me he already had the leadership qualities. I knew they would take time to evolve but I wanted him included in the All Black environment so that he could learn and get a feel for things.'

Norm left the seminar to rejoin his Hurricanes team-mates with mixed feelings. Already it was obvious that John Hart was a different beast to Laurie Mains — more loquacious, with strong commercial contacts, and speaking a language that emphasised off-the-field professionalism as much as on-field endeavour. The All Blacks were no longer just elite rugby players. Overnight they had become corporate stars and role models.

After the Super 12 had finished, Norm was satisfied with his form and that he had done enough to retain his position in the All Blacks. The front row of Allen, Hewitt and Coffin had not been bested during the entire competition, and provided an unyielding platform for exciting new backline stars like Christian Cullen and Tana Umaga. As well, Norm had shone in the loose — connected, it seemed, to his captain by an invisible thread. As Allen hit the ruck he would 'pick-and-go', charging at the opposition in true bull-like fashion until stopped, then Norm would arrive and repeat the exercise. Frank Oliver's no-nonsense forward tactics were ably complemented by Taylor's aim of giving his talented outsides as much freedom as the modern game would allow. They might not win all their games but the Hurricanes quickly earned a reputation as entertainers and crowd-pleasers, their helter-skelter play always proving a handful for the opposition.

Sweetest of the Hurricanes' wins had been the 44-15 thrashing of the Highlanders at Carisbrook, the Wellington front row dismantling their opposition, with Norm in dynamic form. For now, at least, the threat of Anton Oliver had been defused. And so too any threat of demobilisation.

The Hurricanes' inaugural season saw seven of their team selected for the 36-man squad to tour South Africa in August, including the entire front row, blindside Chresten Davis, utility half Jon Preston, Alama Ieremia and the gifted Christian Cullen. A message had been sent to every aspiring All Black: the Super 12 was the proving ground. Make it there and higher honours await — coast, and all bets are off.

But before the South African tour the All Blacks needed to contest the new Tri-Nations with the Wallabies and the Springboks — the second part of the deal that SANZAR had made with Rupert Murdoch. The home and away round-robin would begin with the Wallabies, under their new coach Greg Smith, taking on the All Blacks at Athletic Park. Again, Norm was the reserve to Sean Fitzpatrick.

'We had played warm-up tests against Samoa and Scotland but the boys hadn't really taken them too seriously, despite John Hart beating up the media with how good the opposition would be. I mean, Samoa's best players were now playing for us — Frank Bunce, Alama, Michael Jones, Steve Bachop — so they weren't much of a force. And Scotland were out of season and Gavin Hastings had retired, so we didn't rate them much either. Although that didn't stop Cully [Christian Cullen] scoring seven tries in his first two tests. He was electric. But the real stuff was the Tri-Nations and then the Bok tour. There was unfinished business and the boys were real pumped.'

So much so that on a stormy Wellington day and on a sodden Athletic Park, the All Blacks produced one of their finest performances ever. The Wallabies were thrashed 43-6, conceding six tries and strangely thankful that the damage was not greater. Quite possibly there wasn't a finer All Black team during the decade of the 90s, with the awesome abilities of Cullen, Jeff Wilson and Jonah Lomu let loose behind a dominant All Black pack that rated as one of the finest of all time — Zinzan Brooke, Josh Kronfeld and Michael Jones as the loosies, Robin Brooke and Ian Jones at lock, and an adamantine front row of Olo Brown, Sean Fitzpatrick and Craig Dowd.

'When you consider that Frank [Bunce] and Walter Little were probably at their peak, plus Andrew Mehrtens and Justin Marshall being the halves, then I reckon that was the best team since Buck Shelford was in charge in '88–'89. And it still had Laurie Mains' imprint and background, honed to this really fine edge by Hart. I mean that was what Hart brought. For a while there, he could make the edge even sharper. It was Laurie's team all right but Hart gave it that little bit extra. At least for a while. Until the boys got used to him.'

Norm even found himself playing a bit part in the game — called on for a couple of scrums while Sean Fitzpatrick was having a wound attended to.

'I don't remember much except it being wet and cold, and that most of the hard work had been done and the forwards were starting to get on top. But I do remember afterwards . . . having to stand on the seats in the dressing room because it was flooded from all the rain. That was down in the "dungeons", as we called them — the dark, dingy dressing rooms at Athletic Park.'

Despite Hart's arrival, one aspect of team organisation had not improved — the divide between test team regulars and the rest. A couple of days before the return test against the Wallabies in Brisbane some of this division bubbled over onto the training field, with Norm heavily involved.

'Me and a few of the reserves were being the "c.f."s again — the cannon fodder. Our job was to be the opposition at training, and practices could get quite physical. I mean it had to be if you were trying to duplicate match-day situations. So we're all togged up in our body suits and getting smashed over by the regular forward pack, and there was this lineout drill where the test team get the ball, drive into a maul and then release . . .'

What happened next led to test lock Ian Jones and Norm indulging in a solid fist fight under the noses of the All Black management and in full view of the accompanying press corps.

Norm had been playing spoiler in the maul and deliberately upsetting the ABs' momentum; Ian Jones had given him 'a tap', Norm had 'hooked him back'. And from there it had been all on. Bull Allen attempted to separate the pair, but the real restraint came from the sideline — John Hart screaming 'Norm Hewitt! Don't you dare touch my test player!'

The twin interventions caused Norm to hesitate and in that time Ian Jones landed a blow that was to require stitches. The physical damage healed quickly — the psychological impact took longer to subside. After the practice Hart drew the hooker aside and told him that any repeat of his actions and he would be sent home. The threat was later reiterated in front of the team. Jones escaped any similar censure.

'That was it — that was turning up the frustration factor to max.'

Hart's admonition confirmed the divide that Norm had always felt. It also meant that Ian Jones' final cuff was now unfinished business. The resentment and hostility were personalised — so much so that even into the next year, Graeme Taylor would criticise the Hurricanes hooker for trying to stalk Ian Jones during a Super 12 game.

'Norm was after him, and it was affecting his play. I had to put a stop to it. We needed him to do his job without getting distracted. But I thought it strange at the time. I mean Norm could be a real aggro guy when he put his mind to it — that was one of the things that made him such a good player. He was a hard, hard man. But this was vendetta stuff. Eventually he calmed down, but I thought to myself at the time, "Ian Jones, you've really done something to piss him off this much!"'

In retrospect Norm concedes he overreacted, but the training incident was symbolic. It confirmed that the test-versus-the-rest divide was not only real, but widening under John Hart. And that the All Black coach had his favourites and his non-favourites — and that Norm was very much of the latter variety.

STRANGE DAYS

The 1996 tour of South Africa is rightly regarded as one of the All Blacks' all-time great achievements — the first-ever away series victory against the Springboks, made even more meritorious by the fact that the Boks were reigning world champions. The NZRFU clumsily attempted to label the '96 All Blacks the 'Incomparables', so that they might be ranked alongside the 1905 'Originals' and the 1924 'Invincibles' as one of the immortal teams of New Zealand rugby. While it is doubtful that the moniker will prevail the triumph of the tour will, and the team returned to a rapturous public reception.

And yet it was a strange tour. Four tests were to be played, but only the last three would count towards the series proper, the first being the final stage of the Tri-Nations championship. Although that was not how the players saw it. When the two teams clashed it was as if bull elephants were slamming into each other on the African veldt — the rugby world shook, and both nations held their collective breaths.

'The South African public and press were still really up about winning the World Cup the previous year so there was also another edge to the games. It wasn't just a traditional Springboks–All Black series . . . it was also about the world champions defending that title against the pretenders. Most of the South African media had rubbished Laurie's claims about the food poisoning the year before and the public resented it too — like we were trying to take the gloss off or something. It was definitely the most intense tour I've ever been on because they really wanted our heads. And we wanted theirs right back.'

Compared with previous tours to the Republic, the '96 All Blacks had three major advantages — a squad of 36 players, a maximum of eight games (including the four tests) and neutral referees. At least for the internationals. Home refs would be used for the four midweek games against Boland, Eastern Province, Western Transvaal and Griqualand West.

'I'd heard about the home-town refereeing but never struck it before the midweek games. And, Jeez, it was rough — I could see how previous teams had lost every other series before then. Any little thing you might do was picked up, while the locals would get away with murder.'

Off the field things were also tense. Bull Allen had been told before the tour that he would be the midweek captain, but this responsibility was actually allocated to Taine Randell and Todd Blackadder. Randell, in particular, had a scarfies' sense of humour that was not always appreciated by the old hands.

'Before one game, he pulled the boys together and said: "Look, guys — if you're not going to do it for the All Black jersey then do it for the chicks in the stand." That sure upset a few of them.'

Despite the series win, it is not a tour Norm remembers with particular fondness, the division between international players and dirt-trackers causing real resentment. Because of the way the tour was structured, the midweek team would often find themselves playing in out of the way provincial towns like Worcester or Potchefstroom, and the test team would not always accompany them.

'We'd have to watch and support them but it didn't seem to work the other way round. For a couple of the games, the test team would go off to where the test was going to be played and we'd head off with the reserves to play the opposition. That didn't do anything for team unity. I mean this was the All Blacks playing and the top players couldn't be bothered supporting us. That really pissed us off.'

And there was further insensitivity from the All Black management. At one of the training sessions John Hart attempted some levity by referring to Ofisa ('Junior') Tonu'u as 'my black tracker'. The phrase was often heard and the Polynesians in the team reacted badly.

'It was a real racial put-down. And he [Hart] kept saying it, too. No matter how innocently it might have been intended, the whole "black tracker" thing upset quite a few of us, especially the Samoan boys. I mean race should never be a part of being an All Black — we're a colour-blind team united by the fern on our jersey. So Hart's reference to Ofisa really jarred, and not just with the brown boys. Bull and Toddy were concerned too and they sure weren't Polynesian.'

Norm felt powerless to take the matter any further. If he complained directly to Hart he feared being labelled a troublemaker. And that could mean losing the All Black jersey and all its monetary rewards forever.

'Hart's comments were offensive. But it's not the All Black way to rock the boat. And telling the head coach that he's being an insensitive shit is not going to get you any favours. I should have said something . . . but I didn't. It wasn't my place to. In the end some of the boys finally had a chat to [manager] Mike Banks and that seemed to do the trick.'

But the fact that neither Norm nor anyone else felt confident enough to bring the initial offence to their coach's attention suggests an unhealthy unease within the team. And perhaps a selfishness — each player wary of their place and reluctant to jeopardise it. There was nothing in Hart's demeanour to suggest that he bore a grudge, but Norm wasn't prepared to take that risk.

After the epic 33-26 victory at Pretoria, and with the series won, a number of the reserves and dirt-trackers harboured the hope that they might be called on for the last test at Ellis Park. The test team had played three tests in three weeks and was showing signs of tiredness. Getting them up one last time would surely be a step too far.

But John Hart stuck with the same forward pack and only made the one backline change — Andrew Mehrtens returning for Simon Culhane. Not surprisingly, the South Africans were the more committed team — roared on by 62,000 fans and desperate to avoid a series whitewash. The final score flattered the All Blacks — the 22-32 loss relatively respectable considering that partway through the second half the team had been down 8-29.

'A number of us thought Hart should have made changes, if only to freshen the team. I mean there was nothing to lose, we were meant to be one touring party — although we weren't — and the series was won. But it was that test versus non-test thing again. It was inflexible.'

And so the international season was finished. The All Blacks had played ten tests, and Norm had only five minutes at Athletic Park to show for it. He had watched every minute of every game from the sideline, bar that couple of scrums in Wellington.

'I wasn't sorry to be leaving South Africa, if only to get back to playing some regular footy again. Although whatever feelings I might have had, that '96 test team was pretty special. That was the best team we put on the paddock in the 90s, and much of it was down to Laurie Mains. But you can't say Hart did nothing.

'I disagreed with a lot of the things he did and the methods he employed, but he generally had a good relationship with the senior players and got something extra out of Fitzy and Michael Jones and Zinny . . . the Auckland boys. But he just wasn't too concerned with the rest of us — that's what pissed me off. You were either in the First XV or you were nowhere. Which made it hard for him later on when he needed to bring the new players in. I don't think he'd taken the time to understand them.'

This time Norm was also less impressed with the country itself. The previous year he had been consumed with the World Cup and had had little opportunity to take in the country, read the newspapers, watch the TV news, meet people in the provinces. Despite winning the World Cup and despite Mandela's leadership, South Africa seemed further behind — economically and politically — than it had the year before.

'They might have abandoned apartheid but a lot of the old attitudes were still there. At one after-match I was talking to this guy, a farmer, and all of a sudden he starts talking about "the coons" he's got working for him. All blacks were coons to this guy, but he reckoned that he treated them well . . . like favourite pets. But it wasn't just white on black . . . there was a lot of tribal stuff going on as well at the time — Zulus killing Xhosa, and vice versa. And then there were the "taxi wars" — man, they were something. You could get killed if you stepped into the wrong taxi, while the governmental corruption and crime were always there too.

'When I got on the plane to leave I just thought, "Thank God I live in New Zealand. I don't know how lucky I am."'

CONSOLATION

The feeling was even stronger when he saw Kat waiting for him among the crush of wellwishers at Auckland International Airport. They returned to their home in Wellington and Norm gave himself a fortnight to sleep off the fatigue of the tour and get himself properly rested before rejoining the Southland NPC team.

'I didn't want to go down to Invercargill. It wasn't just that Kat was in Wellington and that the city looked so clean and peaceful after Jo'burg, but I knew the quality of the rugby in the second division would be lesser. There were no end-of-season tours or anything but Anton [Oliver] had been taken to South Africa as the third hooker and it was obvious how Hart viewed him. He was going to be Fitzy's successor, and that would leave me nowhere. So I had to prove myself again and there was no way I could do that from the second division. Or so I thought at the time.'

He had asked Southland to release him from his two-year contract but the union had refused. While the news stories of this exchange reinforced his reputation as a rugby mercenary, there was another side to the story that was not reported. Southland had signed a two-year deal with Norm at $30,000 a year. But at the start of 1996 Southland chairman Brian Beardsley informed him that the union was in financial difficulty and they could no longer honour their commitment. If he played, they would only offer him half the previous year's sum — $15,000.

'It had a bit of a ring about it — like Hawke's Bay reneging a couple of years before. So I wasn't all that impressed. But then they said, "If we go up to the first division the next year, we'll make up that $15,000." It was small beer compared to the NZRFU contract, but the greater incentive was to play well and keep myself in the All Black frame. I could have got out of the contract, I guess, because they had breached the money part. But I didn't need the hassle. I wanted to play some footy.'

Norm did not disappoint. His NPC form was outstanding, winning him the 'second division player of the year' title, and matched by the team winning promotion to the first division by defeating Northland in the final. There had been only one low point in the whole Southland campaign, although the memory lingers to this day.

'I was booed as I ran onto McLean Park to play Hawke's Bay. I'll never forget that. This was the ground where I had captained Hawke's Bay so many times — had led them to wins over the Lions and France, and been a part of some of the best days in the Bay's history. And here I was getting jeered at and hissed every time I picked up the ball. I couldn't believe it. No-one else got that treatment . . . not Matt Cooper or Paul Cooke or Stu Forster . . . just me.'

But it would be Norm who had the last laugh. Southland snatched an improbable last-minute win, and a few weeks later the southerners compounded the Bay's misery by defeating them again, this time in the semi-final.

Norm had intended to play for the New Zealand Maori team on their November tour of Fiji and Tonga, but a persistent sore throat was diagnosed as polyps on his vocal chords. During the NPC he had found that when he barked out orders for scrum and lineout drills, blood would sometimes be left on his lips, and the amount had steadily increased over the course of the season. He was reluctant to have the problem attended to while the New Zealand Maori tour was on offer, but common sense prevailed and he underwent an operation to remove the growth.

It was not the perfect end to the season — a couple of weeks playing rugby with his mates in the South Pacific had sounded good after the long Southland winter. But as he lay recovering, reconciled to a long summer lay-off, he received a call from NZRFU headquarters. Sean Fitzpatrick was injured and had withdrawn from the Barbarians' game against the touring Wallabies in the UK. Would he be interested? Would he what!

Despite the last-minute nature of the invitation he realised the honour he was being paid, and he desperately needed to share the moment with someone. Kat was the obvious choice. The Barbarians management had arranged business-class travel for him, so he converted this to two economy fares, and asked her to accompany him.

'It was a real eye-opener when we got there. There was no real training as such — just a few lineouts and scrums and a bit of a run around. Nick Poppelwell and Darren Garforth were my props, and they were more interested in having a beer than doing any serious preparation. Which suited me down to the ground. Not surprisingly, we got hammered at Twickenham by 39 points to twelve, but no-one really cared.

'The Barbarian Club dinner at the Hilton that night was pretty amazing. Women were barred from attending, so Kat had to go to a separate Ladies Dinner in the Coronation Room, which didn't amuse her. It was just such a stuffy old English thing to do. But that's the weird thing about the Poms. On the one hand, they hoon it up like anybody else. And then the next, it's like we're back a hundred years and it's pinkies raised over the teacups and plums in their voices. All a bit strange for a Maori boy from central Hawke's Bay.'

When he returned from the UK, he found a letter from the All Black coach awaiting him.

'I'd decided to send all the players a review of what had been achieved that season and to look ahead to the next,' John Hart recalls. 'It was personalised for each player so that they would know our expectations of them. I congratulated Norm on what he'd achieved for the year — he'd been a part of the leadership of the midweek team in South Africa and helped Southland get back into the first division. But there were things that I thought he should work on.'

Specifically, the All Black coach pointed to weaknesses in Norm's game: 'One is your aerobic fitness and your ability to get around the field at speed; the other is the ability to throw with accuracy on a consistent basis at lineout time. There has been the odd game where you have let your standards slip, and at Test level that can't occur.'

Norm was surprised at the criticism. He was being admonished for a lack of fitness, a lack of basic speed, and inaccuracy at the lineout — indeed, the better part of the modern hooker's game. And he considered it strange to be getting such information in writing — that neither Hart nor any of the other selectors had taken the time to sit down and personally raise such issues. But, he shrugged, if that's what Hart wants then that's what Hart would get. Those were things he would work on in the off-season. Although if there had been any lack of sharpness he considered a good part of it was due to continually warming the reserves bench.

But it was not the criticism of his rugby skills that unduly worried him. Those things could be remedied. It was the paragraph relating to something else: 'I was impressed with your response to our earlier discussion about the need for personal discipline, particularly in matters related to alcohol and off-field behaviour. You accepted the challenge well and I certainly find it difficult to have any complaint with your off-field performance. However, that is for 1996. The same must be the basis for 1997 and beyond if you are serious about a long-term career as a professional rugby player at the top level.'

'I sat there and thought — you prick. You're out to control my private life too. Earlier in the year we did have a chat about me and the booze — that was true. It was Hart's idea, and his basic line was that I should stay off the turps at any rugby or social function that involved the ABs. I thought it was a bit extreme at the time but what choice did I have? I wanted to be an All Black.

'And as it turned out there had been occasions I'd got on the piss with some of the others — and some of their behaviour had been worse than mine. But it seemed like I was being singled out for attention. It was like "Hewitt, you're a boozer. Mess around and you're out." I didn't see the same rules being applied to anybody else.'

The Hart letter worried away at Norm over the off-season. He resented the message, but even more he resented its delivery. He had not personally acknowledged that he had a drinking problem, and now John Hart was not only contradicting him but demanding exemplary personal standards that went far beyond the rugby field.

It was also evidence of a clash of personality types that ensured neither really understood the other's position. Hart knew Norm had a problem but seemed to think it could best be cured by external control. On the other hand, Norm refused to accept that he had any weakness with regard to drink. The two were at polar extremes, and the manner of this latest communication, by formal letter, only widened the breach.

To this day Hart considers that the issue was managed 'as best it could be given that Norm put up the shutters every time I raised it. When he had his [drinking] binges he lost control — there were flashpoints in his mood. It was exactly the same with another All Black as well. As a rule, it didn't affect their rugby, but my view was that Norm shouldn't be drinking at all. That he had to get help.'

However, no assistance was sought from outside the All Black camp for the problem hooker. If Norm needed help (and Hart would later acknowledge that he knew the hooker didn't genuinely accept that he had an alcohol problem) then he would have to find it for himself. There would be no 'interventions' from family or friends, no demands that he attend counselling, no real attempt to make him address his problem.

The All Black coach had done as much as he felt he could do. And besides, he was the All Black coach — not its manager, and not its social conscience. Hart has said since that he considered it was not his responsibility, that he felt as if he was encroaching upon the players' private conduct as it was. Certainly he didn't have the personal relation-ship with Norm that he enjoyed with other players. Both men knew the other was not really of their world — that they could not step outside their roles or their backgrounds when talking to each other.

For his part, Norm resisted the notion that he even had a problem. And he sure resisted the idea that Hart should have any role in his life beyond the immediate sphere of the All Blacks. As it was, he resented the fact that the standards being applied to him did not seem to extend to other All Blacks. On some occasions he had observed Zinzan Brooke and Craig Dowd conduct themselves poorly in public. But then they came from Auckland, and were perceived as part of the coach's 'in-crowd' — the special place reserved for Hart's favoured test players.

At the end of the letter, John Hart gave his home and mobile telephone numbers and reiterated that his comments were 'designed to be constructive'. But Norm had read between the lines and seen that a character judgement had been made. The day he'd call John Hart would be the day Hell froze over.

CHAPTER TWELVE

Top dog

Norm and Kat used the off-season to look for a new house, eventually settling on a large Highbury villa with spectacular views across both city and harbour. While his new wealth had delivered a more expansive home, it also allowed him to take some financial responsibility for the rest of his family. He invested in his parents' country pub, lent his sister money to buy a new car, and let his Greenmeadows house to his younger brother. If he was going to earn above-average money then he considered a duty of care was placed on him, and that his family should share in his good fortune. And whatever the past troubles between him and his father, the blood links remained strong.

Norm also assumed greater responsibility within the Hurricanes camp. At the early training camps his mana as a senior player and All Black was acknowledged, and coaches Oliver and Taylor welcomed his greater contribution to team meetings and practices. Both men believed that players needed to be more involved in tactics and decision-making, and that the dynamism of the modern game required a more intelligent assessment of on-field options and choices. The combination of this inclusive policy, his All Black status and his strengthening friendship with Bull Allen provided Norm with a security that he had rarely, if ever, experienced. He became Bull's right-hand man — the discipline to Allen's charisma.

'I was always on edge with the All Blacks — never really knowing what the selectors were thinking or if I'd be chosen again. But the Hurricanes were different — they were whanau. It helped that we all got on — Frank and GK and [manager] Tony Bedford got to know everyone's strengths and weaknesses, and took the time to find out what made us tick. So we settled down that second year. Having most of our players back sure helped. We had a really good front row in Phil Coffin, Bull and me, with big Bill [Cavubati] coming off the bench for the last twenty minutes. So that provided the base. It gives a team a real lift knowing that when they run out onto the park their tight five will do the business. With Rigger [Mark Cooksley] and Inoke [Afeaki] we at least had a tight five that could hold its own.'

Graeme Taylor was also excited about how the team was shaking down.

'The sports theorists reckon that there are four stages to establishing a decent team: forming, storming, norming and performing. In '96, we were formed and stormed — and by stormed I mean, that's the time when everyone finds out where they fit . . . when you get the hierarchies established, the rules set, that sort of thing. In '97 we had "normed", if you like. Everyone accepted their position and knew their role. And so we started to perform — play well and play winning rugby.'

Although the team started the '97 campaign poorly, with two close losses to the Waikato Chiefs and the Canterbury Crusaders. It wasn't until their next game, a 64-32 thrashing of Northern Transvaal at New Plymouth, that a hint of their potential was displayed.

'That was the first game we'd played where the forwards delivered ball to [halfback] Jon Preston going forward. Then the backs were just given a licence to run and Tana Umaga was awesome that day. He'd got really fit in the off-season but it was his acceleration off the mark, and the angles he ran, that blitzed everyone. One minute he was there, the next — zip — gone. It was like his "coming out" game — the match in which he announced that he was a star. And having Cully running off him gave us an extra edge.'

It was an important win because it built the team's confidence ahead of their games in South Africa. Northern Transvaal had been a semi-finalist the year before and its forward pack had a deserved reputation for being big and brutal. But the game confirmed a general weakness in South African teams — an inability to properly align and employ their backlines or defend adequately against a fast, wide game.

'They were obsessed with getting forward domination so they kept selecting these big grunters who were strong but bloody thick. We knew that we just had to run them around, and keep them running, and that eventually their forwards would start missing the rucks and their defence would develop gaps. The best way to do that was with helter-skelter rugby — spread the ball, at the breakdown have Bull and I and the other tighties run at them, spread it again, keep them moving, make sure they didn't know where we'd come from next. It wasn't a subtle game plan but it worked because we had outside backs like Tana, Christian and Alex [Telea] and a midfield of Alama [Ieremia] and Jason [O'Halloran] who could position their outsides and make breaks on their own. Alama was the key — a rock on defence and very strong on the charge.'

As long as the tight five established a secure scrum and ensured their own lineout throws, then the potent Hurricanes backline could do the job. But still no-one gave them any chance of upsetting Gauteng at the imposing Ellis Park, or the previous year's finalists Natal at Durban. The conventional wisdom was that the Hurricanes' two early losses had already robbed them of a top four finish.

Two weeks later and Norm was sitting beside a hotel pool in Durban, his head reeling from a night of partying, and reflecting on the most bizarre of fortnights. The team had lost narrowly to Natal the previous evening but secured two invaluable bonus points. His own game had included a try and, despite playing in the losing team, he'd been named 'player of the match' and had the gold Krugerrand in his pocket to prove it.

A week earlier he'd taken pleasure in vexing the loudmouth Louis Luyt, with the rugby chief's formidable Gauteng pack outplayed and out-thought by this mongrel outfit from Wellington. In rugby terms the mini-tour had been very successful, with seven Super 12 points gained and the Hurricanes back in the semi-finals race.

Off the field, however, things had not worked out so well. For a start, Norm's formerly close relationship with Frank Oliver had soured, and over the most petty of causes.

'We used to play a [drinking] game called buffalo . . . it's where you have to drink out of your right hand or scull another. Anyway, we were settled down in the team room at the hotel, having a few beers and watching one of the Super 12 games on TV, when Frank calls Phil Coffin out for drinking with his left hand. So I say to Frank something like, "Fuck off, Frank. He doesn't have to drink — we're not playing buffalo at the moment, we're watching the telly."'

Graeme Taylor remembers the put-down well. For some time he had been uneasy about the relationship between Frank Oliver and some of the senior players, particularly the exclusive 'card school' of Oliver, Allen, Norm and Manawatu loosie Karl Williams.

'They would play euchre everywhere — whenever there was any down time, the cards would come out and they'd have a game . . . in airport lounges, hotel lobbies, buses, anywhere. Cards are a common way for touring teams to kill time and there's nothing wrong with that except that the four of them became such a unit that they started cutting themselves off, socially, from the rest of the team. There's a fine line between coach and players, but I've always been of the view that it's got to be drawn somewhere.'

Certainly Oliver enjoyed the company of his team. Later that year he was quoted in *Rugby News* as saying that 'the forwards are my men. I'd love to be in there with them.' For his part, Norm appreciated Oliver's company, and also the big man's coaching style.

'He was one of the best forward coaches I'd ever had and I related really easily to him. He was a hard man and that's what I wanted to be too. I know what GK's saying, and yeah, he probably did feel a bit out of it, but I looked at Frank more as a father figure than as a mate. I liked the way he was so clear about everything — that there was never any bullshit or bluster. It was always black and white with Frank — there was no grey ever. And he could sink the piss. So we got on extra well.'

At least until the buffalo incident. Oliver took Norm's public rebuff badly, and within seconds the two men had sized up to each other and seemed ready to resort to fists. They were quickly separated but Oliver was furious at the way he'd been spoken to, followed by the physical challenge.

'He called me up to his room and tore a strip off me,' says Norm. 'Said that I had no right to challenge him in front of the rest of the players and who the fuck did I think I was? I guess he had a point and I apologised, but things cooled after that. It was a difficult week, and then to top everything off, along comes the Randle affair.'

THE RANDLE AFFAIR

To this day both players and management remain close-lipped about the incident at the heart of the Randle affair — the alleged rape of a blonde South African woman at the Holiday Inn, the team's Durban hotel. What is known is that the woman met up with some of the players at a nightclub after the Natal game, was regarded as just another rugby groupie, and had consensual sex with at least two, possibly three of the Hurricanes party. This romp took place in the room Randle shared with reserve Hurricanes lock and Western Samoa international Potu Leavasa. Randle observed a good part of the action but denies that he took part, a denial confirmed by others who were present.

Shortly before dawn, a number of the Hurricanes squad began to congregate around the hotel pool. Leavasa went down to join them, provoking an angry reaction from the woman at being abandoned. This also left her alone in the room with Randle. There is general agreement that he asked her to leave, she refused, and so he grabbed her and pushed her out into the corridor. The woman left the hotel, visibly upset at her treatment. Subsequently she returned and alleged to the hotel management that she had been raped. The management, in turn, called the police.

'The thing about rape in South Africa is that it's so common. Unbelievably so. And in most cases, the perpetrators get away with it because their police are so hopeless and they've got higher priorities — like murders and stuff. It's difficult for us Kiwis to appreciate how bad violent crime is in South Africa. It's not so much a problem as a plague. No wonder they all want to get out of the place.

'Anyway, around this time the police were under real pressure to get more active on rape crimes. And in the middle of all that public pressure . . . whammo. Alleged rape — white woman — high-profile rugby player — cops looking for a quick victory . . . Roger didn't have a chance.'

Norm returned to the hotel in the morning after spending the night with businessman Piet Botha and his family, who had befriended him during the All Black tour the previous year. When it became apparent what was being alleged it was Botha who contacted his lawyer, Lester Schoeman, and arranged for Randle's legal defence.

But it was already too late. The media had been tipped off and the police were only too happy to oblige them with selective titbits of information. To make matters worse, the Hurricanes management, inexperienced in such matters, were unable to grasp the politics involved. They telephoned home and awaited instructions from both the NZRFU and the Hurricanes leadership. By the time a formal response had been arranged, it was all too late. The public damage had been done. Randle had been arrested, interrogated, and was soon to be televised fleeing his initial arraignment, his head covered by a coat. No-one protested the young man's innocence — everyone was too stunned by the turn of events.

'It was all pretty dramatic and I was glad that Piet was there because none of us had a handle on it. I knew Roger because he was a Hawke's Bay boy and he always struck me as a quiet, shy type of guy. Wouldn't say boo. He hardly ever drank and was really close to his lady back in Flaxmere . . . the allegations just didn't square with what we knew of the guy.'

The immediate problem was that the woman had slept with other Hurricanes players. There is a suspicion that once this was known, the team management were reluctant to let the entire truth be released for fear of its embarrassing consequences. Leavasa was married, one of the other players involved was an All Black. The team was hastily assembled by manager Bedford, brought up to play with what had happened, and confined to the hotel for the rest of the day.

'Bull and I just looked at each other and shook our heads — we felt so hopeless. At one stage I had to track Roger down because he was so upset about the allegation and had just taken off before the cops arrived. And then we had the Australian cricket team arriving in the hotel the same morning, media everywhere, me looking after Piet's kids while he was down at the [police] station with his lawyer and Roger . . . it was surreal. And because most of us had been out celebrating and had had bugger all sleep, it was like it was all a bad dream. Somehow not quite real.'

Although Randle was allowed to fly out with the team the next day for Australia, he was met at Sydney by Hurricanes CEO David White and escorted back to New Zealand. The rest of the Hurricanes party flew on to Brisbane. Back in New Zealand the young man would be subjected to the most intrusive of media scrutiny, with certain quarters implying guilt — the Durban police had confirmed that semen samples found on the bedroom sheets included Randle's, and the woman herself appeared articulate and plausible. At first. As the media probed deeper they discovered that the complainant had an unstable personality and a murky past. Eventually a settlement was reached, with the woman being paid a sum of money in return for withdrawing the rape complaint. But the public odour remained, and Randle also faced a legal bill of $50,000 and the threat of civil arrest should he ever return to the Republic.

It wasn't just Randle who was shell-shocked. David White remembers the occasion vividly.

'I met a very confused young man at Sydney airport — Roger was physically and emotionally shattered. It was made even more difficult because, technically, Roger was an employee of the NZRFU. And we didn't have plans for this sort of thing happening.'

Neither did the team or its management. A meeting of all the players and team officials was called, to try and sort out the dramatic events and determine an appropriate response.

'We all agreed that things had got out of control,' Norm recalls. 'Oh, we were doing the business on the paddock, but some of our social activities were getting a bit out of hand. And we were getting distracted. So we just said, "Right, let's all go off the booze." Just like that. It was a team pledge: we'll stay off the piss until the Super 12 is over.'

Graeme Taylor considers that the Randle affair and the consequent booze ban were the key to the rest of the season's heroics. But he and Oliver had also decided that they wanted the Allen-Hewitt axis broken — the two senior players too often questioned the decisions of the management team.

'Norm and Bull were very, very close and I considered that their relationship was often to the detriment of the team. They wanted to run everything, and because they were both All Blacks they had considerable mana with the other players. At times, there were conflicts between what they wanted and what we [Oliver and Taylor] demanded. So Frank decided that he would disband the "back seat" for a start — the back seat being Bull, Norm and Phil Coffin. We wanted to have it out a bit more directly but then the Randle affair came along and we weren't going to have that sort of argument in front of the boys or the media. Instead, we just decreed that there'd be an alcohol ban until further notice. Further notice later extended to the whole season.'

Norm was confused by the new directives. Frank had been 'one of the boys' and seemed to relish the social company of the senior players. But it was as if the head coach had suddenly realised that he'd been too close — that the buffalo incident had given credence to the old adage about familiarity breeding contempt. Of one thing, Norm was convinced — he'd crossed a line. Oliver was still fuming as they flew out of South Africa.

In their next game, against the Queensland Reds, the events of the past week seemed to catch up with the Hurricanes. That and the travel arrangements, which had seen them fly from Johannesburg to Perth, then on to Sydney, and finally to Brisbane.

'We were down 15 points in 15 minutes,' remembers Taylor, 'and I was hoping that Ballymore would open up and swallow me. I could just imagine the shit we'd be in once we got home — the Randle incident and then getting hammered by Queensland. Scratch the season.'

And then — the remarkable power of an individual to alter a game. In this case, Bull Allen. With a mixture of mad purpose and frustrated rage, the captain began to seek out the ball and deliberately run at the opposition as if they were his mortal enemies. Within a few moments his solo acts had galvanised the rest of the forward pack, and that energy flowed on through the rest of the team. That night the Hurricanes literally blew the Reds off Ballymore Park, winning 49-27 and securing maximum points.

Both Taylor and Hewitt are agreed that Bull Allen's performance that night was more than just inspirational — it was one of the finest individual performances in Super 12 history. And its effect was to give the Hurricanes the opportunity to turn a so-so season into a great one.

The team came home to an enthusiastic reception from the local media, although the fans were still doubtful — until two stunning displays of running rugby at Athletic Park, when the Hurricanes put first the Bulls and then the Highlanders to the sword. The interchange between backs and forwards, the constant movement and the continual changing of attack angles made for some exhilarating rugby. Fifty-nine points against the Bulls, 60 against the Highlanders — the Hurricanes were the form team of the competition.

Norm was also relishing the team's success. Wellington's media began to make a fuss of their star front row, and the Hurricanes' marketing team was quick to capitalise. There were celebrity events and newspaper profiles, sponsors' functions and personality interviews . . . wherever Norm went he was feted as a hero, a genuine celebrity.

The fans also became aware of his not-so-occasional acts of altruism — finding tickets for an elderly pensioner, giving a pep talk to disabled kiddies, going out of his way to train the Hurricanes' reserve prop, the giant Fijian Bill Cavubati, donating a speaking fee to a kids' charity. Bull might be the charismatic captain and Christian Cullen the star, but Norm Hewitt was not far behind in the public's estimation. He was portrayed as the hard man with a heart of gold — the faithful lieutenant with a ready smile and an eye for a charitable cause.

'I'm not sure I consciously thought about it. I just found that I enjoyed helping people — making a difference. And you could do it so easily — a ticket, an autograph, a few words at a primary school . . . it wasn't hard stuff. That's the great thing about doing anything good, I discovered — both giver and recipient get a buzz. And that was a bit of a shock to me because I'd always been so selfish, always put myself at number one. Now, I didn't need to. It was time to give something back.'

BOGEY-MAN

If Norm thought the Durban controversy had ended, he was mistaken. He began to hear whispers within the Hurricanes camp that his part in events had been unfavourably reported to John Hart. In particular, that he had been drinking again.

'John Hart had his snitches — players who would drop you in it if they were in conversation with him. He was always phoning players and asking questions about their fitness or how their form was, but occasionally he'd ask more general questions, like, "So, what's so-and-so up to then?" I guess it was his way of gathering information on other players. But I felt that sometimes the questions weren't necessarily rugby-related.

'And I guess I was a bit paranoic at the time. I didn't trust him and I don't think he trusted me, so any little rumour I might hear would put me on edge. Anyway, I heard that my drinking in South Africa had been reported by a couple of the Hurricanes players and that Tony Bedford had been asked a few questions.'

His agreement with Hart was that he would not touch alcohol while he was within the All Black camp. What he did while under Hurricanes management was another matter entirely. But those did not seem to be the inferences he was picking up.

For his part, the All Black coach accepted that there would always be a fine line between counselling and directing individual players and interfering in their private lives.

'We had a human resource file on each player,' says Hart. 'The problem was that as All Black coach, I only had the players for a specific amount of time. First they'd be within their Super 12 franchises and then later with their NPC unions. What I wanted to do was get some integration — ensure that any common threads like injury or discipline problems could be sorted out immediately rather than left unchecked.

'My aim, particularly for the top players, was to ensure that we could assist them to become well-rounded individuals — to be able to counsel them in any media or education or personal problems they might be having. Some individuals accepted that help while others resented it.'

Norm was very much in the latter camp. He loathed Hart's personnel policy as intrusive and unwarranted, and although he might see the logic in the All Black camp setting guidelines about playing expectations, he could not accept that Hart had any right to impose standards beyond that orbit. And yet, he reasoned, what choice did he really have? If he openly defied Hart his All Black career would be at an end.

John Hart confirms this perception. 'I made it clear. If he did drink, I wouldn't pick him ... I told him — "If you want to play for the All Blacks, then this is the rule: No drink."'

For his part, Norm continued to deny that he had a problem. Full stop. And he bitterly resented the double standards that were being applied by Hart and the All Black management, regularly observing social behaviour by other senior All Blacks that seemed the equivalent of or worse than his own. But then they were some of Hart's favoured Aucklanders ...

'Some of the senior ABs could get real messy. And while I was no angel

169

when I was under the influence, I didn't see myself as acting any different from the rest. I mean that's the thing about rugby players at that level. You don't leave the aggression on the field — it's a part of your make-up. It's what makes a mediocre player good, and a good player great. That ability to dominate your opponent. And off the field, those contests of strength and will would still be there. So I'd get into a certain mind fix when I drank in rugby company. I wouldn't allow myself to be intimidated. Well, it's one step from stopping yourself being intimidated to intimidating others. And drink would take me that step.'

Norm's reaction to the whispering campaign was shrewd. He could front Hart direct, but that would mean going up against a man he considered smarter and more savvy than he was. It had already been his experience that a player stood no show against a determined coach, and Hart wasn't just an ordinary coach. But he knew that if he let Hart take the initiative there was no telling what discipline might be in store. He would have to find a way of heading Hart off at the pass, without necessarily been seen as challenging the All Black coach's authority.

Norm rang me. 'As an ex-politician, I thought [Michael] might have a good idea of what would be the best course of action. And I guess because I considered Hart to be a bit of a politician, I thought I should fight like with like.'

The result was a letter, faxed to Hart's home address, in which Norm drew a careful distinction between his good behaviour bond while in the All Black camp and his social behaviour outside it.

'I didn't want to piss Hart off, but more fire a warning shot. Like suggesting to him that there was a boundary line between the public and the private Norm Hewitt. And I said that if he wanted to change the rules to govern all private situations then I was prepared to discuss it, but only as a part of any renewed contract with the NZRFU. When I saw [Michael's] letter, I went — "Yeah, that's what I want. Something that would make a Pakeha professional think twice."'

As soon as the All Black coach received the fax, he scribbled a hand–written note across it and faxed it off to All Black manager Mike Banks. 'Mike,' the note read, 'We should have this out with no tomorrow. John.'

The consequence was that Hart met with Norm in Wellington prior to the Super 12 game, and an arrangement was reached.

'Actually, I caved in,' Norm says. 'He said that I had a problem and I said I didn't. So then he says, "Well I'm the coach and I'm not having you embarrass the All Black jersey," or something like that. So I said, "OK, then I'll knock off the booze entirely." I had no real intention of doing so but I was playing well and I didn't want to give the prick a chance not to select me. Suddenly that silver fern had become very important — especially now that it looked like it was going to be taken away from me for something other than a loss of rugby form.'

In fact, the no-alcohol ban was easy to maintain. None of his Hurricanes mates were boozing now that the Randle pledge had been made, so the usual after-match temptation no longer existed. But the tension of the commitment remained. If he felt like a beer, he wanted to be able to have one. Hart's decree denied him that luxury.

Despite his simmering resentment, Norm continued to play the game as if each game was his last. His passion and mobility on the park drew praise from every quarter and Wellington's *Evening Post* rated him their top player of the Super 12 series — outshining more illustrious team-mates like Allen, Cullen and Umaga. He was fit, determined and in a team where he felt both comfortable and valued — it was as if the clock had been turned back and he was captaining Hawke's Bay again.

Meanwhile the Hurricanes continued to draw the crowds to their spectacular brand of running rugby, the highlight of the season a breathtaking 42-45 loss at Eden Park against the mighty Auckland Blues. Against a team choked with current All Blacks, the Hurricanes' audacious risk-taking won converts throughout the southern hemisphere. They had become the excitement team, the personification of what the Super 12 was all about — style, entertainment and personality.

But although they qualified for the semi-finals, the Hurricanes suffered key injuries to key players — first, blindside Chresten Davis was invalided out, and then backline mainstay Alama Ieremia. And against the discipline and cleverness of the ACT Brumbies, the Hurricanes were found out on a chilling night at Canberra's Bruce Stadium.

'To beat the Brumbies we needed our top fifteen on the park and to be firing on all cylinders. They had class players everywhere, especially with Finegan, Gregan and Knox at 8, 9 and 10. Then they had Larkham at fullback and Roff and Hardy on the wings, so they had a great attacking back three as well. The thing I most admired about them was that they were so intelligent — they didn't look to run through you like the New Zealand teams or to physically dominate you like the South Africans, but to create half-gaps and then quickly exploit them. Gregan was the key, and in both our last round-robin game at Athletic Park and then in the semi-final, our loosies ended up getting mesmerised by him. He's the best halfback I've ever seen — his short passing can carve you up — and we got into the habit of watching him instead of attacking him.'

But as the team returned home there was general satisfaction that they had finished third on the table, and that the Crusaders, the Highlanders and the Chiefs had all finished below them. The Hurricanes' franchise was safe, with exceptional crowds following their home games and the team's performance unearthing and promoting any number of stars for higher honours.

Although their efforts were clearly overlooked by the All Black selectors when they named the team to lead off the new international season against Fiji. The only new name was Tana Umaga, Hart sticking by the stalwarts who had delivered him the Springbok series victory the year before. However, from the reserves named that evening, four more players would make their test debuts — loose forwards Taine Randell and Charles Reichelmann, halfback Ofisa Tonu'u — and hooker Anton Oliver. Oliver's selection incensed Norm, and distanced him even further from the All Black coach.

'After the Super 12 final, Hart called me and said that he was worried how much rugby I might get if they included me in the test squad against Fiji. He said that he wanted me to play for the Maoris so that I could get some game time, but that the choice was mine.

'I smelt a rat so I said, "I'll train with the ABs then." Which obviously wasn't the answer he wanted because next thing he gets pretty angry and accuses me of being selfish. Then he says that they [the selectors] have already made their decision and I'll be hooking for the Maoris and Anton will be the reserve to Fitzy.'

Hart concedes that Norm did not accept his reasoning for the switch, but reiterates that his purpose was purely strategic.

'I wanted Norm to be getting some rugby ahead of the Tri-Nations rather than just be sitting on the bench. The Maoris had three games against Ireland A, Argentina and Samoa so it was an ideal opportunity to make sure he stayed match fit. I knew he didn't like the decision but I thought it was for the best.'

But the incident widened the breach between the two men — especially when Fitzpatrick's troublesome knee flared up during the Fiji test and Anton Oliver got some serious game time. Restored to the All Black squad for the two home tests against Argentina, Norm approached Hart to see if he might get one of the tests or alternatively be brought on as a replacement. But Hart refused his request and Fitzpatrick played out both internationals, despite the 93-8 and 63-10 scorelines.

'It was obvious that he didn't rate me. More and more I got the feeling from these sorts of incidents and his general attitude that he didn't want me there or think I was up to it. That if Anton was a better scrummager he would have my spot and I'd be nowhere. It was like when you don't like someone so you don't look them in the eyes . . . that was the treatment I got from Hart.'

Others within the All Black camp had also noted Hart's attitude. In his book *On the Loose*, Josh Kronfeld writes that while he was often confused by Hart's treatment of him, it was obvious that 'some players didn't seem to count for much — Norm Hewitt and Bull Allen appeared not to be highly regarded'.

Little wonder then that the two players preferred each other's company when they were within the All Black camp. Hart clearly had his favourites, and in the 1997 season he again demonstrated a preference for Auckland players like Mark Carter, Reichelmann and Carlos Spencer. Yet who was to say that he was wrong? The All Blacks kept winning — first dusting off the Wallabies 30-13 in Christchurch, then going on to successfully defend their Tri-Nations title with epic away wins in Johannesburg and Melbourne. And it was at Johannesburg that Norm realised his dream of playing a test against the mighty Springboks.

As usual, he had been chosen for the reserve bench and, as usual, he didn't expect to see any action. But midway through the game Sean Fitzpatrick took what was ultimately a career-ending blow to his knee and it became obvious that even his monumental self-will could not get him through the game. Norm watched anxiously from the sideline as the call came to get ready, Fitzpatrick getting slower and slower as the game progressed. From a 7-23 deficit the All Blacks had worked their way back into the game through some individual magic from Jeff Wilson and Carlos Spencer, but a Jannie de Beer penalty took the gap back to seven points.

Enter the ageing and supposedly arthritic Frank Bunce. The All Black centre's Super 12 had been patchy at best, and talkback critics had been demanding his replacement in the test backline. But Hart knew Bunce was a player with a big-match temperament. He latched onto a pass on halfway and ran through a yawning gap while the South African defence scrambled to cover the outside All Black runners. Too late they realised that Bunce could go all the way, and with a final flourish past the bemused James Small, Bunce scored one of the great All Black tries. The Spencer conversion saw the game tied up at 26-all.

'I'd seen Fitzy stumble and then got the word just as a scrum was about to be set. I couldn't believe it at first — here I was in the depths of Afrikaner Hell, in front of 70,000 screaming yarpies, and you could feel the tension as if it was alive. It was an amazing experience — I'd never felt anything quite that white-hot ever before and it's never been matched since. It was like being too close to electricity pylons when you can hear and feel the crack of all that energy just above you. Except this was all around us . . . it was incredible.'

As he ran out onto the field, above the din and chaos of Ellis Park a single loud whoop could be heard around the ground. It was reserve hooker Norm Hewitt screaming out his excitement — releasing all the frustration that had dogged his career over the past four years.

'Some of the players heard and they looked at me as if I was mad. And I reckon, for a few moments there, I actually was. I was so pumped up, so amazingly hyper that I just barrelled into any green jersey I could see. And it was a really physical game too — like there were thirty of us out there literally fighting to the death. That's how intense it was.'

Ultimately the game would be decided by penalties — the All Black tight five gaining a slight ascendancy over their opposites but the Bok loosies of Teichmann, Kruger and Andre Venter having an advantage over the Kiwi back row of Brooke, Kronfeld and Randell.

'Carlos [Spencer] had a magic game that night. And he kicked some amazing pressure goals. When that last penalty went against us and de Beer stepped up, all I could think was what a bummer to draw. And then he missed it — it hit the upright — we scrambled it out and the game was ours. And the most amazing thing was that it felt like I'd just come on the field — the adrenalin made everything go so fast. It was like I'd had an out-of-body experience or something, because I seemed to be running on pure energy and not getting tired at all. And then the whistle went and we'd won. Beaten the yarpies in Jo'burg for the first time since '92. Shit, it felt good . . . as good as great sex. And I thought, "Yeah, this is why I play this game. Nothing matches this."'

The All Blacks' next game was just a week later against Australia at the Melbourne Cricket Ground — a test that many considered to be difficult enough coming a week after the Johannesburg heroics, but in front of a record crowd in sporting mad Melbourne? In fact the venue was the least of the team's concerns. Their main problem was the long flight back and a captain whose knee needed rest and recuperation.

'All week Hart told me that I would be playing the [Melbourne] test and I trained with the playing fifteen, fine-tuned all the various lineout drills and packed down with Olo Brown and Craig Dowd at scrum time. I thought I'd acquitted myself pretty well at Jo'burg and I knew Fitzy's knee wasn't right. But then the day before Hart says that they want to see how Fitzy is on the day. In the end they gave him some pain-killing hypos and he played, but it wasn't his best game and you could tell that it was mental will alone that kept out there. You had to admire him for the effort — there was no way he was going to give me a look-in.'

By half-time the All Blacks had taken maximum advantage of a couple of Wallaby defensive errors and at 23-6 the test was safely in the tucker bag. And then, when it appeared that Norm might yet come on as a replacement, Fitzpatrick summoned a last burst of determination and in concert with Zinzan Brooke created a path for the young star Christian Cullen to put the match beyond the slightest doubt.

'I couldn't believe it. Off the field, Fitzy had been hobbling like some broken down old hobo. And then he goes for a run like that . . . I knew then that whatever gods lived in the rugby world, not one of them was on my side. I had to laugh — it was so bloody exciting and tragic all at the same time.'

In the remaining two Tri-Nations tests the All Blacks comfortably accounted for both the Springboks and the Wallabies — 55-35 and 36-24 respectively. And a feature of both games was the sublime skills of the old hands blending with the effervescence of the new stars — Kronfeld, Spencer, Cullen and Wilson.

'It was a "confidence" backline — from Justin [Marshall] back to Cully at fullback — if those guys were in form then nothing was going to stop them. And if you decided to cover Carlos then maybe Buncey would make the break or Goldie come off his wing or Cully attack from broken play. It was amazing to watch because these were top guns, really athletic guys at the top of their skills. But, Frank apart, they were also confidence players. Their rhythm could be unsettled and if it did then a couple of them might switch off and drift out of the game. But that first half against Australia at Carisbrook [when the All Blacks raced to a 36-nil half-time lead] . . . man, that was something else.'

With the SANZAR Cup successfully defended, Norm returned to Southland for their first division campaign. He had played a couple of games for the southerners between All Black commitments, and believed the team had a chance of retaining their premier status as long as they targeted some of the home games.

'The truth was we played most of our games on good old guts and determination. We didn't have the players or the facilities to challenge the top teams so our idea was to give it a whirl away and get ultra-serious at home.'

Incredibly, one of the 'give it a whirl' performances almost produced the domestic rugby upset of the decade — Southland being pipped 34-32 by the mighty Auks at Eden Park while challenging for the Ranfurly Shield. Norm and the Southland forwards took the fight direct to their illustrious opposites, but it was the Southland backs who shocked the holders with their daring and speed.

'We should have won. In all my time with Southland I doubt if we ever played a better game. It was rip-shit-and-bust stuff, but the atmosphere and the quality of the opposition kept the adrenalin going. And Auckland were having a bad, bad day — they coughed up ball, they made basic errors, their backline nearly strangled itself. We had nothing to lose so it didn't matter. And we almost snatched it in the last moment too when our winger got into space . . . it was a pretty amazing effort.'

Certainly Norm's own form was irresistible. The Southland pack looked to their hooker for both example and leadership and he provided both, Saturday after Saturday. He was enjoying his stint in the south — the people were direct, the rugby was hard and physical, and he was feted wherever he went, the big fish in a small pond. But mostly he was enjoying playing rugby — getting hold of the ball and running hard, matching himself against other hookers and front rows, keeping rival teams honest. Southland's grafting style and spirit suited his own — heartland rugby at its best. And they had beaten Otago in the local derby. The season could almost be judged on that result alone.

And then, as so often in his life, when everything looked to be back on an even keel, when he was starting to feel comfortable with himself again, when Kat and he were talking about getting married and having kids, and when his rugby was at its season's peak . . . Norm incurred a shocking injury that had nearby spectators squirming and looking away.

'We were playing Wellington at Athletic Park and starting to get on top of them. It wasn't much of a day, cold and wet, and our pack felt like it was back home. I went into a ruck, went to ground, got up and started following the ball again when some of the players started shouting out to me . . . "Norm, Norm — your leg!" I looked down and all I could see was this huge gash in my thigh and the blood pissing out.'

But it was not the wound itself that caused the hooker to stagger to the sideline and push away the waiting medics. It was common knowledge that Fitzpatrick was labouring from the effects of his knee injury and that the All Black skipper was a doubtful starter for the tour to Ireland, Wales and England the next month. Norm's outstanding NPC form had been built around the belief that this would be his only opportunity to play regular test rugby — that he had to prove to the indifferent Hart and the other selectors that he was the next best choice . . . that the number 2

Above: *The first ever game of professional rugby. Wellington Hurricanes v Auckland Blues, Palmerston North 1996. Bull Allen leads out the home franchise.*

Below: *Blues wonder winger Jonah Lomu troubles the Hurricanes defence. The Blues eventually triumphed 29-17 but no-one cared. In just eighty minutes, the Super12 had captured the hemisphere.*

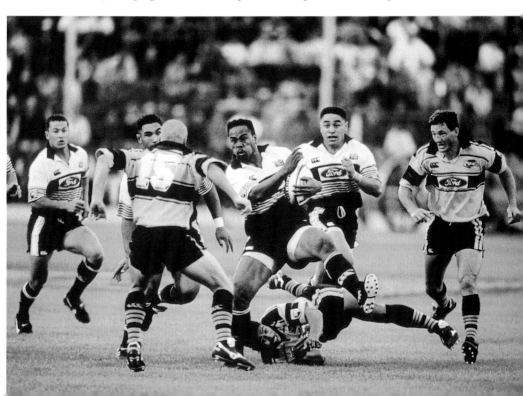

*Wonder of wonders.
Sean Fitzpatrick has gone to
the blood bin and Norm plays
a minor role in the All Blacks'
performance of the decade.
Thrashing the Wallabies 43-6
at Athletic Park 1996. The
props are Olo Brown and
Craig Dowd.*

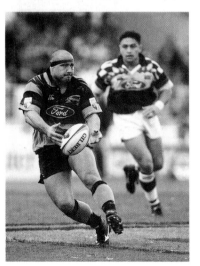

*Part of the 1997 Super12 entertainment machine. Norm in action against the
eventual finalists, the Auckland Blues and the ACT Brumbies. After this, the IRB
law-makers intervened. Rugby was just <u>too</u> exciting.*

*South Africa 1996. John Hart introduced the concept of teams within a team —
and here two of them, 'No Mercy' (above) and 'Big Mex' (below) meet on the
tennis court. It was symbolic of a wider rift within the team between the 'A' team
and the dirt-trackers. The 'No Mercy' team consists of Jon Preston, Bull Allen,
Alama Ieremia, Norm, Glenn Taylor and Simon Culhane.*

Left: *The All Black management team to the UK 1997. From left, Ross Cooper, Sean Fitzpatrick, John Hart, Gordon Hunter and Mike Banks.*
Right: *Crocked captain Sean Fitzpatrick and coach John Hart announce the All Black test team to play Ireland, November 1997. Fitzpatrick should never have toured.*

Bittersweet. Norm takes the field in the surrogate No. 2 jersey to play Ireland at Landsdowne Road.

jersey was rightfully his to wear. And now here he was, holding onto his right leg and watching the internal workings of his thigh, the white of the muscles pulsing deep within.

To this day no-one is really sure how such a freak accident occurred. The official version was that a Wellington player's sprig had unintentionally sliced through the thigh, but Norm has a different explanation.

'The area that was Athletic Park was a rubbish dump in its early days and I'm pretty sure that something in the earth caused the injury. Two days later it was infected and had to be opened up again, cleaned and restitched. There were something like fourteen internal stitches and then another sixteen external ones ... the leg looked like it belonged to someone else — that it had been sewn on from some Frankenstein movie.'

The All Blacks were due to play their opening British tour game in less than a month.

'I've always healed fast. Being youngish and fit helps, but it's more than that — I'm just a typical tough Maori boy. We heal quick. After they'd cleaned out the wound again, I reckoned I'd be right and, thank God, so did [All Black doctor] Doc Mayhew. I was so keen to prove my fitness that I was back running on it a week later. It hurt like hell but I knew Fitzy was down and that this was my big chance. I wasn't going to give that up for any bastard.'

When the touring party was announced and his name was there, Norm breathed a sigh of relief. Although there was a measure of surprise that Fitzpatrick was also named.

'It didn't make sense to me. I knew he was stuffed and so did everyone else. I'd seen them draw huge amounts of fluid from his knee during the Tri-Nations games in an effort to get him ready but this was different again. Fitzpatrick didn't need to tour. We'd won the big prizes like the Bledisloe and the Tri-Nations ... they should either have let him recover over Christmas or left him at home. He wasn't fit to tour and neither was Zinzan Brooke. They were both thinking retirement and the UK tour could have blooded new players for the World Cup two years later. So when I heard Fitzy's name, all I thought was, "What new swifty are these buggers trying to pull now?" Although I couldn't complain — not really. After that slash at Athletic Park, I was bloody lucky to be flying off too.'

CHAPTER THIRTEEN

England

Despite being the form hooker of the 1997 season, and despite Fitzpatrick's chronic knee injury, Norm continued to play in the shadow of the All Black captain. John Hart might have had two assistant coaches in Ross Cooper and Gordon Hunter, but it was to Fitzpatrick and Zinzan Brooke that he would turn when he required technical assistance with the forwards. Indeed, the Fitzpatrick/Brooke axis was a power all of its own, and Hart relied heavily on their experience and leadership. So much so that the All Black coach would ask Fitzpatrick to be his assistant the next season — a clear vote of no confidence in both Cooper and Hunter. Fitzpatrick would decline this request, preferring to play another season, but this would not save the assistant coaches from being dumped — to be replaced by Crusaders coach and former Hawke's Bay CEO Wayne Smith and his assistant, former All Black hooker Peter Sloane.

From Norm's perspective, it was obvious that all was not right in the coaching trio's make-up. But then Norm didn't rate the assistant coaches either. Cooper and Hunter were 'the nodders' — yes-men to Hart's commands. And after Mains' detailed approach and emphasis on technique, Hart's light hand required technical back-up from somewhere. Anywhere. But it remained curiously absent.

'The '96–'97 All Blacks coached themselves. The forward pack had Fitzy, Zinny, Olo Brown, Robin Brooke, Ian Jones . . . these guys had been around for a while and they were encouraged to "take ownership" I think the phrase was . . . yeah, take ownership of their particular area.

'Hart's style was more of a chief executive than a coach. The All Blacks were run along business lines, which I wasn't necessarily opposed to. Except someone had to do the nitty-gritty stuff and neither Hart nor Cooper nor Hunter knew much about the forwards. They certainly didn't have Laurie's talents. But while Fitzy and Zinny were there, it didn't really matter.

'If I had to confine myself to one criticism of Hart,' and here Norm laughs, 'it would be that he forgot the first principle of being a good CEO, which is to delegate. He kept trying to interfere in all the off-field stuff when his job was to get the boys flying right on the paddock. I mean, I didn't trust the prick at all by the time of the '97 tour. I loathed the bastard — so I couldn't take the step back and rationalise what was happening until later. I was too close.'

The naming of three hookers for the end-of-season tour only added to Norm's distrust and sense of insecurity. That Fitzpatrick was touring at all, given his near absence from the NPC, suggested Hart still regarded him as the first choice. And with Hart protege Anton Oliver also in the mix the Southland hooker couldn't be assured he would be playing any games, let alone the tests. Even after the first tour game against the famous Welsh club Llanelli, and despite a barnstorming display that included two tries, Norm perceived an indifference emanating from the coaching staff.

'It was a really weird time because the Llanelli game suggested that I was the number one hooker, but Fitzy was hovering around like a ghost and Anton was there too. And it wasn't just Hart — I felt snubbed by Hunter and Cooper too. They seemed to think that I didn't deserve my spot, that I was just filling in or something.'

'REAL' TESTS

With these misgivings in the back of his mind, Norm approached his first 'real' test against Ireland as if it was his last. Although Fitzpatrick appeared incapable of training, let alone playing, Norm knew his stocks were low and that his hold on the number 2 jersey was tenuous indeed. He went through the usual rituals of an All Black player before an international match — the formal handing over of the coveted jersey in the morning by manager Mike Banks, the lineout drills at the team hotel, the visualising of game situations, the motivational speech by the head coach. Except Norm didn't listen. He had his own psychological sequence, his own gee-up ritual, which included proving himself to the very coach he so disliked.

'Josh was right in *On the Loose*. John Hart talked too much, and most of it was crap. I mean I didn't need anybody to tell me what was required — I had the silver fern on my chest and the number 2 on my back. That was all the motivation I'd ever need. But what we really needed was someone who could dispassionately analyse the game, figure out what we were doing wrong, where we should attack the opposition. We needed more of the basics and less of the drama.'

Although it was Norm's view that an eight-year-old could define the Irish team's tactics. They would go mad in the first twenty minutes, try and suck the All Blacks into a physical game, and hope like hell they had enough points on the board by half-time to motivate them for the second half. Sure enough, the Irish forwards drove into their vaunted opposition from the first whistle and halfway through the first half were leading 15 points to 11, thanks to two tries by their hooker and captain Keith Wood.

'I've played rugby against most of the good hookers in the world but Keith Wood is the best. He's not much of a scrummager — not as good as [Australian hooker Phil] Kearns or Fitzy, but he's a great runner and kicker — a fourth loose forward and a bit more. I backed myself against him in the tight and I reckoned I had the better of him in the scrum and mauls that day, but I really admired his speed and his spirit. By half-time we'd pulled ahead, and then we took them apart in the second half. And then Wood went off injured, so they lost what little spirit they had left.'

But for all the ease of the win — the backs scoring seven tries — the unique atmosphere that is international rugby had captivated Norm. Here he was, running onto the emerald of Lansdowne Park with 52,000 frenzied spectators packed tightly into the old-fashioned arena — the crowd close to the touchlines and vigorously waving their green flags, while small pockets of black and white highlight the groups of All Black supporters. Then a deep, rumbling roar as the local team canters onto the park, led by the balding Keith Wood, some sprinting off at an angle to relieve their nervousness, while others turn and grimly eye their opposition.

And then it's into the semi-circle and Zinzan Brooke is out front, leading the haka. As 'Ka mate ka mate' shudders around that crooked black line, Norm puts every vestige of his concentration into the rhythm of the chant, drawing strength not only from the players around him but from the words themselves, until the final leap of the challenge and the rush into starting position. From the kick-off, he rushes after the ball and smashes into the first maul, confident that he is in the company of fighters who will never flinch, no matter what the opposition.

'That Irish test — in fact, in all the tests I played — I felt like a warrior. I was all primed to play, all hyped up to intimidate and dominate and win. And there was no way I was going to let down the other guys around me or the jersey. The jersey was everything to me — this was what I had dreamed about night after night back in Takapau — running into battle. And for me, at least, it was just that — a war. It has to be at this level if you want to win because the guys you're playing are as big, as strong, as skilled as you are. It's all about desire at this level — desire and mental toughness. And, increasingly, intelligence. That was something I learned later in my career. You've got to intimidate, yeah, but you've also got to be smart. And that was where we started to lose it later in the tour. Justin Marshall was the captain, Fitzy was crocked on the sideline, Zinny was going through the motions . . . we lost the team's rugby brains.'

The next international was against England — the first of two, with a test against Wales sandwiched in between. In an effort to promote the game outside London, the English Rugby Union had decided to host the first of these tests at Old Trafford in Manchester, and Norm's first walk on the ground left him in awe.

'We went for our usual pre-match stroll and I just shivered the whole time. The crowd are close to the pitch but the seating is such that it's like they're all sitting on top of each other and all looking down at you. It was stunning — like being inside one of those amazing English cathedrals. Which, I suppose, it was — because soccer is Britain's only true religion. That's the thing I didn't properly appreciate until my second tour there . . . that soccer is more important to the average Pom than rugby is to us. That's how mad they are about the game — mad to the point that some of them should be locked up. You could *feel* that passion as you walked onto the pitch and looked up at all the red plastic seats and the white lettering that spelled out "Manchester United". I knew that whatever else I ever did in rugby, nothing would match how I felt as I walked over Old Trafford that morning. It was like I was on holy ground.'

It was not just the venue that was impressive. The English fancied their chances of repeating their '93 home triumph and had selected a massive and experienced pack. The front row of Leonard, Cockerill and Garforth had bested everything in the Five Nations, and locks Martin Johnson and Gavin Archer completed a genuinely formidable front five — a tight five that, if anything, the All Blacks underestimated. But it was in the loose forward trio of Dallaglio, Hill and Diprose that England enjoyed a real size and weight advantage, although Norm considered they had erred in not selecting the swift Neil Back.

'It was obvious that they were going to play ten-man rugby and keep the ball in front of their big pack. We knew they rated their pack but I was confident we could match them, and with Josh Kronfeld and Taine [Randell] on the sides, I reckoned that we would be quicker to the loose ball. So I was pretty confident in my preparations despite all the Pom hype about how they would take us apart up front.'

A day before the game, Zinzan Brooke took Norm aside for a quiet word — a conversation that took the hooker completely by surprise.

'He said, all nonchalant like, ". . . and you lead the haka." And I'm going — "What?!?" I couldn't believe it! Me lead the haka against England on Old Trafford . . . it just stunned me. Zinny wasn't really into taha Maori the same way that, say, Eric Rush and I were, and the haka is a big deal for us. It's got to be led right and by someone who understands its importance and place within Maori culture. Up until then, I'd led the New Zealand Maoris with our own special haka and done the occasional midweek one but this . . . this was something else again. I was stoked. Big time.'

And so unfolded the biggest controversy of the tour. The national anthems had been sung, the teams introduced to the Princess Royal, and the first strains of 'Swing low, sweet chariot' were rising above the hubbub. Norm crouched down, raised his arms in front of his chest, and the All Blacks arrayed themselves behind him, adopting their leader's stance. To the sides, flashbulbs popped and camera crews jostled with photographers, but all Norm concentrated on was the wall of white jerseys before him, the English players standing close and defiant, arms linked behind their backs. He began the traditional leader's chant, but before he could utter Te Rauparaha's immortal opening line, a strong English accent rang out across the halfway line.

'Fuck you . . . fuck you, arsehole.'

As the haka continued, the insults from the English players became louder and more numerous — their faces curling in contempt as the All Blacks shouted out the ritual challenge. And then the English line began to advance on the All Black huddle, across the halfway mark, led not by their captain Laurence Dallaglio but by hooker Richard Cockerill, a pugnacious bulldog of a man who was not in the least intimidated by the haka or the occasion. Within seconds, he was face to face with Norm — each snarling at the other like a pair of angry dogs, each daring the other to lose the last vestige of self control and take the first swing.

It was an image that flashed around the sports world. The shaven white mass of Richard Cockerill glowering across at the shaven brown mass of Norm Hewitt — two warriors eager for battle, separated by bare centimetres, inviting confrontation. By the time the haka finished Cockerill was so close Norm could not jump without head-butting him, a thought that flashed through his mind until the Aussie drawl of referee Peter Marshall urged both teams to 'stay back, stay back'.

'I just wanted to slug him [Cockerill]. But I knew I couldn't. Not in front of that many people and an international TV audience. But I knew there'd be a ruck or a maul or a little piece of action somewhere where I'd get the bastard. And yet, I didn't think he or the English players were disrespecting the haka. People who say that miss the point of what the haka is about. It's a challenge — a challenge to war. And the Poms had exactly the right answer to it — you accept that challenge and you throw it back. But, I'll tell you this — I was one motivated Maori boy that afternoon! And I made sure Cockerill knew it too.'

But the English had fighting qualities beyond the temporary fury shown by their Celtic neighbours the previous weekend. Although there was a similar venom to their forward play it was matched by a stronger discipline, and soon the English forwards were securing the vast share of possession. But despite their strength and size, the All Blacks still had an edge in skill and speed and, unlike the English, they could exploit any opportunity to the maximum. By half-time the All Blacks had scored tries to Ian Jones and Jeff Wilson after sudden switches of direction from second-phase play. When Taine Randell dummied his way over to score midway through the second half, the game was safe.

'Actually they had enough ball to win that game twice but they played Mike Catt at first five and he kicked poorly. Once the ball went into the English backline we knew we had the defence to cover them. And we also had Jonah [Lomu] and he frightens the crap out of the Poms every time he touches the ball. I don't know what it is about Jonah and the English but he plays his best against them and they fall over themselves trying to get out of his way. He made a lot of yards from broken play and our first try was due to him setting up the field position.'

As the All Blacks congratulated themselves on a good afternoon's work, the English players began a tour of Old Trafford — since derided in New Zealand rugby circles as a 'victory dance' for keeping the All Blacks to a 17-point margin.

'That wasn't a victory dance — they were thanking their fans for turning up and for all their support that afternoon. I mean, it was pretty immature of the Kiwi media to have a go at them over that because it was obvious what the English were doing. To fill Old Trafford and get that level of public support is a pretty good effort for a game that has to compete against soccer. It was just good PR by the team to acknowledge their fans. I didn't have any problem with that.'

But one thing did disappoint Norm about the British attitude. The All Black midweek team was not being given the opportunity to play club teams — instead being drawn against 'selections' comprising each country's up and coming talent.

'Even Llanelli had Welsh ring-ins . . . it was all a bit silly, really. The point of touring any country is to extend the traditions of the game, to keep those old rivalries going. It would have been nice to play the Leicesters and the Newcastles on their home grounds instead of England "A", or the "English Rugby Partnership XV", as one of them was called. So there wasn't much atmosphere to the midweek games — each one was a sort of trial.'

Especially for Norm. Because Fitzpatrick couldn't train, Norm continually found himself the reserve hooker to Anton Oliver, meaning there wasn't one game on the tour that he did not play or train for. Which went a long way to explain his attitude in the next test against Wales.

HUMILIATION

For the Welsh international the All Blacks were unchanged in the forwards from the pack that had played England, but in the backs Walter Little replaced Alama Ieremia at second five and Lomu was given a place in the starting line-up rather than being forced to come off the bench. The Welsh were not seen as top class opposition, and the fact that the test was to be played at Wembley Stadium rather than their beloved Cardiff Arms Park only reinforced that feeling.

'Wales are a second-rate team, and even at home we were pretty confident of beating them. They were a very unfit team too — at least before Graham Henry got hold of them — so, again, we were confident that we had their measure. But we were surprised that they wanted to play a more open game, and it was a lot more enjoyable for both spectators and players alike.'

By half-time the All Blacks had a handsome 25-nil lead, with Christian Cullen demonstrating his brilliant counter-attacking ability and scoring twice, and another flowing All Black move netting Taine Randell the first touchdown. But in the second half Wales seemed to rediscover their will and began to hold onto the ball instead of aimlessly hoofing it downfield whenever their initial attempts were thwarted. Norm was playing well — solid in the tight, finding his jumpers at lineout time and starting to shine in the loose. Without a doubt this was his best game of the tour so far and he knew it.

'Then the physio came on during a break and said, "You're off in five." And I think I said something like "Bullshit," and he said, "Sorry mate, but that's the call." And I just thought "Bastard!" I'd done my job in all the tests, I'd not let anyone down and was having a good game and then . . . I'm being subbed just as a lineout was being formed. Which pissed me off big-time and it showed as Fitzpatrick trotted out, gammy leg and all, and proceeded to rely on his props to cover his injury. I tossed him the ball in disgust and just kept walking.

'I admit it . . . I sat in the stand, fuming. And you could say that I sulked — but I was bloody angry. The guy shouldn't even have been on that tour and he'd never given me a look-in at any time in my whole career. And I remembered all those sly elbows and the punches and the dirt he'd put in over all the years and . . . yeah . . . I was not happy!'

Norm's mood didn't improve, despite the general air of celebration at the All Blacks' 42-7 win. Nor did it improve when the All Black coach pulled him aside at the after-match, stabbed his forefinger only a few centimetres from the hooker's nose and ordered Hewitt to come to his hotel room once the official function was over.

'It was like I was back at school again and had been summoned to the headmaster's office. It was exactly like that. When I got up there, the two nodders were also in the room and Hart was propped up on the bed. It was like a scene from one of those *Godfather* movies — the Don pretending to lounge around and the two heavies beside him. Anyway, he gets off the bed and says, "Who the hell do you think you are?" and he's angry. His face is flushed all red and he's saying that what I did was despicable, that I showed unbelievable disrespect to Sean Fitzpatrick and that I was lucky to even be on tour, let alone be a test player.

'And I knew I hadn't imagined the cold shoulder all tour. That all his dislike of me was just pouring out of his mouth and that this was what he really thought of me — him and his two mates — and that I was just a toerag to these guys. And because he was angry, the truth was really coming out.'

John Hart confirms the general tenor of the conversation.

'I was really upset. There were two issues as far as I was concerned. First, that substitutions were now part and parcel of the modern game and that players should get used to them. There had been the earlier incident that year when Justin Marshall had been subbed by Byron Kelleher at the Carisbrook test against Australia. I was concerned that, publicly, such dissent was not a good look for the All Blacks.

'And, second, I thought that Sean Fitzpatrick was a great player and that although there was obviously a problem with his knee, he didn't deserve to have Norm's refusal to acknowledge him or to have Norm storm off the field like he did.

'I don't often get upset but I was in the hotel room [that evening]. After I'd finished taking him to task, pretty vigorously as I recall, he started to cry. He was just a softie underneath. It was one of the assistants who said that he should apologise to the team.'

Norm disputes that he cried as a consequence of the dressing down.

'If there were any tears they were of frustration and anger. Hart was basically saying that I wasn't worth All Black status, and at one time I thought, "I'm going to deck this little prick. I'm going to deck him." Even my father didn't talk to me like Hart did that night, and during it all neither Hunter nor Cooper said a word. I certainly left feeling humiliated and I did get emotional when I later made my apology to the team. It was like being stripped of rank in front of all your army colleagues — it made me feel like I was a nothing, a nobody. I can't remember much of what I said to the team — something like "I apologise for my behaviour but I don't apologise for wanting to play test football."

'And Fitzpatrick sitting back and thinking that somehow he was owed this apology. It was an incredibly humiliating occasion and I felt it every second of the remaining days of the tour. It was like I was a leper or something. I later raised it with Fitzpatrick and Zinzan Brooke, about Hart's general treatment of me. They said they would talk to him but I doubt if they did because nothing changed. Besides, Fitzy and Zinny were the senior prefects to Hart's headmaster. Their loyalties didn't lie with the likes of me.'

KRONFELD'S CALL

Back in New Zealand, public and press sympathy were squarely on Norm's side. Former All Black test captain Andy Dalton said the hooker had every right to be angry at being replaced, given his standard of play and the fact that he'd spent a record 38 internationals on the bench watching Fitzpatrick play. *Dominion* sports editor Russell Gray lambasted Hart's decision as 'petty', and commented that few spectators or viewers would have been aware of Hewitt's feelings of umbrage 'had Hart not run off at the mouth'.

'It was also strange,' Gray wrote, 'that someone who wants problems kept in-house and, rightly, demands loyalty from those around him, should make his displeasure public.'

Talkback reaction was much the same. The guy had been playing well and Fitzpatrick was obviously injured. It didn't make sense.

The only player comment on the matter was later provided by Josh Kronfeld in his rugby memoir *On the Loose*. The flanker's sympathies clearly lay with his fellow player and sometime room-mate on that English tour.

'To me Norm was a small powerhouse. He could perform like a hurricane at times, and yet he often showed the patience of a stone statue. How [he] survived in the All Blacks as long as he did I'll never know. He was a committed and loyal understudy to the great Sean Fitzpatrick [and] his passion for the game and love of the All Black jersey were unadulterated. He suffered some serious injuries but fought back several times. I admired him for that, and in some ways he was a mentor to me in my career as an All Black.'

About the telling-off by Hart and Norm's consequent apology to the team, Kronfeld was in no doubt. 'I'm still not sure where Harty was coming from in respect to the [Wales test] incident . . . I don't think many of the players had a clue as to what had happened. And I wasn't alone in thinking it was making a mountain out of a molehill — and [that it left] Norm humiliated and angry.'

Kronfeld also raised the apparent double-standard in Hart's actions — that halfback Justin Marshall had escaped any consequences following a similar display when he was replaced during the Bledisloe Cup test at Carisbrook. Indeed, that had been a more serious transgression, with Marshall visibly and audibly upset as he stomped off the park, a variety of swear words being broadcast into TV viewers' homes.

Hart later excused Marshall's actions — writing in his autobiography *Change of Hart* that a blow to the sternum had affected his halfback's passing game and hence Ofisa Tonu'u had been brought on. In other words, Marshall wasn't performing. The difference in the Welsh test was that Norm was. His form at Wembley Stadium did not warrant replacement. Yet Hart was prepared to indulge Marshall's defiance.

'Justin wanted to see the campaign out and I can understand that.'

With Norm, it was a different matter entirely.

From that night on, Norm lost his immediate will to wear black. All the expectation, the pride and the passion that had been the silver fern began to slowly leak away. He found it difficult to look his team-mates in the eye — not so much because he had shamed himself, as because he had been shamed — that he did not deserve to be an All Black, let alone a test player. And that he did not belong. A division had been imposed between him and the rest of the touring party.

'Hart didn't want me there — the selectors didn't want me — the senior players like Fitzy and Zinny didn't give a stuff . . . it was like I was the bad bastard at school again . . . like I was back in the juniors. So I went back to being that Maori boy again — I didn't look people in the eyes, I didn't say anything, I just went dumb. And when I put the jersey on again [for the second test against England] and led the haka again, it felt like nothing. That I was going through the motions. All I wanted to do was get out of that environment and get back home.'

It was by no means a given that Norm would play the second test at Twickenham. But Fitzpatrick had tested out his leg in a midweek game against England 'A' and had struggled from the first scrum. When Norm's name was read out for the last test he knew that his was a reluctant selection, and also that this would be his last All Black tour. Not only had he become irredeemably alienated from Hart and the selection panel, but the fun and excitement had gone out of such expeditions.

'All I ever wanted to do, I guess, was play rugby, go on tour, party. Work hard, play hard. But the new professionalism — or at least, professionalism as it was interpreted by Hart and [manager Mike] Banks — did away with all the old traditions. The backseat challenges had been banned, the dirty-dirties parties, the card schools . . . the sort of things that I had previously enjoyed. We were a professional unit now and so we got a bit dull, as I far as I was concerned. I mean, I know people will think that I was a bit of a dinosaur, but getting on the piss with your mates is part of what rugby is about. At least, I thought so at the time. And here I was banned from drinking, not wanted by the management, and ignored by the senior players that I respected. I just felt . . . lost.'

Norm wasn't the only one with his mind on home as the team ran out onto Twickenham to confront the English. Within fifteen minutes the team trailed 3-20, the English playing with fire and passion and no little skill.

'We were shell-shocked even though we expected them to come out hard and we knew they had a good pack of forwards. But they played some good footy in that first quarter and that really boosted their confidence. I always thought we'd come back at them — I guess because I just wouldn't accept that the Poms could beat us. But it took us a while — we had to go back to the basics, secure some ball, work their forwards around, create some go-forward for our backs.

'In the second half, that allowed Jonah and Goldie to start running at them and once both Merts and Walter [Little] had scored, we should have put them away. But then we slackened off again and lost the intensity and that allowed them to get the 26-all draw. I don't know what it is, but last tests of the year always seem to trip the All Blacks up. In that particular game our loose forwards were overshadowed and I thought Zinny coasted the whole tour. Also, they had recalled Neil Back so he gave them some added zip at the breakdown. Dallaglio had a great game that day — he's a real tough bastard and tends to play a bit like a Bok loosie. All elbows and knees.'

Although the All Blacks had retained their unbeaten record for the year — the first unbeaten season since the Buck Shelford era of 1988/89 — the team felt as if they had lost.

'Kiri Te Kanawa came into the dressing rooms afterwards and did a bit of singing but I wasn't very interested and I don't think many of the guys were. Bull [Allen] had come in for Craig Dowd at prop [for the Twickenham test] and I got the feeling that Hart was looking at Bull and I as somehow partly to blame for the result. But then Hart only had to look at me by that stage and I was in trouble.'

It would have surprised most observers that Norm's self-confidence could be so fragile. He was a square 110 kg of muscle, with an iron determination on the paddock and a deserved reputation as a hard man. But it seemed that his very essence had been challenged — that the pride he took from being a rugby player, and a good rugby player, had been stripped away. Rugby gave his life purpose, it was his *raison d'être*. And being in the All Blacks reinforced that often fragile self-esteem. Now, it seemed, he was not really good enough after all — he was an interloper who had been found out, a substitute, a plastic All Black.

But despite his own harsh self-evaluation, the influential *Rugby News* saw things very differently. In summarising each player's contribution to the UK tour, the rugby weekly praised Norm's effort, commenting that he 'took his chance well. Stepped into the biggest boots in the game and let no-one down. Lacked Sean Fitzpatrick's scrummaging expertise, but added a new dimension with his running. Threw accurately to the lineout and . . . established another great hooker's rivalry with Richard Cockerill.'

But the media comment had no effect on the big hooker. In his own mind, he had not made the grade — not been worthy. And that judgement ate at his self-confidence all summer long.

CHAPTER FOURTEEN

Decline

O ver the summer, Norm went through his usual off-season rituals — a couple of minor operations to remove the bone chips from an elbow and scar tissue from an ankle, strength training in the gym, endless kilometres on the running machine and sprint exercises at the park. He would have preferred to go on holiday with Kat or head up to Mahia and go fishing with his old Hawke's Bay mates, but there was no time. The off-season was an illusion — the period when you not so much recovered as caught your breath from the year before and prepared for the one ahead. The last test against England had been on 6 December, and the Hurricanes camp would convene at the end of January. There would be squad practices, 'friendlies' against other New Zealand Super 12 teams, and then the first game of the new competition in Cape Town in late February. Rugby was no longer an elongated winter sport — professionalism had made it a year-round job.

Yet despite the injuries, the travelling, the bust-up with Hart and the enforced time away from Kat and his family, this was still the game he loved. More significantly, it was the only life he knew. Whenever he thought about the various stresses, he consoled himself with the thought that he was being paid six or seven times the average annual wage to play what was, after all, just a game. And, courtesy of rugby, he had a good home in Wellington, a seemingly infinite supply of sponsors' products, the respect of the sporting public, a sense of whanau within the Hurricanes, and Kat to come home to at night. Life wasn't so bad after all. No matter what had happened in England the year before, and his depression on his return, the summer was doing its healing trick. All things considered, life was pretty good.

True, there was still the Hart cloud looming on the horizon, but that was counterbalanced by the encouragement in the All Black coach's letter of early January, which congratulated him on his performances during the recent northern tour.

'It is a credit to you,' Hart wrote, 'that after such a long time on the bench behind Sean Fitzpatrick, you took the necessary step to Test Rugby [sic] so well. This happened because you recognised last year the importance of self-discipline in your life. The challenge for you, regardless of the uncertainty over Sean's future, is to re-establish yourself based on 1998 Super 12 form as the leading contender for this year's Test series. You should take *nothing* for granted.'

Norm sniffed at the promise. Yeah, well, if form had been the sole criterion then he would have played a few more tests by now. But maybe Hart meant what he said. In the same letter, there had been urgings to concentrate on fitness and speed. In the areas of scrummaging, taking the ball up and lineout accuracy, the All Black coach pronounced himself well satisfied.

But the optimism did not last long. At an early-season All Black camp in Queenstown, essentially just an introductory get-together so the players could meet Hart's new assistants, Wayne Smith and Peter Sloane, Norm asked if he might get some more playing time now that Fitzpatrick's chronic injury seemed likely to force his retirement.

'You've had your chance,' Hart shot back. 'Now it's Anton's turn.'

The response floored Norm. It not only ran counter to the criterion of Super 12 form that Hart had outlined in his letter of just a few weeks earlier — it completely demotivated the Hurricanes hooker. What was the point in playing to the max if the All Black selectors were already turning a blind eye? Jesus, what was the point, fullstop?

One answer might have been that the Hurricanes needed Norm and Bull and the other All Blacks in their midst to be playing their best for that team's campaign. But such altruism was not yet a feature of the Hewitt character. In his mind, the top team was the All Blacks — they were the peak to which all New Zealand rugby players aspire. Remove that peak and the most powerful of motivations, straight out self-interest, was also removed.

'I know, I know. I should have put the [Hurricanes] team first. But that's not the way rugby really works. When you get to Super 12 level, you've always got an eye on the black jersey. Players who say they haven't are either lying or know they'll never be selected. Top level sport is about being the best you can be. It's a very selfish philosophy but it's as true of rugby as single-sculls rowing or America's Cup yachting or women's hockey. Every player aspires to get into the "A" team — to be at the great events of that particular sport, be it the Olympics or the World Cup or whatever. And I was no different.'

During the off-season Norm had ministered to his own doubts. Inevitably, he came back to the same answer. *Don't give the bastards any reason to drop you. Play your guts out.* But that would no longer be enough. Anton Oliver had been anointed Fitzpatrick's heir and Norm would be back on the reserves bench no matter how well he played. But his determination to be the best refused to die. He'd give the selectors no option — he'd force his way into the ABs. Even though a good part of him no longer wanted to be there.

'It would depend on what mood I woke up with on the day. Some days I'd get all motivated and all determined that Hart couldn't ignore me. On other days, I'd flag it away. It was a real yo-yo existence. But being back with the Hurricanes helped. Just being amongst the guys again sorted out my head.'

Sure enough, when the Hurricanes reconvened his fellow team members were still buoyed from their performances of the previous season. Most of the same squad had returned, Frank Oliver and GK were back as the coaches, and public expectations were building with every day. When the Hurricanes won their first three games — impressive away defeats of the Stormers, the Bulls and the Chiefs — a good part of New Zealand started believing that this would indeed be the Hurricanes' year. Watch out the Blues.

And then, as if to mock such confidence, the whole Hurricanes campaign turned in just half a game. In front of a packed Athletic Park, the team were giving the Queensland Reds their usual object lesson in helter-skelter, running rugby.

'We'd stuffed them — had them on the ropes. I think we were up by 20 or 25 points at one stage. And then they abandoned the game plan [Queensland coach John] Connolly had given them and starting running the ball back at us. And all the natural class of John Eales, Tim Horan and Daniel Herbert started coming to the fore. But it was their little Aboriginal first-five [Shane Drahm] that did the real damage. He was like an electric eel that day.'

Both the partisan crowd and the Hurricanes were stunned by their sudden reverse — the ebullient backline suddenly made to look fragile. When the lanky Eales kicked the final conversion the Reds had won 41-33, with the home team denied even a consolation bonus point.

'That game was, effectively, our season. You could feel the boys start to doubt themselves after that and, if anything, we played even worse a week later. Thrashed by the Sharks at Palmerston North. It was pathetic.'

Neither Oliver nor Taylor had any answers to explain the team's sudden demise, and then injuries began to claim vital players with their replacements unable to make the step up. The local media started to turn.

'The real reason was that the other teams had worked us out. They knew we were a rip-shit-and-bust side. We'd smash into rucks and mauls, adopt the old "pick-and-go" and then when the defence was thin enough, the backs would be given the ball. But the new defensive techniques that the Canterbury Crusaders had started — with the forwards not committing to breakdowns but staying on the fringes — found us out. And we didn't really have the brains to change. We just kept on running into flat defences and our runners would get smashed on the fringes and the ball turned over.'

To make matters worse, their inspirational captain Bull Allen was also suffering a loss of form, his usual broken play charges curiously absent.

'I reckon Bull had the same problems as I did. It was obvious that Hart didn't want him either so he'd lost a good chunk of his motivation too. The same was true for me — I was playing shit at the start of that season. I just couldn't get myself up.'

Meanwhile, off the field, Norm was becoming heavily involved in the team's promotional activities, discovering a particular empathy for children's charities. His affable public face was appearing on billboards, promotional literature and in feature articles in newspapers and magazines. He had started to involve himself in writer Alan Duff's 'Books in Homes' scheme — a laudable community initiative but one that began to distract him from his playing focus. Ironically, the Hurricanes' popularity had started working against them. Everybody wanted a piece of the team, and because of Norm's seniority, his friendship with Allen, and his previous experience with the community work trust, he was regarded as a natural for any public relations work.

'If I'm honest, I was also believing a bit too much of my own publicity. I was a celebrity in Wellington and all over the lower North Island and that was a boost to my ego at a time I figured I needed it. And then I started overcompensating — thinking that I was a bigger person than I really was. In rugby there's a saying about being "bigger than the game". It means that someone has become a bit of a wanker because they're reading their own hype and getting sucked into the bullshit. A lot of All Blacks suffer that disease and, at the start of '98, I reckon that was me too.'

Then Bull Allen was injured in the Hurricanes' improbable victory over the ACT Brumbies in Canberra. The team was now a strange parody of conventional rugby wisdom — they could win their away games all right, it was the home contests that ran them ragged. The immediate consequence of Bull's injury was that Norm took over the captaincy of the Hurricanes, and that placed fresh demands upon him. Although he was up to it — or, at least, he assumed he was. He could speak in public, knew the right way to hold a fork at the dinner table, and could indulge in sufficient small talk to keep the sponsors and their spouses happy.

But on the field, still the Hurricanes would not gel. They were comprehensively defeated by the Crusaders at Napier — yet another home game thumping — then lost to the NSW Waratahs before rediscovering some of their old form in an 80-point thriller against the Blues back on Athletic Park. It was a game that restored some of their lost public prestige, yet also a game that reminded the team of what they might have been.

Although Norm's own form had improved, it was clear that the cumulative damage to his knees and legs over past seasons was robbing him of his dynamism. He could still break the occasional tackle, and his stocky frame was effective in taking the ball up, but the leg speed had gone. He had become a grafting player, indispensable in the tight but not the fourth loose forward that the modern hooker was supposed to be.

THE COCKEREL COCKERILL

This was the rationale that Hart and the All Black selectors offered when they announced their New Zealand and New Zealand 'A' teams for the June trial. The younger Anton Oliver, a transplanted loose forward, had more speed in the loose, they said, and the All Blacks were looking to play a faster-paced game. Although there were still many critics who considered that Oliver's lack of scrummaging ability and errant lineout throwing made him the inferior choice to the Hurricanes captain. Nevertheless, most media accepted Hart's logic that the 1999 World Cup had to be the primary focus over the next two years, and so youth and promise would have the advantage over age and experience. Especially given that the new choices — Oliver as hooker, Mark Mayerhoffler as centre, and Taine Randell as No. 8 and captain — would have the chance to gain good experience against the weakened English touring team.

Despite the retirement of Fitzpatrick, Zinzan Brooke and Frank Bunce, the New Zealand rugby community did not feel particularly wary about that year's All Black schedule. There would be just the seven internationals — two against an under-strength England (their reputation further tarnished by a 76-nil thrashing by the Wallabies) and then the usual home-and-away Tri-Nations competition, with an extra test against the Australians rounding out the year. It was not an unduly onerous schedule, certainly not in comparison with previous years, and the lack of an end-of-season tour was seen as a positive in terms of refreshing players ahead of the World Cup year. The previous month's Super 12 final between the Canterbury Crusaders and the Auckland Blues indicated that New Zealand rugby was a dominant force — especially given that the nucleus of the previous year's All Black team was still very much intact.

Although a measure of pique affected his assessment of the '98 All Blacks, Norm was surprised that Taine Randell had been given the captaincy. He had been unimpressed with Randell's efforts for the midweek team during the '96 South African tour, and nothing that he had observed since suggested that the young man was ready for such responsibility.

'I thought of Taine as a follower rather than a leader. I mean he was head prefect material all right, but only because there would be a headmaster and other teachers around him. But All Black rugby isn't school. On the field, you've got to have the respect of your fellow players and you've got to be a real hard head. Taine wasn't that kind of leader. I guess that their only other option was Robin Brooke at that time, although Todd Blackadder would have been my choice. Hart had only picked him as the blindside reserve because Michael Jones was there. Although 'Ice' was well past it by then. Hart just didn't want to let him go.'

And captaincy was now something that Norm was applying his mind to. Not only had he led the Hurricanes in the second half of the Super 12, but his appointment to lead New Zealand 'A' against the English confirmed that he had skills beyond the mere physical. Norm saw it a little differently.

'It was the consolation prize. I knew that. But if I was going to captain the team, then I was going to give a hundred and ten percent. What I really wanted was to beat the Poms by more than the ABs would beat them the next Saturday. And that was pretty much my motivation to the team: "The selectors don't think you're up to it. Prove the bastards wrong." That sort of stuff.'

And then a deluge occurred, a rain squall that bucketed down on the host city Hamilton and turned Rugby Park into a slippery quagmire. At that point all bets were off. The English had a useful forward pack, if a mediocre back division. But the weather and ground conditions essentially took both backlines out of the game, and Norm was a relieved captain to escape with a narrow 18-10 victory.

'The Poms didn't win a game all tour — not even against the Academy XV. But for a while there I got real worried because they had some useful forwards and a good front row in Rowntree, Cockerill and Vickery. We got shown up a bit that night with some of the boys deciding to do their individual thing instead of playing as a team. Still, at least I could say that I'd now led teams that had defeated the Lions, France and England. That wasn't too bad.'

However, it was not good enough to win him any game time in the first test at Dunedin. Although the Carisbrook international would be robbed of any meaning when English lock Danny Grewcock was ordered from the field for, ironically, stamping on Anton Oliver's head. From then on the All Blacks scored at will — the final 64-22 scoreline representing New Zealand's highest-ever win over an England team.

'The boys weren't all that fussed about the result because we'd let them score three tries and they had competed well in all the set pieces, despite being a man down. It was ironic that Grewcock should go for stomping because it didn't affect Anton at all. If you're going to put some filth in, then you expect a return. I don't think Grewcock even touched him in the end.'

That night Norm deliberately set out to disobey Hart and drown his self-pity in the local brew. It didn't look like he would be getting any game time in the next test either, despite Hart's discovery of the new substitution rule that allowed for non-injury replacements. However, he could not go drinking with the All Blacks — that would be to unnaturally tempt fate. So instead he went out on his own until he was adopted by some locals and ending up at a favourite student watering hole, 'The Gardens'. He was surprised to see a good number of the English party downstairs in the public bar and went over to join them. The night deteriorated from there.

Within seconds Richard Cockerill was baiting his opposite with the record number of tests that Norm had spent on the bench, saying that now he was going to be doing it all over again, but this time to Anton Oliver. 'You've got splinters up your arse,' Cockerill taunted. 'What's it like walking around with all that wood up your arse?' Although Norm attempted to laugh it off, the jabs found their target. He returned fire, accusing the English players of being 'a bunch of poofy playboys'. They were more interested in drinking tea with their pinkies raised, he said, than learning how to play a decent game of rugby. Cockerill and the others took the rejoinders in good humour and invited him to stay on. The beer continued to flow.

'It wasn't long before we were totally pissed, and when the pub closed we decided to get a mini-van back into town to check out the night-clubs. But we were giving each other shit all the time — especially Cockerill and I — so once we were in the van, we started pushing and wrestling. Two big hookers rolling around the mini-van trying to get a headlock on each other . . . it wasn't pretty. Anyway, when we got into town, we poured out of the mini-van and exchanged a few blows. It wasn't anything major — we were too pissed to do each other any real harm.'

They were quickly separated by the other players and staggered off in different directions. Norm was supposed to be rooming with Auckland flanker John Carter, a man he disdained as one of John Hart's 'pets', so he decided that arriving back at the hotel in his present state would be tempting fate. Instead, he located another late night bar and drank until breakfast.

'We had a recovery session that Sunday morning but I flagged it away. I just crawled into bed instead while Carter was out and tried to get some sleep. It wasn't until later in the week that the issue broke in the papers. Apparently, a couple of scarfies had spotted us and yabbered away to the media. Although I wasn't the only one in trouble as it turned out. Quite a few of the boys got into trouble that weekend . . . getting pissed, spewing up in public, doing a bit of petty damage, that sort of thing.'

It was also the weekend when one of his All Black colleagues was alleged to have got a blowjob down a Dunedin alleyway, and had been spotted and reported to the All Black management by a member of the public. Comments were made within the All Black camp and John Hart privately expressed his disgust. Although it's an issue that Norm avoids to this day.

'I reckon private lives are private lives. No-one's got the right to judge. Although when I heard about that and some of the other troubles reported to the management, I was glad of the company. Planting a Pom didn't seem such a big deal after all.'

In fact, it wasn't the minor scrap with Richard Cockerill that was the problem. It was the breaking of the drinking embargo and his pledge to Hart.

'I fronted up and told them the truth. That I'd gone out and got pissed. There was a sort of disciplinary committee put together by [All Black manager Mike] Banks and it included Hart and a couple of the other senior players — Ian Jones and Robin Brooke, I think. From memory, Craig

Dowd and Zinny were alleged to have misbehaved too, but there was no doubt that I was in the deepest shit. The committee was convened too late to affect the team for the second test, otherwise I reckon I would have been a gonner. Hart was not a happy man.'

VOID

Norm took his customary seat on the reserves bench for the second international at Eden Park, aware that his place in the camp hung by the thinnest of threads. It was his assessment that had Hart been aware of his Dunedin misdemeanours before the squad's assembly in Auckland and the subsequent disciplinary hearing, he would unquestionably have been dropped from the team.

And yet a part of him had ceased to care. His frustration at being consigned again to the reserves, and his simmering resentment at Hart's tactics and intrusions, ate away at his caution. Given his private deal with the All Black coach, his behaviour in Dunedin had been reckless, even defiant. But the yo-yo moods continued — one morning mortified that he had jeopardised his All Black career; the next, dismissive of any repercussions. All he wanted to do was play rugby and now even that simple pleasure seemed about to be denied him.

And then, a rare stroke of luck — even if it was dependent on the misfortune of another. Anton Oliver pulled a calf muscle in the first half of the Eden Park test and was struggling to get around the field. At half-time, and with the All Blacks only 14-7 to the good, Hart gave him the word. He would start the second half.

'We'd been playing poorly in the forwards — the boys listless and the Poms getting amongst us, especially in the tight five. So I was pumped when I ran out there and made contact with Cockerill almost immediately. Gave him the eyes . . . just to let him know I was there. And we gave each other shit at the next scrum, slagging each other . . . having a bit of fun.'

From the sideline it was obvious that the injection of Norm and loosie Isitolo Maka had rejuvenated the forwards, with both players taking the fight to the English and upping the team's energy levels. And then Norm got trapped in a tackle, his body going one way, his left knee the other. As he stood up, he could feel a searing pain behind his kneecap, his lower leg losing sensation as it flopped out in front of him. He thought he'd dislocated his kneecap, so he banged it hard and manually attempted to correct the damage. But at the scrum immediately afterwards his leg refused to plant properly and he limped to the sideline, demanding that the physio strap it tight. The strapping secure, he tried to jog down the touchline but the knee would not support him, the damage too severe. The tackle had torn his medial ligaments and shredded the accompanying cruciates — he had just suffered the kind of injury that ends rugby careers.

'I was gutted. I sat in the medical room under the stand — Anton Oliver beside me — and just stared at the wall. I couldn't believe it — from being all fizzed up a quarter of an hour ago to this . . . I couldn't believe it.'

Incredibly, initial medical opinion suggested that he may not need an operation to repair the damage. If he let the knee heal itself — stayed off it for a couple of months — then maybe he would be back playing by the middle of the NPC. Cursing his luck, he returned home to Wellington and Kat, inconsolable.

Two weeks later he sat down at home and watched the All Blacks begin their worst losing streak since 1949 — starting with a 16-24 reverse against the Wallabies at Melbourne. All through the game, feelings of helplessness and despair welled in him as he switched the television off and on, off and on — not wanting to watch the game yet unable not to watch it.

'I thought it would be easy — I'd get in a few beers, watch the game in the lounge, relax. But the more I drank the worse it got. I was, like, all jittery and angry at the same time. Feeling sorry for myself big time. So I kept drinking — tried to deaden all my feelings.'

In the build-up to the next test, against the Springboks at Athletic Park, Norm decided he couldn't even bear to be in the same city as the game. He considered going home for the weekend, but realised that for his rugby-mad family the Bok game would be compulsory viewing. And how could he explain to them how he felt — that watching the game would be like watching his whole purpose in life ebb away? If Oliver failed, then the new reserve hooker Mark Hammett would play. And he rated Canterbury's Hammett. That guy would only need one opportunity to prove his merits. It was not so much that the door had shut tight on his future All Black career as that he could still see the faintest of lights. Despair, he felt, he could handle. It was the hope that was the real problem.

'I got more and more depressed and I couldn't get out of it. It was like being sucked down in a spiral. I mean, it sounds pathetic now but rugby was my reality. It always had been. And I was crocked, limping around on a knee that didn't seem to be getting any better, and convinced that if I was playing for the ABs then I could be making a difference. But I was also thinking that maybe I'd never get back, and I couldn't handle that. I could see that between Hammett and Hart, I was stuffed.'

He refused to confide his feelings to anyone, even Kat. Instead, he would drive himself to a nearby bottle store, buy a slab of beer, and drink all 24 cans over the course of an evening. Most days he wouldn't drink, and some optimism would return. He'd attempt to repair the damage with Kat or concentrate on his rehabilitation. But then a mate would call around with a dozen, or there would be a rugby game on the telly, or his knee would flare up again . . . and he would back in the black hole and binge drinking.

Others began to notice the change in his personality. His sister Tracy refused to call around anymore because the atmosphere at the house was so grim and dark. Kat complained to mutual friends that she felt as if she was living with both Jekyll and Hyde, while his relationship with other members of his family, friends and other rugby players either deteriorated or fell away entirely.

And yet he could still switch on the charm in an instant. Other friends noticed nothing out of the ordinary — at the dinner table Norm was his usual high-spirited company, always ready with a rugby story or a considered explanation as to why the All Blacks were playing so badly. But with every rugby international GK's 'Boris' would return — downing beer after beer, throwing empty cans at the TV screen, yelling in frustration at the muddled tactics that were being played out before him.

Slowly, though, the knee was coming right, and he decided to test it in a game for the Wellington development team. But he lasted only a few minutes, the knee sore and unresponsive, his leg refusing to support him properly. He was back to square one. Finally, a second medical diagnosis prescribed corrective surgery. The same orthopaedic surgeon who had restored Michael Jones' career, Barry Tietjens, was booked to undertake the procedure.

'I was so pissed off. If they'd only given me the operation straight away, instead of farting around thinking that it would cure itself, then I would have been three months closer to recovery.'

But if he followed all the post-operation advice and stuck to the rehabilitation guidelines he stood a good chance of at least playing again. And next year was the Super 12 and the chance of taking over as permanent captain of the Hurricanes. There was also the prospect of the World Cup. The glimmer of hope refused to fade.

CHAPTER FIFTEEN

Fall

Although the knee was healing and the All Blacks' run of losses suggested any number of openings for form players the next season, Norm's relationship with Kat did not have a similarly optimistic outlook. At the end of the academic year she had sat her final exams and flown out on the traditional OE adventure. Her plans had confused Norm — couldn't she delay the trip a year? Let him get through the '99 season and then maybe they could go together? But it was a lukewarm offer. For the first time, their age difference had come to mean something — Kat eager to experience new places and new people, and Norm wedded to his rugby and indifferent to the prospect of more travel.

The binge drinking only accentuated the distance between them. He had become morose and moody, aware that his relationship with Kat was coming to a natural end but unwilling to accept the inevitable. He began to accuse her of being grasping and ungrateful — saying that she had accepted the gifts and travel that came from being his partner but now that his future was less bright, she was deserting him.

'Looking back, it was unfair to accuse her of any of those things, but I didn't have any sense of perspective. Kat was leaving and I was staying exactly where I was — if anything, going backwards.'

On the rugby front, though, things were not quite so hopeless. Although any fitness work was restricted by the knee, surgeon Barry Tietjens considered him at least six weeks ahead of the rehabilitation schedule, and he was racking up improved numbers in the gym, regularly bench-pressing 170 kg. His captaincy for the next Super 12 season had been confirmed and both Oliver and Taylor were involving him in their team planning and strategy. But for all their inclusion and enthusiasm, there remained just one goal for the next year: to make the All Black squad to the World Cup. Against Kat's departure, the truer perspective had been measured.

A step in the right direction was achieved when he was named in the 37-man All Black squad for the SAS training camp at Hobsonville in late January. It was Hart's idea — an initiative designed to build team spirit and test each individual's mental strength when physical exhaustion had set in. Hart also used the exclusion of three leading hopefuls — Jonah Lomu, Joeli Vidiri and Isitolo Maka — to send a message to other prospects. If you aren't prepared to put in the work, then forget it. For Vidiri and Maka, it was the end of their All Black careers.

'It was a big call leaving Isi [Maka] out. And it exposed the Pakeha coach mentality when dealing with Island players. The point is that each culture — Pakeha, Maori, Samoan, Tongan — has their own way of looking at things and doing things. It was something I'd begun to appreciate as captain of the Hurricanes. That although rugby is a great racial unifier, a coach or a captain has to get inside the head of each player, and culture is a huge factor.

'The Pacific boys are different when it comes to training — they're a group people, so Isi needed someone to look after and guide him during that off-season. To keep him up to it. He came back from summer a real blob, and so did Joeli and Jonah. But just like Hart knew we would need Jonah at the Cup, we also needed Isi. He was the form No. 8 during the '98 season and had an ability to commit defences and punch holes off the back of the scrum. The All Blacks missed that sort of power at the World Cup while the Aussies had exactly that sort of player in Toutai Kefu.'

Although few of the SAS training squad gave the recalcitrants a second thought. Each potential World Cup pick lived in their own zone — determined that they should not suffer a similar fate. There was no group loyalty. It was every player for himself.

'I really enjoyed the camp. It was hard yakker — the hardest I'd trained since the bad old days under Laurie — but it was my sort of training. I was doing army things and ever since I'd been a kid I'd had a fantasy about joining the army. The army is very much a Maori thing, I reckon. It's a natural place for us because it's about being a warrior and having that group camaraderie, the whole whanau thing.'

That the camp was an endurance test could be measured by the amount of weight players lost over the four days — Norm shedding 6 kg, yet feeling that he had made his point. If they needed toughness, if they needed mongrel, then he was their man. But there was no time to relax — on the last day he flew out of Auckland for Queenstown to join the Hurricanes for their pre-season game against the Highlanders.

'None of the ABs who did the SAS course were going to be playing — I doubt if we could have. But it was a team bonding thing to join our respective camps and, as captain, I needed to be there with the boys. We were all pretty pleased to have survived it and so when we got to Queenstown, we had a few beers ... Alama, Filo, Christian ... the Hurricanes boys who'd been up at Hobsonville. It was nothing too serious — just a couple of pints and a bit of a yack.'

However, stopping at a couple of pints had never been Norm's style. He left the team's hotel and went into town, caught up with some of the Otago All Blacks, and had a few more. When he had exhausted their company, he staggered off in search of any other bars that might still be open.

But this latest binge was renewing his depression. After his earlier exuberance Norm was now on the classic downer, and Kat's absence seemed a void. And there was something else playing on his mind too.

A couple of weekends earlier Norm had invited some of his mates up to his Brooklyn home to watch a couple of videos, have a few tinnies and generally catch up ahead of the new season. Christian Cullen, Tana Umaga and others had dropped by, as well as a few other friends who were not involved with the Hurricanes, including Norm's brother-in-law Tony.

'It was a typical guys' night — no chicks — a lot of laughs and a lot of beer. And then there's this knock at the door and Tony's grinning because, unknown to the rest of us, he's phoned up a couple of strippers for the lads. Apparently he had a part-time job as a bouncer once and got friendly with a guy who ran a massage parlour. I was a bit pissed off to start with because suddenly there are a couple of prostitutes in my home, but then, I'm just as plastered as everybody else so I think, "Ah, what the hell. Let it go."'

There was immediately a problem when the older of the women recognised one of the players and realised she knew his parents in a completely different social setting. Embarrassed, she stayed outside and waited for the younger woman to complete her performance. But the younger woman was flying high on drugs, and completely oblivious to the fact that this was not the time of the month to be throwing herself around quite so frenetically. When this was pointed out to her, she picked up her clothes and fled the house.

'It was all a bit weird. Real sleazy. You couldn't have imagined anything less sexy, but it's all over in a couple of minutes and the boys go back to their drinking. Yeah, thanks Tony, I say. Don't do it again.'

Norm thought nothing more of it — it was the kind of incident that he would likely dismiss in the morning as fragments of something he'd dreamed. The party broke up — some of the guys went home and others crashed at the house.

'I'm still up — having a domestic tidy-up, can you believe it — when there's this knock on the door at five in the morning and a couple of cops are standing there saying they've received a complaint from the massage parlour that one of their girls was assaulted. I couldn't believe it. So I tell them what the score was and they seem to accept it and off they go.'

Only to return a few hours later with substantial reinforcements — an overuse of police resources that has Norm shaking his head to this day.

'When I opened the door I could see a paddy wagon, two uniform police cars and two plainclothes cars, about half a dozen cops . . . it's like one of those police siege scenes out of a movie. And this time, the cops are saying that the girl who was stripping said that she'd been gang-raped, sexually assaulted with bottles and a whole series of other indecencies performed on her. Then the police swarm all over the house with all the forensic equipment — dusting for fingerprints, taking carpet samples, all that drama. And next thing, Christian and I are down at the Wellington Central Police Station, put in separate interview rooms, told we don't need lawyers, and interrogated.

'It was freaky. Even though it was all bullshit, it seemed that I had to prove myself rather than the other way round. I felt like a criminal.'

After the interview Norm telephoned his old Taradale coach, Detective Sergeant Keith Price, explained the situation and asked him to intervene. Price rang back after talking to the detectives involved. His reply chilled the big hooker.

'It was the "Caesar's wife" argument. Because I was a prominent rugby personality they were giving the case their special attention. They were basically saying that they normally wouldn't take a druggie prostitute with no physical evidence of sexual or physical assault too seriously, but because it was us they were going all the way.'

Price then advised Norm to contact private investigator Trevor Morley, a former policeman with a deserved reputation for ferreting out the facts in such cases. Morley duly reported back that police investigations had confirmed the players' stories and the prostitute had withdrawn her complaint. But the incident left a sour taste in the lead-up to the SAS weekend. And Norm had a horrible feeling that it wasn't over yet.

DAMAGE

And so a strange combo of moods accompanied Norm's drinking that night in Queenstown — all his earlier optimism, tempered by new doubts as to whether Hart was just jerking him to put pressure on the incumbents Oliver and Hammett; the grief that accompanied his broken relationship with Kat, and a nagging feeling that the last of the stripper story had yet to play out.

'I was sitting in this bar, all alone, just getting more and more wasted and feeling more and more upset. The whole world was against me . . . that sort of shit. And each drink only made it worse. Eventually all the bars were closed and I started staggering back to the team's hotel. I saw this block of units as I was walking along, and it sort of looked like the place, so I went to slide open the door of the nearest unit but it was locked. So I hammered on the windows to be let in.

'The lights go on and there's this guy who's obviously just woken up, gesturing through the window and shouting at me to piss off. At about that time, I realise that I'm nowhere near the team's hotel so I stumble off again. But then I stop, and think, "Who the hell did that bastard think he was?" And next thing I'm running back towards the chalet like I'm on the charge in a rugby game, and right in front of me is the sliding door with the plate glass window — and bam — I put both my fists right through it.

'I knew what I was doing but I didn't. As I took my hands away from the smashed window, I looked down and there's this huge gash on the underside of my left arm and glass all over me . . . some was sticking into my stomach and some in my back . . . and next thing I'm sitting down on the footpath and watching all this blood pump out. I didn't panic or anything . . . I just sat there and thought, "Ah fuck, so this is how I'm going to die." And I didn't give a damn. Right there and then, I was quite prepared to bleed to death. I didn't care if I lived or died.'

Fortunately, others did. The couple renting the chalet dialled 111 as soon as they were able — shocked and frightened that a stranger should try to smash his way into their home, the invader leaving a trail of blood from their front room out onto the porch and down the path. Within minutes, both police and ambulance officers had arrived — their most immediate concern the large drunk man sitting in his own blood in the gutter, his right fist clamped over an angry red gash. At first the man seemed reluctant to accept any help, but finally the paramedics prevailed.

'I wasn't feeling anything — the combination of alcohol and shock, I suppose. And as they put me in the ambulance, it was all a dream — the flashing lights, the uniforms and everything. Just unreal.'

A couple of fire service personnel who attended the incident would later claim the rugby player was lucky he had not bled to death. Which was partially true. Norm had been lucky. Despite the lacerations to his fists and arms, the glass had not cut any arteries or sliced any of the exposed tendons. There was a deep, 8-cm-long wound up from his left wrist and the white of the tendons was immediately visible, but that was all and the ulnar artery was intact. He was put into the ambulance and driven down to Invercargill, although any surgery would have to wait until the alcohol in his system was at manageable levels. On midday Saturday, Kew surgeon David Schluter began a routine two-hour operation to repair the night's damage.

In his notes, Dr Schluter made the comment that 'this 30-year-old was pushed through a window last night after drinking'. It was a story Norm had invented in the immediate aftermath of the event to reduce his embarrassment. By the time he was prepped for surgery it was obvious that the accident would have significant consequences beyond the immediate damage. He was sobering up quickly, and coming to realise that his senseless act would likely snuff out any chance of being in the World Cup squad. Although maybe there was a way out, he figured. Maybe if he spun a story about falling or being pushed through the plate-glass door.

'I came up with this bullshit story because I couldn't face it. I wanted to run away. And I knew there would be trouble, although at that stage I didn't appreciate how much.'

Norm woke from the general anaesthetic, registered the heavy bandage over his left arm, and immediately telephoned Hurricanes manager Tony Bedford for assistance. Bedford was singularly unimpressed.

'You got yourself there,' was the gruff reply. 'You get yourself back.'

Norm scrambled around for his clothes, negotiated a price with a Southland cabbie, and tried to console himself on the three-hour trip back to Queenstown. Maybe things could be hushed up, he thought. Yeah, maybe things weren't so bad — he shouldn't panic. Yeah, but what about the arm? How was he going to explain that then, eh? When he arrived at the hotel the team were returning from their Highlanders game and a hasty meeting was convened with the management to review his situation. Despite Bedford's earlier dismissal, the manager had squared matters with both the couple at the chalet and the police. The couple had accepted a sum of money to pay for the damage to their chalet, and were unwilling to press charges. Norm would need to apologise to them personally and make good the restitution but otherwise that area was OK.

He felt even more heartened when All Black manager Mike Banks rang that night to express his personal support and note that Norm was not the first All Black to be experiencing emotional problems and that he would definitely not be the last. Any relief Norm might have felt at the managers' attitudes turned out to be misplaced, however. At a team meeting the next morning, he apologised to the players for letting them down. It would not happen again, he said. But if he expected understanding he was in for a nasty shock.

'No-one believed me. You could tell by the body language. There was total silence after I'd finished, a few raised eyebrows, people looking away from me, that sort of thing. It was "Yeah, right. The guy's a boozer — he won't change because he can't change."'

The players' reactions stunned Norm. These were some of his closest mates and they had written off his promise to steer clear of the drink. It wasn't so much that they were annoyed that he wouldn't be there to lead them onto the field, but that they considered his pledge to be worthless — that whatever he might or might not be as a rugby player, at the core he was just another drunk.

Meanwhile, news of Norm's early morning exploits was reverberating around the national media. It was Sunday — a day when news is short and news editors are searching for a good story to kick off the new week. By that evening, Norm's fall from grace had become that story. When he returned to Wellington it was to the knowledge that, far from being fixed, the Queenstown incident was developing its own momentum. He was summoned to appear before the NZRFU the next day.

'On the Monday morning I met with [NZRFU contracts manager] Bill Wallace, Tony Bedford and a few others, and basically they said that I was in the shit and to put myself in their hands. I felt so stink that when they said I should front up to the media and apologise, I didn't object. I just wanted it all to go away and if I could say a few words to a couple of journos and get out of it, then that's what I'd do.'

With Norm's blessing, the union arranged a media conference for that afternoon to manage the fall-out and, hopefully, put the issue to rest. A week earlier Australian cricket star Ricky Ponting had taken part in a similar circus after being involved in a nightclub brawl. The public apology had suddenly become the new PR fix-it. Front up, take it on the chin, get on with it. At heart it was a deeply cynical ploy designed to massage the bad news away and transform blame into sympathy.

A statement was drafted, the media advised, and Norm given some time to learn his lines.

'It was a bunch of crap. Mostly all about how I'd let *them* down — the NZRFU. It was one long apology to the fish-heads and then, almost as an afterthought, to the players and the public. But I didn't feel any responsibility to the union. At heaps of after-matches, I'd seen any number of them pissed out of their heads. It felt like I was being set up to publicly prostrate myself before my employers. There was no way I was going to do that.'

He asked for some private time and excused himself from their company. At which point he telephoned me.

'[Michael] had gone through a similar sort of thing when he'd resigned from Parliament. And if I was going out, I wanted to at least say what I wanted to say. I reckoned that I was being set up and, OK, maybe I deserved it, but I wanted someone who knew me and knew the situation. He faxed me the finished words and then I was escorted into one of the union committee rooms where there were rows of reporters, TV cameras and photographers' flashlights going off all the time . . . it was over-whelming. I felt like I was being hunted.'

Up until that moment, Norm had considered that things could still be squared — that the fall-out could be managed with the minimum of fuss. He was worldly enough to appreciate the merit of a stage-managed press conference, and hopeful that it might extricate him from this mess of his own making. Besides, against being humiliated by Hart after the Welsh test, a gaggle of press people didn't rate.

'I thought I'd read the statement, get up and bugger off. I didn't feel anything when I sat down. And I hadn't really appreciated what Michael had written . . . I'd given it a quick flick and gone "Yeah, sweet as . . ." and that was it.'

But when he came to speak the words, he found that they had changed. That uttering them required him to consider the import of what he was saying. And when he started with the apology to his family, for shaming them by association, the full impact of what he had done, where he was, and why he was there, slammed home.

'It was like I was a kid again — a small, scared third-former at Te Aute — and all I wanted was my mum. I know it's pathetic but there you are. Suddenly I missed her and my family and I knew that I'd cut myself off from them and nearly everyone else that mattered. That everyone who was important to me had been relegated and that my selfishness was consuming everything. And it was embarrassing ... because I was starting to appreciate this, for the first time, in front of all these media. And I couldn't help myself ... I started to cry. And once I started, I couldn't stop.'

For the next 48 hours, the New Zealand media was consumed with the spectacle of one of rugby's hard men breaking down in public, his big hands brushing away the tears as he struggled to read the prepared statement. The story led the television and radio news bulletins that night, dominated the 'Holmes' show, and featured on the covers of all the metropolitan dailies the next morning.

The public response was instant. Despite snide remarks from some sports journalists, most New Zealanders were sympathetic to the big man's plight. He had publicly admitted to an alcohol problem, confessed that he needed help, and taken the first steps towards getting that help. The tears had been real, the distress genuine, and his contrition painfully obvious.

'I didn't consider what the [public] reaction might be. I was just numb from it all — it was like all the pressure that had been building over the past couple of years had just been released and I had nothing left. I felt drained. When Mum came through the front door and said she was going to be staying until I was all right again, it was such a relief. Mum just took over — she was brilliant.'

So too was a new friend — aerobics star Arlene Thomas. The two had met through mutual friends and frequented the same Wellington gym. Norm was wary of getting involved again so quickly after Kat and, for her part, Arlene enjoyed the idea of a hassle-free relationship that allowed the occasional movie or meal together with no strings attached. But in the wake of the Queenstown debacle, Arlene's unflappable optimism cut through the big man's reserve and their friendship began to build into something more.

John Hart had also offered his support. When Norm's mother answered the phone on the night of his apology, he presumed the coach was calling to cut him adrift. Instead, Hart congratulated the hooker on taking the first step towards curing his chronic alcohol problem. However, he warned, the first step is always the easiest. The really hard work lay ahead, and every day would be a test.

'The NZRFU insisted I see a shrink — actually both a psychiatrist and a psychologist. Even Paul Holmes pitched in. He rang to say that he'd had an alcohol problem, and recommended AA. So I even went to a meeting with them. I would have walked on hot coals if I thought something was going to do me good at that point.

'You see, I was still looking for the quick solution. If I do this, this and this then maybe it'll all go away. That sort of stuff. I'm not sure that, deep down, I was really convinced that I couldn't handle the booze. Everyone was telling me I couldn't — and there was a hell of a lot of evidence to back them up — but for me, it was like playing a game of footy and you're down 20-nil. OK, if we watch their halfback, pressure their scrum and kick for position . . . then we can win this game. I thought it'd be that easy.'

BLACKMAIL

If Norm thought his troubles would soon pass and the media find a new personal tragedy to fixate on, he was about to be horribly disabused. Two nights later, just before midnight, a man who claimed to be the pimp of the prostitutes who had appeared the fortnight before turned up at his door. They needed to talk, he said.

'He tried to blackmail me. He said that both TV3 and [TV1's] *60 Minutes* were interested in the girls' story, that he knew "the whole truth", but that $20,000 would make all my problems go away. If he didn't get the money, then that was what the TV stations were going to pay him for the girls' stories.'

Norm had noticed camera crews filming the house from the road the day before, and he wondered if the two events might not be connected. He told the pimp that he'd think about the sordid offer and get back to him. Don't wait too long, the pimp warned. The media had their cheque books open already.

He could inform the police, Norm reasoned, but it would only be his word against the pimp's. And given the nature of the earlier investigation, he was wary of involving them again. As he fretted over what to do next, an old mate rang to offer support — an old mate with business connections to the red-light district. Desperate, Norm explained his problem with the pimp. Forget about it, his mate said. He'd sort it out. And he did.

Although there was another sting to this particular tale. That weekend's *Sunday News* led with the lurid headline 'Cops quiz All Blacks over sex claim — call girls' allegations rock NZRFU'. Underneath were splashed photographs of Tana Umaga, Christian Cullen and Norm. The body of the story may not have matched the headline but the damage was by association — his reputation further blackened. Not only was Norm Hewitt a vandalistic drunk, but he associated with prostitutes.

'I felt dirty, and that my stink would somehow rub off on my family and Arlene. I knew I was guilty of bingeing, but not this other sort of crap. But there was nothing I could do. I was the media punching bag for that week, or so it seemed.'

Despite this feeling of siege, the public perception had actually moved the other way. Any number of press editorials and columns praised Hewitt for fronting up to his drinking problem — from former All Black great Chris Laidlaw to best-selling author Alan Duff. Duff recalled how Hewitt had been an inspirational ambassador for the 'Books in Homes' scheme over the past couple of years, freely giving his time to encourage and motivate children from disadvantaged backgrounds. Over at NZRFU headquarters a flood of supportive letters and cards were overwhelming administrative staff — praising the hooker for his honesty and wishing him the best in his counselling.

Finally, the weight of that support began to tell.

'I was in the darkest hole for the week after the press conference. I couldn't see where I was, or where I was going, or what to do next. Mum and Arlene were there but it was like they were a long, long way away. I couldn't sleep properly and the thing that I most wanted to numb me was drink. That's how I'd coped in the past and now that crutch was gone too.

'But then all those letters and cards and flowers to my home . . . from people I didn't even know, including the couple from the chalet . . . it did start to make a difference. I began to climb out of that hole, and I reckon everybody played a part in pulling me out. It made me feel so humble. That so many people could give a damn when I didn't deserve it. It was amazing.'

But John Hart had been right. The more difficult days did lie ahead — when the public sympathy had passed and the world returned to an even keel. The initial crisis might be weathered, but what of the next time, and the time after that? And always the thirst was there. Just awaiting its chance.

CHAPTER SIXTEEN

Journey

There was no electronic anklet nor any guard stationed outside his home, but Norm felt as if he was under house arrest. His fall from grace continued to lead news bulletins and sports features, and journalists pestered away, looking for any fresh angle that might prolong the story. When a daily newspaper featured a photograph of Norm stepping outside his back door, taken with a zoom lens from the gully opposite, he knew it was time to leave. He would have to escape.

'The media just kept coming. Everybody wanted a piece. Some idiot even said that I had a responsibility to come clean. What did he think I'd done at the press conference, eh? I felt as if I was being hunted.'

One evening his old Te Aute mate George Ormond called. It was a short conversation — get in the car, mate, and come up here to the farm at Mahia. There was someone that he needed to meet. Within minutes Norm was heading north. But a couple of hours later, as he neared Waipukurau, he began to feel uncomfortable. Not just as he reviewed the circumstances of the past few days, but uncomfortable with himself. As if he couldn't be trusted even when alone. He called another old friend from his Te Aute days — Bill Haukamau.

'Billy was Gavin Hinds' best mate at Te Aute, although we hadn't really got on at school. But after Gavin died, we had him in common, I guess. It brought us closer. So I gave him a call on the way and said I'd pay his wages for a couple of days if he'd join me. I didn't want to be alone — even for that short drive from Waipuk to Mahia. I needed someone with me.'

Although Norm didn't know it, Bill's life was also at a crossroads. He was working at the local abattoir, living with the mother of his two young daughters and seriously thinking of getting patched up with the Mongrel Mob.

'Billy was one angry man. He had a quick temper and was a real tough hombre. Heavily tattooed, not much of a family man. I liked him because of Gavin, but we both had our own personal troubles at the time. It was funny how we ended up on the same journey at the same time.'

When they arrived at the Ormond farm in northern Hawke's Bay, George welcomed them both and suggested that they all drive to Tauranga the next day. There was someone they needed to meet.

'I went for a jog that afternoon and sorted through all the shit in my head. I wasn't too keen on taking off again but George was like a brother and he was doing his best for me. He'd become a Mormon since his school days — had converted through marriage — so he didn't drink or smoke or anything.'

That night George told Norm that he had been charting his mate's steady decline but had felt powerless to intervene. But he knew someone who could help. A Maori mystic by the name of Selwyn Jones — a champion kickboxer and hellraiser in his day but subsequently a strong believer in the old wisdom that lay within tikanga Maori. Since then he had devoted himself to helping street kids, prison inmates and any other Maori who had lost their way.

'Selwyn was heavily into the spiritual side of things. He reckoned that most of Maoridom's problems were because we'd ignored our wairua and that was a big part of what it was to be Maori. I just nodded — sounded all a bit like Maori AA to me — but I tagged along. He was going around various marae giving lectures on the old ways so we joined him at Huria marae, which was just outside Tauranga.

'I don't know why but I felt immediately at home when I stepped on that marae. Apparently it was connected to Kahungunu, but it was more than that. Selwyn was a great teacher — he took us through all the carvings and explained their significance. I felt a bit embarrassed when he asked me if I spoke Maori, and I said "No, not really." But he said that was OK. Anyone can learn te reo, it's the tikanga that makes a Maori, not the language.'

Despite being intrigued by his new acquaintance, Norm was still keen to get back to the farm at Mahia or even back to Wellington. He felt anxious and it seemed as if constant movement was the only solution. But he decided to stay and listen to the lecture at Huria marae. They'd welcomed him as whanau not manuhiri. The least he could do was listen.

'The lecture lasted five or six hours but it was like it was over in a flash. It was incredible — I was fixated by the whole story Selwyn told and the whole sincerity and spirituality of the man. It was like he was talking direct to me — to my head and my heart at the same time. And he was saying that life is a journey and that we have responsibilities to ourselves but, most importantly, responsibilities to others. And the way he said it . . . wrapped within tikanga Maori and the old ways. It cut right through me and I knew he was right and where I'd gone wrong. I'd been self-centred and mean and forgotten my place and my role. Well, he gave that back to me. Let me put all my shit to one side. Made me realise how I'd mistreated women and that I had a role in protecting them — made me see not only where I'd gone wrong but how to put it right.'

Norm credits his epiphany to Selwyn. But whatever Jones' influence, the conversion would not have taken root had not the rugby player's search been so desperate. It had taken the Queenstown incident and its aftermath to jolt Norm awake — to make him understand the emptiness of his existence and how far he had fallen. And it was a measure of his innate determination that he was prepared to try any suggestion, any path that might put him back on track. Whether it was the psychologists and the psychiatrists of the rugby union, the AA, the religion of his friends, or the mysticism of Selwyn Jones and the marae, Norm was prepared to try them all. But at Huria he found the combination that suited him best — a personal mix of tikanga Maori, spiritualism and peace.

'The journey', as he still likes to call it, this brief road trip to Mahia and Tauranga, had an even more powerful effect on Bill. He returned to Waipukurau, told his partner and daughters that he loved them, married his partner, swore off both booze and drugs, and converted to the Church of Jesus Christ of Latter-day Saints.

'What happened to me was huge, but what happened to Bill was way bigger. It seemed that we were both struck by the same light at the same time, and all we did on the way back — George, Billy and me — was talk about what we'd been doing wrong and how we were going to change it. I mean, it sounds dramatic, but that's because it was. We weren't "cured" or anything. I knew that every day would still be a struggle and that there'd be times when we would be down and then the demons would really be back.

'But at least we knew how to fight them off now. We knew what to do and how to do it. For me, it was through karakia to Atua [prayers to God]. That's how I could find the strength to cope — to get me through. That, and knowing what my purpose was. How I had a responsibility for those weaker and more vulnerable than me.

'The biggest thing that hit me at the time was that it wasn't my drinking that was the problem. My drinking only released those things that lived within me. If I stopped drinking, they'd still be there. No, it was all the disrespect I'd shown to women over the years. That's what really got to me. How I'd treated my mum, my sisters, my girlfriends, any woman . . . even Arlene.

'I was driving home, had just passed through Pahiatua, when I gave her a call to tell her I was coming home. And was hoping that she'd be there when I got there, I suppose, as well. I told her that it was as if I had this big smile in me. I couldn't explain it any other way. And it was interesting that I rang her to share the feeling. It told me how I really felt about her.'

A NON-PERSON

Despite the epiphany at Huria marae, the practical realities soon returned. He still had to make a living, and rugby was as much a part of his being as it had ever been. The Hurricanes were training without him, and both coaches and team had been relying on his on-field leadership. When they lost their first Super 12 competition game in a listless performance against Queensland, his guilt immediately doubled.

Second five-eighth Jason O'Halloran had taken over the captaincy but it was not a happy choice. While he had the team's respect, O'Halloran was an insulin-dependent diabetic who had to watch his diet and refrained from a good part of the team's socialising. As Norm had discovered the previous season, captaincy was as much about man management as about tactical decision-making on the field of play. That required getting to know each player on a personal level, and the nature of O'Halloran's lifestyle militated against that kind of relationship.

'Jason was an extremely good player,' Graeme Taylor says. 'A very heady player — always thinking and able to give his outsides like Alama, Cully and Tana the half-gap that they needed. But he was quite a shy guy off the field — he would get to bed a bit earlier than the others because of the diabetes, and we probably erred in putting the captaincy on him too. But there was no-one else. With Bull gone and Norm missing, there was a real gap.'

The Hurricanes marketing team had begun to treat Norm as if he was a non-person. In the team's first home game against the Stormers, he was removed from the match programme's pen portraits despite still being a member of the squad. And when he was asked to make a public appearance on behalf of the kids' charity Ronald McDonald House, the Hurricanes' marketing team sought to bar his participation — the event was to take place in a downtown sports bar, and the association was deemed too raw.

'I just told them to get stuffed. I had never liked all that corporate PR bullshit but it was their hypocrisy that really upset me. I could talk to the patrons at the piss-up, but not for a charity. No way.'

Despite being excised from the match programme for the Stormers game, Norm found his way onto Athletic Park as a second-half replacement for Davin Heaps. It was a game the Hurricanes were expected to win, but the Stormers outplayed them for much of the time — Bok pin-up boy Bobby Skinstad particularly prominent — and the final 22-24 scoreline flattered the hosts.

'We were under quite a disadvantage that Super 12 season,' says Taylor. 'We had so many new draft players — I think ten or eleven in all. They were quality guys like Andrew Blowers, Ofisa Tonu'u and Glen Osborne, but at that level combinations are important and only time together produces that. Look at the Crusaders and the Brumbies over recent years — their advantage is their teamwork. The Hurricanes never had that luxury — each year we were forced to build a new team.'

In such an environment, Norm's skills were sorely needed. Not just as a captain, but as a top hooker who could hold the scrum together and organise the lineout. Against bigger and taller packs, the Hurricanes were often at the losing end of the possession contest. Crusaders' reject Stu Loe had been drafted in as the prop replacement for Bull Allen, but solid grafters like Mike Edwards and Ace Tiatia were unlikely to trouble the men mountain from South Africa or dull the ruthless efficiency of the Kiwi front rows. Against that, the Hurricanes' loosies were in outstanding form — Andrew Blowers making a mockery of his dumping from the Blues, and Kupu Vanisi and Filo Tiatia also staking claims for higher honours.

Midway through the Super 12 campaign the Hurricanes were still in with a chance of a semi-final berth, despite their early losses to Queensland and the Stormers. A last-minute away draw to the champion Crusaders raised their hopes, then a remarkable 34-18 thrashing of the Sharks in South Africa further revved the optimists.

'That was the game where the outside backs clicked,' remembers Norm. 'Alama [Ieremia] had a foot injury for most of the early part of the season and the backline didn't work without him. He was the key — solid on defence and a real threat on attack. He also gave Jason [O'Halloran] confidence. They were chalk and cheese, those two — Alama the big gregarious Samoan, and Jason the weedy, quiet white guy — but they had this weird chemistry when placed together. Anyway, that Sharks game the forwards did their bit and Cully, Tana and Alama just carved them up. They really fancied themselves, the Sharks, so they got a hell of a shock.'

But despite his impressive form O'Halloran regarded the captaincy as a continuing burden, and with Norm returning to the fray Oliver and Taylor restored the hooker to his leading role. It completed a remarkable recovery — from a disgraced drunk just two months earlier to 'Captain Hurricane' against the Chiefs. But the elevation was not universally applauded. In rugby union and media circles, Norm was not regarded as having done sufficient penance. And his abstention from alcohol was cynically regarded by many as just a ruse to regain the selectors' favour.

'I overheard a couple of NZRFU fish-heads talking at an after-match. They'd obviously had a bit too much to drink themselves because they were talking a bit too loud and unaware of me standing behind them. Anyway, they were both saying that I'd fallen off the wagon a couple of times before and I'd fall off again. At the time I felt very angry, but when I thought about it, I could understand why they doubted me. I hadn't exactly been Mister Reliable. But this time, I knew it would be different. This time I had a reason bigger than me to stay off the piss.'

Although there would be no fairytale conclusion to Norm's reinstatement as captain. The team suffered narrow and successive losses to the Blues, the Chiefs and the Brumbies — the last two games in front of their home fans. The Hurricanes' season was effectively over, and so too the coaching prospects of Frank Oliver and Graeme Taylor. Oliver would resurface as an assistant coach for the Blues, but Taylor would be cut loose entirely — dumped even as the assistant for the Wellington NPC team.

'GK and I have had our moments but I could understand his bitterness at the treatment he got. The problem with the Hurricanes in '99 was that we had a run of key injuries to key players, no real depth on the bench, and then the overall handicap of all those new draft players having to fit in. I don't think the problem was with the coaches, but they still got it in the neck. It was as if there needed to be some sort of public execution to explain the poor season, so GK got the first bullet and Frank the ricochet.'

HATE

Despite the Queenstown incident, the subsequent injury and the performance of the Hurricanes, Norm was still disappointed not to make the All Black squad for the shakedown game against New Zealand 'A' and then the early tests against Tonga and France.

He had dropped to third in the pecking order behind Anton Oliver and Mark Hammett. For the first time since 1993 he was no longer a member of the All Black squad, and it hurt. He had been a member of one of international sport's elite teams, and still considered himself good enough to represent his country. But the selectors felt differently — both his age and his lack of pace counting against him. He was the old warhorse who hears the signal to charge but can't quite answer it in time.

Initially he shifted the blame. It was Hart's fault that he wasn't in the squad; his new assistants Wayne Smith and Peter Sloane were biased in favour of the southern franchises. A moment's reflection allowed the truth to come through. He was one of the strongest scrummagers in the game and his set-piece performances might well be superior to those of the younger men, but that was not enough. The All Black selectors were looking for runners — hookers who could not only do their job in the tight but get out and support the ball carrier.

'No one doubted Norm's ability in the tight,' says Hart. 'But all his injuries had caught up with him and slowed him down. There was no question that his spirit was willing, but our view was that the other two were quicker around the track.'

Norm refused to accept the logic of his rejection. He would give Hart no option — he would play his guts out in the remaining games and make the selectors rethink their priorities. Again, that innate determination never to be beaten — never to give in —pushed him forward; a determination that may have been honed in the early years at Te Aute, but was a part of the Hewitt character from his first breath. This time there was an edge to his will. The game at Christchurch, for New Zealand 'A' against the All Blacks, would be as much about defiance as about advancing his claim to the silver fern.

'You get pissed off when you're dropped. I know players put a brave face on and say that they can understand the selectors' view and hope to play their way back in. But that's bullshit. It's like a kick in the guts when you're dropped. They're telling you you're not good enough, and you resent that. At that stage, you've got two choices: you either get hard and prove the bastards wrong or you bugger off. A lot of All Blacks don't survive their first dropping — they're not tough enough, mentally, to come back. Their whole world caves in.'

So, too, might Norm's world had it not been for the Queenstown incident and his subsequent reappraisal of what was important and what was not. There had been a significant change in Norm's preparation and playing style since Queenstown.

'I didn't hate any more. I'd psyched myself up in the past by getting a real good hate going before I stepped out onto the paddock. The other team were my personal enemies and each game was a war. It was all about domination. An intensity that sure made you a madman on the field.

'You wanted to do them harm. If they got in your way you blew them away. If you could step on their hands in a ruck or get away with a good stiff arm out of the ref's vision then that's what you did. Anything to dominate, anything to intimidate the other team. At the top level, rugby is as much about war as it is about skill. If you don't have the passion, if you're not prepared to do some damage — then you won't make it. That's the attitude that made me hard — that's what made me an All Black. I hated the other team with a passion.'

One of the frequent criticisms directed at the All Blacks in recent years is that their players, particularly the forward pack, lack 'mongrel' — the ability to intimidate an opponent, to physically dominate and hurt them. When the World Cup team was later savaged for its failure to return with the William Webb Ellis Trophy, the collective refrain was that the All Blacks had 'gone soft' — that the modern game had robbed the All Blacks of the physical aggression that had allowed them to dominate the game since the 1950s.

'Where do people think that aggression comes from? Short of having fifteen psychopaths in black jerseys, the players have to get themselves into a state of war before a test match. It's harm or be harmed. Even the pure types like Michael Jones would go over the edge in a test match — sure you might see the legit big hits, but I saw Ice hurt people, give them the sly elbow or stamp on their hands while they were lying in the ruck.

'I reckon that's half the reason why the All Blacks and the Springboks are lagging a bit behind the Australians at the moment. The Aussies actually aren't all that physical on the field. You play a team like the ACT Brumbies and you know you're not going to be in for all that physical an encounter — the challenge is primarily mental. You've got to keep concentrating or they're gone.

'And with all the live TV, the touch judges getting involved all the time and then having a commissioner citing players for dirty play, then a lot of the biff and aggro has gone out of the game. Sure, there are still subtle ways to put the filth in and Fitzy was the master of that. I learned a lot from him. But the filth will only take you so far. The game is becoming more like chess every day. I used to joke that playing some teams, like the Brumbies, made my brain hurt.'

Despite the fact that rugby administrators are now taking a firm stand against the overt punching and kicking that marred first-glass games at the start of Norm's career, he maintains that many spectators still get a thrill out of players hurting or being hurt.

'You hear the oohs and ahhs around the ground when there's a big hit or someone is almost cut in half from a gang tackle. You still get the odd coaching instruction to "look after" a certain player, and you know what that code means. The whole idea of turning defence into a weapon of attack involves doing as much damage as possible within the laws of the game. People love that as much as they love the running and the high-speed switches and dummies. Aggro is part of the game.'

So without the desire to impose his physical presence on the field, Norm had to find another incentive to perform. His determination would get him only so far. If he was to retain a playing edge, he needed something else. Something external.

CHAPTER SEVENTEEN

Captain

Despite not being selected in the All Blacks for their internationals against Samoa, France and the Tri-Nations, Norm was still determined to play his way into the 1999 World Cup squad. He knew Anton Oliver and Mark Hammett were the preferred choices, but rated them as suspect under pressure. The first chance to test that theory was in the All Blacks' warm-up match against New Zealand 'A'.

The official word was that the World Cup squad had not been settled but privately most players regarded Hart's mind as being made up. The All Black coach had somehow survived the previous year's five-match losing streak, and with seemingly even more control over the All Black environment. That included making sure they would not be embarrassed by their New Zealand 'A' opposition. This suspicion was fuelled when the Crusaders' inspirational captain, Todd Blackadder, was withdrawn from the New Zealand 'A' team in the lead-up to the trial match and transferred to the All Black reserves.

'We were set up to lose,' Norm recalls. 'With Todd gone, I was appointed captain and so I revved the boys up about how the pricks were trying to shaft us. They couldn't afford for the ABs to lose. My message was simple — get in their faces. Show no respect.'

Under lights at Jade Stadium in Christchurch, the All Blacks survived the encounter and scored three tries to one in their 22-11 win. But Norm was unimpressed. The 'A' team's front row of Gordon Slater, Con Barrell and himself had gained the measure of their opposites, while he considered both All Black locks, Robin Brooke and Ian Jones, to be showing their age.

'There was nothing to pick between the two packs — if anything, we had the better of them. If it hadn't been for the individual class of Jeff Wilson and Christian Cullen — and our fullback Adrian Cashmore making a couple of errors — we might have rolled them. At one stage the ABs had a 19-3 lead and then completely lost the plot. I came off thinking they were soft and that the AB teams I'd played in would have put their foot on our throat and not let it off.'

Only three of the 'A' team subsequently made the World Cup squad — Rhys Duggan and Scott Robertson, with Bruce Reihana called in late to replace an injured Carlos Spencer. It's a statistic that confirms to Norm that the All Black selectors had made their minds up long before the international season began. There were also complaints coming out of the All Black camp after the match that some of their players had been unnecessarily roughed up — further proof to Norm that the ABs needed to harden up. This was international rugby, not touch.

But he didn't have long to dwell on such things. The 'A' team had a full programme over the coming month, with a game against the touring French and then a home-and-away series against an Australian Barbarians selection. The French were duly despatched 45-24 at Hamilton, with Todd Blackadder back and leading the side from the front.

'That French team was piss poor. They had no spirit. It was like they didn't want to be there. When the ABs thrashed them 53-7 in the test I thought, "Well, scratch that team as a threat at the World Cup." But like everybody else, I forgot that they left their best forwards at home.

'Part of the reason they won that World Cup semi went back to the "A" game at Christchurch. The ABs would lose concentration. They didn't have anybody on the field to focus them. But as to why they lacked leadership . . . I don't think Harty can escape criticism on that score. He appointed Taine [Randell] captain and he tried to run them by remote control. That's not how you learn to lead or take responsibility.'

If the French were pathetic, it was a different game against the Australian Barbarians. With Matt Burke in outstanding form, the Australians secured a deserved 33-24 win at Melbourne. At scrum time the Aussie pack embarrassed their counterparts, with Andrew Blades having much the better of young Crusaders prop Greg Somerville. But a measure of revenge was gained a fortnight later when New Zealand 'A' won 40-17 at Whangarei.

'The difference was that the Aussies let their test reserves play in the first game but pulled them for the second. There was no Matt Burke or Phil Kearns or Andrew Blades to worry about at Whangarei, but their pack was still pretty useful. That's the thing I've noticed over the past decade — the real progress in Australian rugby has been in their forward play. They've always had good backs but it was their forwards who set up their World Cup wins in '91 and '99. I'd reckon we had better backs and more depth in our backs that year. We still do. We just don't coach them properly. They've got no patience.'

Ross Cooper was the 'A' team's coach for the '99 series, and Norm observed at first hand why John Hart might have pulled Crusaders' supremo Wayne Smith into the All Black set-up.

'Ross was a nice guy. But in my book he had serious coaching deficiencies. He didn't have the technical skills of Laurie Mains or the vision of John Hart. Maybe it was that his style never worked for me — he was more the gentle persuader and I got frustrated that we weren't spending enough time on getting our set-pieces right.'

And maybe part of it was that Norm knew his chance for higher honours was gone — that the 'A' team's performance in Melbourne had confirmed to the selectors that the best team was the one they had chosen; that the proud boast about New Zealand's rugby depth was no longer true. Certainly with the All Blacks' securing of the Tri-Nations the selectors had no reason to doubt the ability of their selections. Until one rainy night in Sydney, at the new Olympic Stadium.

'I watched that game on the telly and was surprised how easily Australia dominated the forward exchanges. But it was more than the All Blacks being flat. I mean, they didn't lack for motivation — the Bledisloe Cup was on the line, it was a world record crowd — just putting on the silver fern should have been incentive enough. But there was something missing. Like they didn't have a Plan B, or if they did no-one on the field was strong enough to impose it on the others.'

But the All Blacks had ceased to be Norm's concern. He felt aloof, even uncaring, about their plight. His failure to be chosen was taken as a rejection of both his skills and his person. It was an entirely human reaction to being looked over — the national team did not demand the same loyalty now that he was no longer within the tent.

But the journey earlier in the year and the fact that he still loved the game softened the blow. There were other challenges apart from the All Blacks. There was the Maori team to lead, and the Wellington Lions in the NPC. At least having the captaincy of both teams salved his ego, and played its part in sustaining his appetite for the game.

SECOND BEST

Returning from the Maori tour of Fiji was a culture shock in more ways than one. Not only was the camaraderie of the Maori squad missing from the Lions set-up, but the Wellington NPC team was a bewildering mixture of personalities and cultures. Ten days after the Suva test, Norm led the Lions out onto Eden Park for their opening match against Auckland, knowing they were woefully underprepared and hoping to avoid a massacre. Although the team didn't receive the 70-point hiding that Canterbury had handed out a couple of seasons earlier, it was close — 45-6 to the Queen Street boys, with the Lions lucky to get six.

'We were in trouble, and that was no reflection on Goss [coach Graeme Mourie]. The problem with having the Hurricanes drawn from different regions and having so many draft players was that there was no proper team spirit. That flowed through to the NPC, unlike teams like Waikato and Auckland that had a solid core of Super 12 players. And it was worse with our All Black stars like Christian and Tana being kept out of the NPC on John Hart's say so — I thought it would be a miracle if Wellington even made the final four.'

Realising the scope of the problem, Norm secretly called the Maori players in the Lions squad together — Dion Waller, Mike Edwards and Norm Broughton prominent — and asked for their help.

'I'd just come back from leading the Maori team and I needed lieutenants I could rely on, and real quick. Players who would assume leadership roles and back me up. And to a man, they responded. It was our Maoriness that provided that early togetherness. And then I worked on the other cultures in the team. I made a big deal of the fact that we had Pakeha, Maori, Samoan, Tongan, English, Dutch and Fijian players in the Lions — and that recognising and respecting their culture was important.

'I think that's where Wellington teams have gone wrong in the past. Coaches and managers haven't respected the diversity of cultures. Haven't tried to get inside each player and see what makes them tick. And the quickest way to do that is to respect a player's culture. Recognise it in the team. Make them feel at home.'

Although there were definite signs of improvement the early results were patchy, with home wins against North Harbour and Counties-Manukau followed by an away loss to Northland and a scratchy effort against Taranaki. It looked as if Wellington had produced yet another underperforming NPC team — as erratic and soulless as its predecessors.

Until the team's Ranfurly Shield game against Waikato — a game no-one gave Wellington a ghost of a chance of winning. The final 30-24

*This is personal. England hooker Richard Cockerill confronts Norm in the midst of the All Black haka at Old Trafford 1997.
A year later and they would be brawling in a Dunedin mini-van.*

Nadir. The aftermath of Queenstown, February 1999. Norm is led to his public execution by NZRFU director Bill Wallace and flanked by Hurricanes manager Tony Bedford.

Left: *Ritual humiliation at NZRFU headquarters.*
Right: *Norm breaks down. The media conference was to be an insincere 'mea culpa' until he thought of the shame he was bringing on his family.*

An unexpected epiphany. The travellers return from their journey —
Bill Haukamau, Norm and George Ormond.

The rugby team that Norm places above all others in terms of spirit and camaraderie.
New Zealand Maori celebrate their 18-15 victory over Scotland.

Gaining the respect of the world champion Wallabies at Sydney, May 2001 —
if only the NZRFU had a similar outlook. NZ Maori regarded themselves as
having been robbed of a win by South African ref Tappe Henning.

scoreline in favour of the holders did no justice to the Lions' efforts at Rugby Park that afternoon — Waikato scrambling against a fired-up Wellington pack led from the front by its captain. Despite the loss, Norm walked from the field in a buoyant mood. The team had proven itself before a disbelieving rugby public and won the respect of its supporters.

The rugby press were less convinced. Waikato had shot out to a 22-8 lead and coasted — so ran the media wisdom. 'Taranaki had been far more confrontational, more a test of manhood,' reported that week's *Rugby News*. 'Wellington only tested Waikato's resolve.'

But Norm knew something that the scribes did not. He had felt the new spirit in the team — a togetherness that had been absent earlier in the season. It had shown in the play of No. 8 Filo Tiatia, who had left the field following a blow to the head but returned heavily bandaged to play one of the matches of the season. If it had not been for David Holwell's erratic place-kicking, Norm was convinced they would have won.

'That's probably a bit tough on Dave but he was having the yips at that stage. Later he sorted out his kicking and won a lot of games for both the Lions and the Hurricanes. But I wasn't too upset we lost. I knew better was to come.'

And so it proved. Over the next three weeks Wellington comfortably accounted for all the South Island unions — Southland, Canterbury and Otago. Still the pundits refused to give them credit. The balance of the All Blacks were drawn from Canterbury and Otago, and defeating them with their stars absent was a somewhat hollow victory.

When the Lions took Waikato apart in the semi-final by 38 points to 17, the captain bulldozing over for one of Wellington's five tries, the rugby critics were finally forced to take notice. The Waikato team was barely changed from that which had retained the Ranfurly Shield a few weeks earlier, and contained no fewer than eight past or future All Blacks. This time *Rugby News* had to confess that the Norm Hewitt-led tight five 'were imposing and hard, bullying Waikato not just in rucks and mauls, but off the ball and after the whistle too'.

'I made sure the boys weren't going to be intimidated. We were back up at Rugby Park for the semi-final and no-one was giving us a show. So I put it to the guys that if we were going to win our front five had to really do the business. We'd been criticised all season and labelled "past it" and "soft". That sure stirred the boys up. Kevin Yates and Mike Edwards could be real hard buggers when they put their minds to it and both Dion [Waller] and Inoke [Afeaki] were geared up to do some damage. We let the crowd motivate us too. They can be a mouthy lot in Hamilton so it was good to silence the cow bells. It was payback time.'

Yet without the All Blacks — now engaged in pool play at the World Cup — there was an air of phoniness about the NPC. Wellington's achievement in making its first-ever final was devalued by the fact that thirty of the country's top players were absent. This also led to a lack of interest that was reflected in the crowd sizes for the semi-finals — 14,000 for the Hamilton game, 13,000 for the Auckland-North Harbour semi a day earlier.

'I knew if we won the title the next Saturday people would dismiss it. But I didn't care what the public or rugby writers thought. I only cared about the team, and for us getting to the final was a big deal. It represented a huge step from where Wellington rugby had been at the start of the season, All Blacks or not.'

Although the first division final was played at Eden Park in front of a respectable crowd, the attention of most fans remained directed 12,000 miles north to where the All Blacks were due to take on Scotland in the World Cup quarters. As he led the team out onto Eden Park, Norm looked across the field at the Auckland team and counted all the All Blacks John Hart had left behind. He wouldn't have minded if a few more of the Auks had been training in the Murrayfield mist.

'We knew we could match the Auckland forwards but it was their backs that worried me. We were frail out wide and Jason was really the only experienced player we had. Jason Spice and David Holwell were both promising young guys but they were still getting used to each other. We had to keep it tight if we were going to win — not give the Auckland backs any latitude.'

Sure enough, it was the Wellington outsides who wilted in the heat of finals rugby. Knowing that O'Halloran was the playmaker, the Auckland defence concentrated on closing down the midfield and then pressuring the inexperienced back three of Colin Sullivan, Ali Koko and Brad Fleming. Boasting five former All Blacks in their backline, including Eroni Clarke and Craig Innes in the centres, and possessing the mercurial skills of first-five Orene Ai'i and winger Doug Howlett, the Aucklanders closed down most of Wellington's attacking options.

That the final score was only 24-18, and that Wellington might have won had not a couple of awkward kicks been spilled, provided a measure of compensation when the final whistle blew. Graeme Mourie was especially proud of the team's effort, declaring that the team had 'played out their guts on that field', while the rugby media praised the efforts of the tight five for dominating their opposites and giving Wellington set-piece superiority.

But Norm was shattered by the defeat. He had expected the team to win, confident that the Lions forwards would have the measure of their opposites and that the backs would rise to the occasion. But he had not figured on a tenacious Auckland defence, or the freakish efforts of Michael Jones, summoning one last game-turning performance from his battered body. And Auckland had played safe, no-frills finals football. They had abandoned their usual running game in favour of halfback Tonu'u kicking into the box and the chasers pouring through to pressure the Lions' inexperienced back three.

As the winners' medals were presented to the victorious team, the Aucklanders celebrating with upraised fingers and high fives, Norm scowled. The game had been within their grasp and they had let it slip. Next year, he told himself. Next year, we'll get you.

REFLECTION

As he looked back on the '99 rugby season, Norm could be forgiven for feeling a quiet sense of satisfaction. From the rubble of his relationship with Kat and the public humiliation of Queenstown, he had fought back to captain the Hurricanes, New Zealand Maori and the Lions, and had almost led the latter to glory. He had also found a true rugby home within the Maori squad, and his leadership had brought fresh dynamism to the Maori tradition. On the home front, his relationship with Arlene was blossoming — a mature relationship based on respect and an understanding of each other's needs.

Even more importantly, he was at peace with himself. There was still the odd temptation to drink — most strongly felt whenever he was in rugby company — but he did not succumb. He was also learning to deal with the old anger without resorting to the booze — had learned to direct his energy in positive ways, either through prayer or by devoting time to Ronald McDonald House and other kids' charities. He now regarded his rugby profile as more than just a commercial opportunity. It was a chance to give something to others who needed help. The message of the March journey had been fully absorbed.

Yet there were a number of people within the rugby community who remained sceptical about this new Norm Hewitt. For all his good works, Norm's commercial activities continued to ruffle feathers. The new rugby world had not only created a divide between professional and amateur players, it had also alienated many officials from the top players. Here they were, they reasoned, getting paid next to nothing to administer the game at grass-roots level, while players like Norm Hewitt got six-figure salaries and exploited the business that surrounded their beloved game.

Certainly Norm found that his captaincy and high public profile provided him with an opportunity to increase his earning power beyond the NZRFU salary. He would arrange individual sponsorships for himself and other Lions players, negotiate personal endorsements, and even made a small fortune trading surplus World Cup tickets. They were all legitimate extensions of the new professionalism, but that didn't stop the accusations that he was lining his and other players' pockets at the expense of the game.

'It was crap,' Norm retorts. 'Rugby is a very unstable career. You can be earning good money one minute and the next you're crocked or have been dropped. No-one gives a stuff about you then. You're yesterday's news.

'And it's impossible to have a career or a full-time job and be a top-class rugby player. The daily training, the travel, the touring . . . no employer wants to know us. The game is far more intense than when I first started playing — far more time-consuming than even three or four years ago.

'So I had no problem trying to get the best deals for myself and my players, given that our earning power is finite. They were my charges and I was going to look after them. After we quit the game, a lot of us won't have a career path or qualifications. We're going to have to start from scratch. So, for the moment, rugby is our job. By getting players a better deal, we're also reducing the financial incentive for them to head off to Japan or France or the UK.'

Although even for Norm the lure of an overseas contract was strong. He had been approached by the English club London Irish during the '97 UK tour, and they had kept in contact. In addition, former Hurricanes mates Jarrod Cunningham and Steve Bachop were with the club and enjoying the cosmopolitan environment. Despite the fact that he was no longer a top drawer All Black, the money being offered was tempting — £80,000 a year, and another £20,000 if the team performed to expectations. In addition there would be match payments and win bonuses — the overall package worth around NZ$300,000.

'Initially I said no. I looked at the $165,000 I was getting from my NZRFU contract and my other commercial interests outside rugby . . . then all the other stuff like the unfinished NPC business, my family, whether Arlene would like it . . .

'But then Goss started umming and ahhing over the Hurricanes captaincy for the next season, and the way he was talking I wasn't even sure I'd make the squad. I'd asked him straight questions during the NPC season about the next year, and what my prospects were, but all he would say was that it depended on my form.'

Norm interpreted Mourie's caution as reluctance. He had been used to Oliver's gruff, no-nonsense style, but his new Super 12 coach was altogether a different personality — aloof and measured. The two had not hit it off during the regular NPC season, despite the team's impressive run towards the end.

To any observer of human nature it was obvious the two men had different personality types and came from different rugby cultures, and both were determined to stamp their impression on the team. It was an unequal struggle — coach against captain — but Mourie was the new boy in town and despite earlier stints with Wellington as a player and a coach, his appointment as the Hurricanes' head coach was something else again. As a former All Black captain, with a playing reputation as a thinker and strategist, Mourie was determined to play a different style of game to that of his predecessor. In contrast, Norm was the old warhorse with a practical understanding of team dynamics and the players' respect. For the moment, they needed each other.

Eventually Mourie made the call. Norm Hewitt would lead the Hurricanes out onto the swish new Wellington stadium for the 2000 Super 12. It was the final factor that convinced Norm that London Irish was not a goer. Yes, he might be better off financially if he took the contract, but he'd travelled enough over the past thirteen years and there were enough new challenges just outside his front door. The grass was definitely greener at home.

The capital's *Evening Post* described the appointment as 'completing one of the best comebacks since Lazarus'. The paper's rugby writer, David Ogilvie, had observed the rehabilitation of the Hurricanes captain from close quarters. In the wake of the Queenstown incident, the hooker had 'had a long way to go to regain his equilibrium and the confidence and respect of his team-mates. He's fought long and hard to do that.'

Yet Norm knew his appointment was only the start of it. It was one thing to lead a team — another entirely to lead them with distinction. That test still awaited him. But off the field it was the same story. One day at a time.

'There were a lot of times over that Christmas I felt like having a beer or a glass of wine. Part of me was saying that it would only be the one. Just for the taste, not the alcohol. But it wouldn't have just been the one — there would have been another and another until I was pissed. And no matter how you rationalise things, it still doesn't make saying "No" any easier. For that reason alone, I wanted the rugby season to start again tomorrow. Then at least I could distract myself. So, yeah, I'd come back. But I still had one hell of a long way to go.'

CHAPTER EIGHTEEN

Maori

The history of Maori rugby provides a unique insight into the often vexed relationship between Maori and Pakeha. Although that relationship has traversed most paths over the last two centuries, from hostile to politically correct, the rugby field has been one place where the races have generally accepted each other as equals — where qualities of courage, initiative and skill have made redundant both colour and culture.

Certainly relations between the races have had their moments, and it has only been in the past generation, with the renaissance of the Maori language and Crown recognition of the Treaty of Waitangi, that this country's bi-cultural heritage has been acknowledged and encouraged.

Maori rugby has been an important part of the renaissance. In recent years it has become a shopfront for the Maori people — a symbol of pride both at home and abroad. Yet its beginnings, in the wake of the land wars of the 1850s and 1860s, were less auspicious. Perhaps not surprisingly, it was the kupapa (friendly) Maori — invaluable to the colonial government in its eventual military success — who were the first Maori to take up the new craze of rugby football. The game appealed on any number of levels — as a physical challenge, as a test of strength, as a contest of skill and daring. Most importantly as a sport that celebrated teamwork and where the concept of whanau was critical in terms of delivering final victory.

In addition, the game was accessible to all comers — whether Maori, half-caste or Pakeha, landed gentry or labourer, tradesman or toff. Rugby was a sport that exemplified the pioneering and egalitarian spirit of the new country. There appears to have been little evidence of any racial discrimination in the selection of the rugby teams of early times, the first recorded Maori representative being Winihana, who represented Wanganui 'Country' in 1872. Jack Taiaroa and Joseph Warbrick were two outstanding Maori players who toured New South Wales in 1884 with a New Zealand representative team. They were also key members of the 1888 Natives, a team comprising mostly players of Maori descent.

The 1888 Natives' tour of North America and Great Britain was not only the first true international rugby tour but an astounding feat of athleticism and endurance. The team — whose story is ably told in Greg Ryan's *Forerunners of the All Blacks* — played 107 matches in just five months. The tour also created New Zealand rugby's first international 'star', Tom Ellison, who is credited with the invention of the notorious wing-forward position, and also the positioning of the five-eighths in the backline.

Since that time the strength and influence of Maori rugby has waxed and waned — often losing its better players to the rival code of rugby league yet still producing the backbone of many an All Black team. It has also contributed some of the greatest players ever to wear the silver fern — George Nepia, Johnny Smith, Mac Herewini, Waka Nathan, Sid Going and Buck Shelford to name but a recognisable few.

The New Zealand Maori's first 'official' international match — in the sense of a team chosen exclusively from Maori players and sanctioned by the NZRFU — was in 1921 when they held the touring South Africans to a one-point margin at Napier. But that and subsequent contests against South Africa would also provide the game with some of its most shameful moments. All Black teams which toured the apartheid republic did so without Maori players, and even when this discrimination was relaxed in 1970 those players chosen were still required to tour with the status of 'honorary whites'.

At home, things were only marginally better. No New Zealand Maori game was scheduled against the 1937 Springboks, and they were only allowed to play against the 1956 tourists after the most extraordinary of official lectures. Just before kick-off the Maori team was warned that their conduct must be exemplary or they would jeopardise any future games against touring teams. Demoralised by this last-minute edict, and power-less to respond to any on-field provocation, they were duly thrashed 37-nil. The game still ranks as New Zealand Maori's worst-ever defeat.

However, other nations enjoyed their contact with Maori representative teams. During the 1920s, representative Maori teams toured Australia and played 'test' series against New South Wales, the only Australian state then playing the game. The Queensland union had failed to survive the interregnum of the Great War, and New South Wales was rugby's only flag-carrier from 1919 to 1929.

In the 1990s, the Australian Rugby Union would retrospectively recognise all New South Wales' fixtures played during that period as *bona fide* Wallaby tests. This led to one of the great quirks of All Black football — the 1922 All Blacks losing their series against Australia by two tests to one, but the New Zealand Maori team defeating the same Wallaby combination in the same year by the same margin. For a brief moment the Maori team could claim to be the best in the world!

During the 1960s and 1970s, New Zealand Maori not only played touring teams but also undertook regular tours of the Pacific Islands — 'missionary' ventures designed to stimulate interest in the game in Tonga, Western Samoa and Fiji. In turn, the NZRFU hosted the Islanders, with 'tests' against the Maori the highlight of their itineraries.

And yet Maori rugby was very much a thing apart. There were annual contests between Northern and Southern Maori teams for the Prince of Wales Cup, but for most rugby followers, and even the players themselves, these matches were little more than curiosities — deemed of lesser importance than inter-provincial matches.

BEING MAORI

As a young boy growing up in central Hawke's Bay, Norm Hewitt regarded Maori rugby as an irrelevance. His dream was to play for Hawke's Bay and then the All Blacks — against those priorities Maori rugby was as inconsequential as his own Maori background.

'My father is Pakeha and my mum Maori, but I wasn't really conscious of any difference in race until I was at primary school. Then some of the kids would tease me for being a half-caste, and although I didn't know what that meant, I knew it wasn't good. As a kid, all I could work out was that Mum was darker in colour than Dad and had a helluva lot more relatives. I do remember my first tangi though. That totally freaked me out. I had to hongi the dead guy in the coffin, and I had nightmares for weeks after that. If that was what being a Maori was all about, then I wanted no part of it.'

But being Maori was not a matter of choice. When his parents decided he should follow his older half-brother, Robert, to Te Aute College he became immersed in Maori culture whether he liked it or not. And he didn't.

'The whole thing was foreign to me — the emphasis on whakapapa, te reo, the haka, waiata and tikipuna . . . none of it seemed real or relevant. As far as I was concerned Te Aute was all about rugby and sport. That and all the other "life skills" I picked up there, like drinking, smoking, drugs . . . fighting. Money, dope and rugby meant something, but not all that taha Maori bullshit.'

Norm's defiance of authority included the school's cultural ambience. In particular he resented the fact that the same rich/poor split that had been so much a part of his rural childhood seemed to be duplicated at Te Aute. The sons of chiefly Maori families seemed 'more equal' than their peers. To Norm's eyes, they had greater sway at the boarding school than a labourer's kid of mixed parentage. His initial indifference to his Maori heritage quickly developed into a matter of personal policy, despite his pride at making Te Aute's 1st XV and playing in their traditional games against St Stephen's, Hato Paora and Church College.

'I even failed School Cert Maori despite the natural advantage we Te Aute kids had. I got it the second year, but only just. My favourite subject was horticulture — anything academic, including learning te reo, was too much for me. I kept thinking: "So is learning Maori going to get me a job? Nah." Mind you, I think I used that argument for just about every subject I took.

'But because my older brother was from two Maori parents and I had Pakeha blood through Dad, I did notice that I was whiter than Robert and whiter than most of my school mates. As a junior, some of the seniors used it as an excuse to bully me, but that was the hostel hierarchy. If it hadn't been that, it would have been something else.'

When he left Te Aute Norm deliberately linked up with Napier's Technical Old Boys rather than MAC or Clive, clubs with strong Maori and Te Aute links. After his first senior game a couple of MAC players challenged him at the after-match, demanding to know why he was turning out for a Pakeha team. Norm shrugged his shoulders — Maori, Pakeha, it made no difference to him. Rugby was his only culture.

'I was selected and played a few games for Hawke's Bay Maori, but they were just practice games to me. It didn't mean anything — I wanted to get into the Hawke's Bay Colts or the senior rep team. And that was pretty much the view I had of most Maori rugby. It was just another team and another game — another step to get where I wanted to go.'

Ironically, it was his promise as a young rep hooker that brought him to the attention of the New Zealand Maori selectors, and his first game for the Maori was as a replacement in their 63-9 thrashing of New Zealand Universities at Rotorua. But it was not until 1991 that he played in his first Prince of Wales game. He remembers the game well — not only did he lead the underdogs to a win over Buck Shelford's much-vaunted northern combination, but there was unusual media interest in the match. This was to be Buck Shelford's comeback match after his controversial axing from the All Black squad. Would the great man win back his place for that year's World Cup?

'That was also the day the selectors experimented with Steve McDowell as hooker [for the North team] — I guess they were looking for a back-up to Fitzy for the World Cup. But, boy, the whole day was a disaster for those guys. Buck got caught in the bottom of a ruck and stamped on and had to leave the field, and Steve was hopeless. Great prop, useless hooker. Maori boys don't give a stuff about reputation when you're at the bottom of one of their rucks and the South had a real mean pack that year — "Boom" Graham, Gordy Falcon, Jamie Joseph, Phil Coffin — Jeez, I was glad I was playing for them, not against them.'

A year later and Norm was looking forward to the Pacific Islands tour at the end of the NPC season — the New Zealand Maori team's first visit to the island nations in over a decade. But that was before the Shoreline Hotel incident in Dunedin and the consequent disciplinary action.

'I was gutted because Maori rugby was starting to mean something to me by then. I'd got used to the different feel of being in a Maori team and was starting to respect the culture a bit more. Most of that respect was because of the guys involved. And Maori rugby also appealed to me because it was so physical. It was always a real contest for domination.

'But I reckon the turning point for Maori rugby was that Lions game in '93. It was a huge buzz to play at Athletic Park in front of a huge crowd, and to almost beat them. Until then I wasn't sure that Maori rugby had much public respect, and I guess I was as much a part of that problem as anyone else. But in the days leading up to the game we developed a real closeness, and it was our Maoriness that made it all happen. We became brothers and it was just so natural. No effort at all.'

Although it was a qualified brotherhood. All Black status and the silver fern were the ultimate goal, and for most All Blacks of Maori descent their ethnic team was of secondary importance.

'I was a Maori New Zealander. That's how I saw myself and still do. I wasn't into all the blame-guilt bullshit. For me it's all about getting on with today and making yourself better for tomorrow. But that didn't mean

I wasn't proud of my Maori heritage. I am and I've become more so with each year. But it's only one part of me — an important part, yeah, but part of the whole.'

From the middle of 1993 onwards, Norm's priorities were those of most Maori players at the top level — he was an All Black first and a Maori All Black as time and rugby commitments allowed. He played in their 'test' win against Fiji in 1994, but would not play for them again for another three years.

'Even then it was only because John Hart insisted I get some game time ahead of the Tri-Nations. And shit, I hated him for that decision. But once I got back into the Maori camp I was OK again. I felt comfortable. And it was a good Maori team too . . . we beat Ireland A, Argentina and Western Samoa all in the space of a fortnight. But I was still impatient to get back into the AB camp. I think that was the way most All Blacks of Maori background looked at it . . . New Zealand Maori were a team of convenience.'

Although not for all players. For some, New Zealand Maori represented the pinnacle of their rugby careers. Jamie Joseph was one of those players. Despite being a veteran of twenty tests for the All Blacks, playing for the Maori team was something else again.

'My father [Jim Joseph] was a Maori All Black, and all the time I was a kid I wanted to be just like Dad. The Maori team was *the* team. I actually got into trouble over that attitude when I was playing for Otago in 1991 under Laurie Mains and he blew me up for putting the Prince of Wales game before the Otago team. But I didn't care because I wanted to get selected for the Maori All Blacks. Once I was in the All Blacks though, the Maori teams always came second. I didn't like that. I thought they could have made sure that the Maori teams played when their All Blacks would also be available to them.'

STATUS

The attitude of the NZRFU toward Maori rugby has always been a strange mixture of paternalism and indifference. On the one hand, traditionalists respect Maori rugby for its history and style. On the other, there is a view that selection for any national team on racial grounds is inherently discriminatory.

Current Maori coach Matt Te Pou admits as much. 'It is racism, but it's positive racism. Given the problems with our people, especially our youth, the New Zealand Maori team is a positive role model. It's an international statement too — that we're Maori and proud to be Maori.'

Te Pou was appointed assistant to Chas Ferris for the Maori 'test' against Fiji in 1994, and took over the senior role a year later. He's justly proud of the team's achievements since that time. But he also qualifies his enthusiasm against the reaction of some in the rugby fraternity. 'Sometimes Maori rugby is seen as a threat rather than an opportunity. There's no real forward planning — we don't know who we're playing from one season to the next. I think we're also seen as a bit of a threat internationally. No-one can quite work out where we fit in.'

Regardless of this ambivalence, Te Pou is convinced that Maori rugby will continue to have a place in the wider rugby framework because it is part and parcel of modern Maori culture. The team draws both its strength and its justification from being the representative team of the Maori people.

Norm has a different take on that issue, and one that is surprisingly political.

'When I was made captain of the Maori All Blacks, quite a lot of the press asked why there even was a Maori team. Even though they were sporting journos, you could see that quite a few of them personally believed the team was racist.

'But my view is that Maori have a right to our own team. Because of our tradition going back to the 1888 Natives, and also because of the Treaty [of Waitangi]. People might say that the Treaty shouldn't have anything to do with rugby, but it does. It has something to do with every aspect of New Zealand life. It was the partnership that Maori signed with the Crown back in 1840.'

To suggestions that rugby could scarcely be considered a Maori taonga, or treasure, Norm smiles.

'Why not? It's a part of what makes up our culture — our identity in the world. I can't remember whether it was Sir Peter Buck or Apirana Ngata, but one of them said that rugby saved the Maori race — that when it was falling apart — people were dying of disease and the old ways were falling apart — rugby was the glue that kept Maori hapu and iwi together. That's probably overstating it, but rugby was very important in allowing Maori to take their place in wider society. It allowed us to win the respect of Pakeha, and provided a positive outlet for the warrior spirit. I reckon Maori were made for rugby. It suits our personality.'

However, Norm acknowledges that many in the rugby community still regard Maori rugby as an inconvenience. It's an attitude he struck first-hand when he was chosen to captain New Zealand Maori in 1999.

'The NZRFU treated us like second-class citizens. Everything seemed to be an afterthought. As an All Black and a Super 12 player I was pissed off that the Maori rep team got substandard everything ... accommodation, training gear, management, PR, the works. For almost every Prince of Wales game I ever played in, the organisation was a shambles. Some of that was probably down to the organisers, but some of it was also down to the status of Maori rugby. No-one knew where we fitted in.'

As a player Norm had generally accepted his lot — it wasn't his place to challenge the system. But when he was appointed Maori captain in 1999 his focus changed. He would no longer go with the flow. The team were his charges now and something had to be done about their status.

'We were due to tour Fiji in July — during the Tri-Nations — so that meant players like Taine Randell, Robin Brooke, Kees Meeuws and Darryl Gibson weren't available to us ... but that was cool. We still had a good team ... any number of past or future ABs like Caleb Ralph, Bruce Reihana, Norm Berryman, Glen Osborne, Rhys Duggan — I mean add Karl Te Nana and Glen Jackson and we probably had the second best backline in the world that year. The forward pack was Deon Muir, Glen Marsh, Troy Flavell, Mark Cooksley, Dion Waller, John Akurangi, Paul Thomson and me. When you consider that we had Ron Cribb, Leon Macdonald, Todd Miller and Dallas Seymour in the reserves, then that's how strong we were. Phenomenal really.

'Anyway, I raised the issue of where we lay in the NZRFU hierarchy. Essentially, I argued that New Zealand Maori deserved to have equal status with New Zealand "A". But [NZRFU chief executive] David Moffett and [contracts manager] Tony Ward weren't convinced. I got the feeling that Moffett thought he was doing us a favour just letting us go to Fiji. But my argument was that rugby had gone professional and that ran right through the playing ranks — from the All Blacks, to New Zealand "A", the Academy team, Super 12 — why should New Zealand Maori be treated any different? We were professional players. We were representing the NZRFU and Maoridom. It wasn't so much the money as the status. "Look at the 1888 Natives," I said, "look at the gifting of the silver fern to the All Blacks from Maori" ... but I got nowhere.'

Indeed, the reaction to Norm's lobbying was direct and personal. He was advised that if he continued to claim special treatment for the Maori team then it may well impact on his own career and those of his charges. He approached Sean Fitzpatrick, recently appointed as the NZRFU's player liaison, to intercede on the Maori team's behalf.

'Fitzy just sat on the fence. He told me that he could see our viewpoint

and that he could see the union's. But Fitzy was the fish-heads' man —
their tame players' rep. They were the ones that paid his salary.'

Matters came to a head when the team were presented with contracts
to sign on the eve of their departure for Fiji. Far from improving the
Maori team's status, the NZRFU was offering players an allowance of $50
a day.

'I couldn't believe it. $50 a day was what we used to get as amateurs.
And it wasn't taxed in those days! So how were players with families and
mortgages and financial commitments meant to get by on $350 gross a
week?'

Norm conferred with some of the other senior players, particularly
Dallas Seymour and Glen Osborne, and a consensus quickly emerged. The
players would refuse to sign the contracts. In return it was pointed out that
a refusal to sign could mean no tour. A fall-back position was reached: the
players would sign, but refuse the allowance. It would be their protest.

In the middle of all this Matt Te Pou and his assistant Jim Love tried to
focus the team's concentration on the upcoming itinerary. But their
sympathies were firmly with the players.

'For that Fijian tour we had players stepping off the bus after having
played for New Zealand "A", on good professional wages for representing
their country, and then going straight into the Maori camp — another
representative team — and getting next to nothing. It didn't sit right with
any of us. It wasn't so much the money as the principle of the thing.

'Both Jim and I also got quite frustrated too because we could see that
Norm and some of the other senior players were doing the right thing —
by going through Fitzy and the official NZRFU contacts — but still getting
nowhere. We were caught in the middle of a very unpleasant situation,
with the team getting progressively angrier and us meant to be leaving on
the next plane. Fiji were going to be tough enough without this sort of
carry-on.'

As each hour passed the attitude of the Maori players hardened.

'We made some exceptions,' Norm recalls. 'A couple of the poorer
players needed any cash they could get. So [manager] Mattie Blackburn,
Matt Te Pou and some of us pooled our own money so that the boys with
the most urgent problems could get by. But, shit, we were angry. We'd been
fobbed off by the union and now there was this last-minute demand to
sign [for the daily allowance] or else.'

It was no surprise when the spat went public. The team's kaumatua,
Whetu Tipiwai, let it slip in an interview with a Maori radio station, and
within hours every mainstream media outlet was leading with the story.

Captain Norm Hewitt's defiant stance featured heavily. Soon talkback lines were clogged with callers — some condemning Hewitt for trying to blackmail the NZRFU, others supporting the players' principled stance. The night before the team flew out, a crisis meeting with the union's chairman, Rob Fisher, was arranged.

'Fisher said that this [the public fuss] was the first he'd heard of a problem. I believed him because it was my experience that Rob was an upfront guy. He was pissed off that we'd gone public but he promised to look into it while we were away. But as I got on the plane I thought how bloody typical it was that the chairman of the NZRFU didn't know what had been happening in his union's name with Maori rugby. It proved to me how far down the totem pole Maori rugby really was.'

When the team arrived back in New Zealand it was to the welcome news that their daily allowance had been increased from $50 to $200 a day. But Norm was more pleased that the team had stuck together over the issue — that an 'all for one' spirit had allowed them to present a united front.

'There was only one back-slider on the no-allowance agreement and that was [Counties lock] Jim Coe. I was disappointed with Jim because we'd all agreed and he'd been a part of that decision. We let it be known among the Maori boys when we came back, so I guess Jim got the occasional reminder whenever teams with Maori players in them played Counties.'

FIJI

Fiji were the 1999 Pacific Rim champions, and they intended to use the Maori visit as preparation for the World Cup. Their Kiwi coach, Brad Johnstone, had assembled his top players from various parts of the globe and there was a general air of optimism among the host officials.

Matt Te Pou fully expected the full-strength Fiji to test his team's unbroken sequence of wins. After a hard-fought 20-nil victory over a Fiji 'A' combination, his caution was confirmed. But he considered that the Maori team had bonded well after the allowance upset, and his captain was proving a real asset.

'Norm's always been a leader. I could sense it the moment I met him back in '94. He automatically assumes responsibility for himself and others — the team becomes his cause. And whether it's scrum training or social stuff off the field, you'll find Norm contributing. He was a great lieutenant to [former Maori captain] Errol Brain in those games against Ireland "A", Argentina and Western Samoa in '97 when we beat all three sides in just ten days. Initially he didn't want to be there because John Hart had dropped him out of the All Black squad. But that feeling only lasted as long as it took to get into camp. Then he gave 110 percent — as he always does.'

As for Norm, while he accepted that the revitalised Fijians would test the Maori, he was quite confident of his team's abilities. He had even appropriated a new haka for the occasion — 'Tika Tonu', one of the famous old Te Aute haka. It was a sure sign that he intended to stamp a very personal mark on the Fiji game.

'We knew the Fijians fancied their chances. They'd just come out of the Pacific Rim competition, and playing them up there is bloody tough — the grounds can be like concrete, and you don't have time to get used to the heat or the humidity. They're also a real home-town team — like all the Pacific boys, they grow an extra leg in front of their fans and play as if they've been snorting cocaine all day. All hyper and aggressive. If you let them get any early confidence you're in big trouble.'

Despite New Zealand Maori's 20-nil win over Fiji 'A', the nature of that game had reminded them that physical intimidation was also a major part of the island game. Within the first few minutes of the international, Fiji seemed to justify all their supporters' enthusiasm. Sevens genius Waisale Serevi taunted the Maori defenders with some early runs, and the home side led 10-nil within as many minutes. Norm regathered his troops and reminded them to stick to the basics.

'We used our tight five to drive at them through the middle and then played for field position. It was a case of being patient because it had been hosing down before kick-off and continuity was becoming harder with the slippery ball and greasy field.'

By half-time New Zealand Maori had wrested back the initiative to lead 20-13, and they began to exploit their set-piece advantage in the second half. In addition, the Fijian runners were finding that the combination of a slippery surface and fierce marking was too much for their skills. The second half became a Fijian nightmare — the Maori backs coming into their own and slicing through the deteriorating defence. Norm found himself an unexpected beneficiary, scoring tries on either side of half-time as he ran off the mauls.

And then, the perfect end to the perfect match — another storming attack down the left of the field, the defence in disarray, first-five Glen Jackson receiving the ball from the resultant ruck and kicking wide and high to the opposite wing. The squat figure of Norm Hewitt sloshes through the puddles, eyes fixed on the ball, grasps it in his fingertips and in virtually the same movement slides over for the final score.

'I don't think I could ever do that again! I was at full tit just trying to get there, the ball was slippery, the conditions treacherous, but somehow it stuck. The boys gave me shit after that one. But, hell, it felt good. Three tries, 57-20 against Fiji on their home turf. The biggest ever Maori "test" victory.'

From the Maori XV, Osborne, Reihana and Duggan would be added to the All Black squad for that year's World Cup, with Flavell, Cribb and Macdonald selected a year later.

'If there was one consolation for missing the World Cup that year it was being with New Zealand Maori. I've got a lot of time for Matt and the team environment is spot-on. We enjoy each other's company, we respect and add to the Maori tradition, and we strike the right balance between culture and rugby. In the past, I've been in Maori teams where we spent too much time on karakia and not enough on scrum practice.

'But the common factor is enjoying each other's company. Characters like Glen Osborne — a real Hori. One day he'll be shearing sheep in the boondocks and the next playing a top match like only Oz can. He was a great one for nabbing all the little jams and butters and shampoos and things from the hotels and taking them back to all his nieces and nephews — he'd have a whole suitcase of them by the end of a tour. And we were all proud of who we were and what we represented — the style, the culture, the language — we were Maori. And we were winners.

'It's different from playing in the All Blacks. We were a more communal team, we treated each other better without all the senior/junior divisions and there was no corporate crap or hidden agendas.'

But there were signs in 2000 that the unbeaten sequence was becoming a burden. The team were fortunate to defeat the touring Scots — again in wet conditions that made it difficult to play constructive rugby — and they were becoming conscious that there are some strange burdens to being winners, as a fear of losing replaced the earlier Maori joy of just throwing the ball around and running hard.

'The team is conscious that it is a flagship for the Maori people,' says Te Pou. 'In fact, rugby is a bit of everything for Maori — a substitute for war, a place on the international stage and a unifying factor for our people. Very high standards have been set by Maori teams over the past twenty years. The bar has been set — that's going to be a big thing for future Maori sides. And players like Norm who are determined and professional and proud — they've shown the youngsters the way. And that goes for off the field as well.'

CHAPTER NINETEEN

Mutiny

I n the wake of the All Blacks' 1999 World Cup failure, a collective madness seemed to seize the rugby community. The semi-final loss was bad enough, but the manner of the defeat incensed the team's supporters. The forward pack was gutless, the coaching ineffectual, and the players themselves overpaid simpletons . . . expletives deleted, such was the tenor of the criticism in both the talkback jungle and the mainstream media. 'Guilty!' screamed the cover of the monthly magazine *Rugby World*, a picture of the accursed accused, coach John Hart, splashed across its front. A foreign observer visiting New Zealand in those days after the World Cup might have assumed that the All Blacks were a group of sporting Quislings who had wilfully sabotaged the aspirations of an entire nation. It was the Kiwi tall poppy syndrome at its most hysterical.

'I couldn't believe the reaction,' Norm recalls. 'One moment the boys were super-heroes, and the next . . . it's like they're all child molesters or something. I felt really sorry for them because I knew what they were going through. Every top sportsman gets knocked some time in their career — some journo is bound to put the boot in. But to have a whole country after you — that's just sick.'

As the media pillory continued John Hart was singled out for special attention, and the lunatic fringe followed their lead. Death threats were made against Hart and his family. Although Norm had no particular affection for Hart or his methods, this kind of reaction was beyond sanity. One night, after watching one of Hart's horses being booed at

Addington Raceway, he sat down and wrote the man a letter.

'I was very surprised [to receive the letter],' recalls Hart. 'But it was a measure of the guy and I appreciated his support. It certainly wasn't an easy time for us — the family or the team.'

Hart had resigned immediately after the All Blacks' play-off loss to South Africa, but the damage was not so easily contained. Manager Mike Banks was required to fall on his sword, so too NZRFU chairman Rob Fisher. Within months Saatchi and Saatchi dynamo Kevin Roberts had also resigned from the NZRFU board.

Norm observed the drama with mixed feelings. Part of him was delighted at the demise of the corporate culture that had cocooned the All Blacks. And his earlier misgivings about the All Blacks' mental toughness had also been proven — when the pressure went on the team's lack of poise and leadership had been ruthlessly exposed. But he had also been a part of that special brotherhood and he knew too many of the players not to be affected by the team's demise. Some were personal friends, and he could not but feel sympathy for their plight. Certainly they didn't deserve the kind of vitriol that was being thrown their way.

'It was a weird feeling. If I'm honest, there's a part of you that gets bitter after you've been dropped. You almost want them to lose for not picking you. So that's why a lot of All Blacks can't watch a test if they're not playing. It produces too many conflicting emotions. You want them to win, but if they lose you've got a better chance of getting back.

'Top sportspeople are very selfish. That's been my experience. You don't get to the top unless you're self-centred — unless you're prepared to make the sacrifices, professional and personal, to achieve your goal. It's not quite so bad with a team sport like rugby because the team becomes a goal in itself. But if it's between you and someone else to wear the silver fern, well . . . you don't give a snot about them. Because they sure don't give a toss about you. You'd chew your nuts off to represent the All Blacks — that's how irrational it can get.'

Although Norm considers that a lack of perspective is not confined to the top players.

'In my experience, the ugliest people in rugby — apart from the fish-heads — are the fans who live their life through their team. If you lose, it's as if you've personally let them down. It doesn't matter how much effort you put in, or the knocks you got or the blood . . . whether the ball bounced wrong or the ref was a jerk . . . you still lost. So you let them down. And you're a jerk. And they let you know it, either calling out during a game or jeering as you walk off. Sometimes I've walked off and just wanted to smash some of them — do a real Cantona and deck the bastard who's swearing at you. And then the next week, the same wanker is all over you because the team has won.

'That's why players are wary of fans. You never know if you're dealing with a real person or a nutter. Generally, the kids are great — it's their parents who are off their head. Kids are more loyal and forgiving. I like to make a fuss of them because I'm aware of their hero-worship and what I was like at their age. Even when you've had a nightmare of a game, the kids will pat you on the back.'

During the 1999–2000 summer Norm discovered that being the Hurricanes captain was as much about public relations as leading the team at practice or on the field. He was obliged to appear and speak at any number of functions, from school galas to private clubs to sponsors' cocktail parties. Each time he was conscious of the performance that was required to satisfy the audience's expectations. He had crossed the line from private citizen to public personality. To those who had known him in earlier days, the transformation was remarkable — from being the stumbling simpleton of the amateur Hawke's Bay rep team, he had become a leading figure in one of the most successful rugby franchises in the world.

But the change had not come without some personal cost.

'It's hard to explain, but you feel on edge every time you step outside the house because you know you're on show. I'd experienced that in Hawke's Bay but it was different. I was just a footy player. No-one expected anything of me except to run, tackle and throw the ball into the lineout. But as the Hurricanes captain, you're part of not just the management team but the marketing team too. You're a businessman, not just a rugby player. So you're never off. Even when you're asleep, you're still the Hurricanes captain. And part of me loved that, and part of me hated it.'

The capital, in particular, had embraced rugby like never before — the Hurricanes were not only their team but also a potent symbol of Wellington's civic revival. The new Westpac Trust Stadium — an all-seated facility only a brisk walk from the downtown restaurants and bars — had already captured the public imagination. But the off-season recruitment of wonder winger Jonah Lomu pumped up the volume many times over. Wow! Christian Cullen, Tana Umaga, Jonah Lomu . . . a back three made in Heaven.

'There was an amazing buzz all over Wellington that summer. People would stop you on the street, shake your hand and wish you luck. It was amazing. And when the squad went down to the stadium and had a decent look and walked around the ground, I knew that it was going to be an amazing place to play. It's because all the seats are raised and face the centre of the ground . . . it's like all the spectators' excitement is projected out onto you. When the Wellington stadium is full there's no other place quite like it in world rugby. I've played them all but the stadium is something else again.'

JONAH

In hindsight, it was obvious that the supporters' expectations had been set too high. Despite possessing the holy trinity of Cullen, Umaga and Lomu, and a class midfield in Alama Ieremia and Jason O'Halloran, the Hurricanes' forwards lacked the size, strength and class of their Super 12 competition. The problem was going to be getting enough ball to unleash the firepower out wide.

In addition, the Hurricanes squad lacked a more crucial component. Player depth. The bench was not just weak — it was a liability. An apparently deliberate policy of picking players from within the Hurricanes franchise meant that almost all the talent was drawn from only two first division unions, Wellington and Taranaki. Like many, Norm wondered if some of the Taranaki players were up to it. They were demons in the NPC and on their beloved Bull Ring, but the Super 12 was up another skill level again. Even then gaps remained, and it took former English test prop Kevin Yates, South African Joggie Viljoen, Otago open-side Kupu Vanisi and North Harbour tearaway Matua Parkinson to plug the more obvious ones.

The Hurricanes also had a new and untried coaching combination — former All Blacks Graham Mourie and Bryan Williams. While their playing pedigree was undoubted, it was no guarantee of coaching ability. And despite the Samoan influence in the Hurricanes' backline, Williams in particular was having trouble connecting with his new charges. Norm observed the stand-off and hoped it would sort itself out. It never did.

By his own admission, Graeme (Goss) Mourie was still learning his way. He was a more cerebral character than his predecessor, and was looking to impose a more patterned structure on the Hurricanes' play. The 'rip-shit-and-bust' tactics of previous years were firmly rejected.

'We didn't really have the players to fit Goss's game plan. Our forwards weren't able to dominate the set pieces, and we needed better control if we were going to make the new tactics work. But Goss was the coach and that was his strategy. He was really into all the technological stuff — the videos, the player charts, the computer programs that could plot a game and be replayed with the touch of a button.

'I had my doubts. I still do when it comes to all that computer stuff. It can be total crap because it relies so much on someone feeding in the data, and there's the first opportunity for error. The other thing is that computer analyses give false impressions about a player and their influence on a game. For example, was the tackle effective or not . . . what was happening wider out that influenced your decision . . . who called that they'd take the player but didn't . . . that sort of stuff. I'm not convinced, eh. You come off knowing if you've played well and the programme sometimes says you were shit. Or vice versa. I think a lot of players think too much about playing for the computer than getting stuck in.'

As for Mourie, he was glad of any assistance that allowed him to make the transition to coach.

"I didn't know anything about coaching [before I took over the Lions] so I had to learn pretty quickly.' One way was to rely on the franchise's senior players to make mini-leadership decisions. Looking back, Mourie concedes he might have expected too much.

'Leadership is lacking in the [modern] game. In the past you've had players who were club captains or provincial captains, so when they all came together, there was a good ground of experience. But most top players these days hardly ever play club, and if they do, they don't captain their team. In the Hurricanes we didn't have any provincial captains in the franchise apart from Jason [O'Halloran] and Norm. Norm was the obvious choice — he's got the personality and disposition to lead, and that's relatively rare these days.

'I know it's not the PC thing to say but the increasing influence of Polynesian players is also a factor. They are marvellously skilled players but leadership is not their thing. They don't feel comfortable with responsibility, and we've got to do something about that.'

Norm recognised the need for firm leadership, but after the previous season he was also aware that he couldn't do it alone. He needed back-up. Central to his plans was his old mate Gordon Falcon, the big Maori No. 8 who had been recruited back from the ACT Brumbies. Whatever their past differences, the two former Magpies had rekindled their friendship and Falcon agreed to serve as his captain's enforcer — on and off the paddock. The No. 8 became his captain's *de facto* lieutenant.

'The problem though was that Gordy was carrying an old injury which stopped him training properly. It was a miracle he could play eighty minutes, especially with his back the way it was. But, Jeez, he was tough.

He would put in the big hits, but he also had the experience to anticipate where you needed defence and shut the attack down straight away. He had soft hands too — could put players into gaps that weren't apparent until after he'd actually made the pass. [Australian coach] Rod McQueen wanted him as part of their World Cup squad and you could see why. But just like Jarrod Cunningham turning down England, Gordy turned down McQueen. Huge calls . . . their loyalty to New Zealand was too strong. Anyway, he only played the first couple of games for us and then injured himself again and that was it. We missed him bad.'

But such problems were in the future. For the moment, Norm basked in the public and media attention, confident that his team were genuine contenders. And when he led the team out onto the new stadium for their opening game of the 2000 Super 12, the reception was electric.

'We ran out of the tunnel and then the roar of the crowd hit us. It was like body surfing up at Ocean Beach — this amazing adrenalin. All I wanted to do was sprint down the field like a mad bastard. It was an incredible buzz, and as I looked around I thought to myself: "So this is how the gladiators felt." The packed crowd, rock music blasting out of the speakers, surrounded by my men, waiting to go into battle . . . a huge Sharks pack opposite.'

The game highlighted the Hurricanes' future strengths and weaknesses perfectly. At set plays the forwards struggled against their larger opponents, while the defensive pattern showed alarming lapses in concentration. But with the ball in hand, the Wellington loosies and midfield backs could turn defence into an attack with the flick of a pass. And the speed of Cullen, Umaga and Lomu was something else again — an athletic magic that converted half breaks into tries and the crowd into screaming dervishes.

And yet at half-time the Sharks actually had the lead, courtesy of some forward grunt and a runaway try from their halfback. In the dressing rooms Mourie stressed the need for the team to concentrate. The South Africans' defence was fragile — but it was the pushed 50/50 passes and occasional outbreak of white-line fever that was keeping them in the game. Be patient. In the second half the Hurricanes quickly assumed control, and finished with a satisfying 40-23 victory.

'It was a good lesson to us all. You can be on top for phase after phase and have all the territory and possession but if you lose your concentration for one moment, or one player doesn't do their job . . . wham. You're standing behind your own goal posts. But the other thing to come out of that game was how important Gordy and our midfield were.

Jason and Alama were great attackers in their own right and if defences drifted out onto Jonah or Tana or Cully then the guys inside could make the break. Although we had the biggest name in world rugby playing for us on the wing, it was the Petone white boy and his Samoan mate that were the real difference. Without Alama or Jason, the backs lost structure.'

Nevertheless, Norm was thrilled that Jonah had made the transfer from Counties to Wellington — and not just for the off-field excitement the big man generated.

'I've always had a lot of time for Jonah — both as a player and as a person. I mean how he's survived all the attention without it messing up his head staggers me. He's not a big head at all. He's exactly as you see him . . . a huge Tongan guy who loves his footy and his music and can switch on the after-burners whenever he gets the ball. The thing about Jonah is that he can drift a bit during a game — if the game isn't flowing his way he can go cold. So the key is to get him involved and keep him involved.

'As a person, he's honest, humble, and very much a team player. If there are any commercial tensions around him they're not of Jonah's making. He's been very smart on that score . . . appoint a manager and let him deal with the business side of things. Sometimes I think [his manager Phil] Kingsley-Jones needs to pull his head in a bit and place less demands on the big guy, but that's not my call. You can't argue with Jonah's success.'

THE STAGGERS

There was no better proof of Lomu's ability than in the next Hurricanes game against the Queensland Reds, as he swatted players away on rampaging runs, opening up try-scoring opportunities for those Hurricanes trailing in his wake. In a fit of pique, Reds coach John Connolly labelled Lomu 'half a winger' — drawing an immediate retort from Wallaby great David Campese that if Lomu was half a winger, he'd hate to see the finished version.

But for Norm the important thing was that they had two wins from two, and maximum bonus points. This could be the Hurricanes' year. It was a feeling that did not dissipate despite a loss to the Highlanders at Carisbrook. Tana Umaga had stuck out a careless forearm with the match evenly poised and was marched from the ground. But there was still a measure of satisfaction to be gained as the front row of Yates, Hewitt and Slater had the better of their All Black opposites. When the Chiefs and the Cats were then defeated, the whole Hurricanes franchise was abuzz. Although their captain was worried.

'We'd lost Gordy with a leg injury, and it was serious. Plus we had hung on for grim death against the Cats, and it was only the individual brilliance of Tana that saved us that day. He was everywhere. Each game was wearing the tight five down and our bench wasn't of the same calibre. That's the thing about the Super 12 — it's week in, week out stuff. You have to grind out a game every six or seven days and your body doesn't have time to recover from the knocks. So you need a good bench to take the pressure off — either as replacements during a game or if someone is injured. Then we lost to the Blues at home in a pretty gutless performance, and the pressure really started to build.'

Particularly since their next game was against the champion Crusaders. The word was that new All Black coach Wayne Smith would draw heavily on the successful Crusaders franchise, including installing their inspirational leader Todd Blackadder as the new All Black captain.

'The AB selectors communicated through the coaches during the Super 12. So a couple of times during the season Goss would pull players aside and say something like, "the selectors are impressed" or "they want to see you concentrate on such-and-such an aspect of your game". That sort of thing.'

Norm had not yet abandoned his All Black ambitions. By all accounts Oliver's form had deserted him at the World Cup, and his replacement Mark Hammett was not displaying convincing form in the opening weeks of the Super 12. Maybe he still had a chance.

'Goss came up to us at training and said the selectors were impressed with Gordon [Slater's] form, and obviously Yatesy wasn't being considered because he was a Pom. And then, almost as an afterthought, he turned to me and said they thought I was going pretty average. That sure let the air out of my tyres in a big way.'

Until he reminded himself that he would be playing one of the selectors' preferred choices in the Hurricanes' next match against the champion Crusaders. At which point the motivation quickly returned. The Canterbury franchise were the darlings of the new All Black coach, not surprising given that he had taken them to two Super 12 championships. What better way to extract a measure of revenge.

So began one of those weird symmetries that arise in top-class sport, where one team seemingly has 'the mockers' on their opposites — an unnatural ability to defeat their rivals no matter what the form book, the TAB odds or the stars on parade suggest.

'We really wanted to beat the Crusaders. They were not only playing through champs but the buzz was that Smith would be stocking the All

Blacks with Canterbury players. And that Todd Blackadder would probably succeed Taine Randell as All Black captain. We'd also played badly against the Blues the week before, so we owed our supporters and ourselves.'

The result was a smash-bang affair, with the Crusaders conceding an early lead then battling back into the game. Yet again discipline problems beset the team, with a yellow card given by referee Paddy O'Brien against prop Mike Edwards and 10 points conceded while he cooled off in the sin bin. The second half started much as the first had, with Christian Cullen zooming over. Again the Crusaders battled back, and when Todd Blackadder stretched out and planted the ball across the line it looked as if that was it. But again the Hurricanes' backline worked its magic and Jonah Lomu went over for his second try. It was 28-22. Seven minutes left. The Crusaders charged back onto the attack, launching wave after wave as Norm marshalled the defence superbly. Until O'Brien's persistent pinging of the Hurricanes got the better of him.

'I screamed out that he was a cheat. Actually I think I called him "a fucking cheat", and I was bloody lucky not to walk. By now the refs were definitely getting a mindset about us and I was getting a bit paranoid.'

Graeme Mourie was not impressed. He had already taken Norm to task for publicly saying that his forwards would 'not back down' despite their super-aggressive approach attracting the referees' ire.

'Refs read newspapers too,' says Mourie. 'He'd told the media there would be no stepping back and that didn't help. Captaincy requires a bit of cunning, and that includes off the field as well.'

Nevertheless, the Hurricanes' defence held. After they'd resisted another frenzied assault the ball bobbled free, referee O'Brien blew the full-time whistle and the crowd roared its approval. The Hurricanes were back in the title hunt. Both Mourie and Hewitt agree that it was one of the team's gutsiest performances, and demonstrated that even the Crusaders' legendary defensive capabilities could be thwarted by the freakish talents that lurked out wide.

But one team did have an answer. The Hurricanes were soundly defeated at Canberra, the ruthless efficiency and organisation of the Brumbies eventually overwhelming a tiring defence. Again Cullen, Umaga and Lomu had cut loose early but the Brumbies adjusted their defence, began to control the ball, and slowly strangled the life from their opposition. The over-aggressive play of the Hurricanes' forwards had also contributed to their defeat, with Inoke Afeaki sin-binned at a crucial stage of the game.

'It was Tappe Henning who was in charge, and I was becoming real suspicious of South African refs around that time. I still am. In the next game [against the New South Wales Waratahs] we struck Andre Watson and he pinged us every time we even looked at the Aussies. It was crazy stuff.'

Indeed it was. Three yellow cards and a red card to Jonah Lomu at the end of the first half for a dangerous tackle on Waratah centre Nathan Grey. It was bad enough that the Hurricanes would be required to play the entire second half with fourteen men, but when first Norm and then Inoke Afeaki were marched off to the sin bin, the team coped with just thirteen players for twenty minutes of the second half. And coped magnificently.

'Sometimes a team will relax if the other side lose a man. In modern rugby one man down means a helluva lot. If you put the phases together properly you can soon create an overlap. But sometimes the reverse is true. A team can lift itself, and that's what we had to do. I told the boys that it was backs-to-the-wall stuff. We were not going to let them score. And we had a good lead too so we could concentrate more on defence and not on having to score points to win the game.'

Australian rugby commentators watched, first in disbelief and then with a grudging respect, as the Hurricanes resisted the fully manned Waratahs. TV comments man and former Wallaby front-rower Chris Handy showered particular praise on captain Hewitt. Norm was 'an angry ant', 'a hero', 'a little battler' as he directed his troops against a team that contained no fewer than nine Wallabies and a considerable array of attacking talent. Twice the Waratahs secured scrums on the Hurricanes' line, against seven Hurricanes forwards and with the feed. Twice 'Captain Hurricane' stole tightheads and the danger was averted. When the final whistle blew, coach Mourie wasn't sure if he should laugh or cry. The team's disciplinary record was pathetic, but their courage and spirit could not be faulted.

However, this time the damage would stretch beyond the field of play. Jonah Lomu received a two-match suspension for his efforts, and then Tana Umaga and Gordon Slater were given leave by the Hurricanes management to be with their partners for the birth of their respective children.

'The funny thing is that it was sex that stuffed us in the end. With Jonah out, we needed everyone on deck. But Tana and Gordy knew where their responsibilities lay. A part of me was thinking: "Your priority is the game, mate. Forget all this PC bullshit." But that was because I knew we would be rooted without them.'

And they were. The Hurricanes lost their last two games — both in

South Africa, against the Stormers and the Northern Bulls. The Bulls had not won a game all season, and the Hurricanes only had to defeat them to secure a Super 12 semi-final. But the combination of Joost van der Westhuizen's return, the loss of the key Hurricanes players, and a scrambled game strategy saw the chance slip away. Thinking they needed to score four tries to secure the winning bonus point, the Hurricanes took chances and were punished. As it transpired, a simple win would have been enough.

'That's rugby,' Norm shrugs. 'In the end, we weren't quite good enough. The media blamed all the yellow and red cards, but that was crap. If Gordy Falcon hadn't been injured, if the boys hadn't been quite so randy nine months before, if the refs hadn't prejudged us . . . then we would have been there. The forwards played bloody well — our top eight could really do the business. But that's the lesson of Super 12. Unlike test rugby, you're only as good as your bench. Injuries happen when you're playing week in, week out — you've got to have nine or ten other players who can make the step up. If not, you're stuffed.'

REBELLION

It was a disappointing end to the Super 12 — the loss to the Bulls tumbling the side to eighth on the table. It was doubly disappointing because the team possessed the talent to have seriously challenged for the title. Kupu Vanisi had been the outstanding loose forward of the competition, Spice and Holwell had developed into a reliable halves combination, and the front row of Slater, Hewitt and Yates had done the job upfront. In Waller and Tito the Hurricanes were also developing a good locking combination, with Filo Tiatia and Inoke Afeaki powerful runners off the back.

But the modern game is all about decision-making, patience and intelligence. In seeking to make up for their lack of physical size, the forwards had raised the ire of the match officials. Norm had employed the tactics he had always employed — if opposing players were deliberately infringing or slowing down the ball at the break-down or on the wrong side of the ruck, retribution was immediate. But such retribution was out of place in the modern game with its hawkish match officials, citing commissioner and video camera.

'Rugby is a brutal game. It's all about collision, intimidation, domination. Sure, technique and skill are important, but in the rucks and mauls, in the tackle situation, at the lineout, if you don't dominate your opposite then you're not going to win. So there's a fine line between being aggressive and being over-vigorous, and I was pissed off that, because of our reputation, we were getting constantly penalised for what other teams were allowed to do to us.'

But the players were not allowed to dwell on their failure. The international season was soon upon them, with tests against the visiting Scots and then the Tri-Nations. The make-up of Wayne Smith and Tony Gilbert's first All Black squad indicated that Norm was no longer a contender — Anton Oliver and Mark Hammett were retained as the hookers and Todd Blackadder appointed the caretaker captain. Players from the Crusaders and the Highlanders franchises dominated the All Black squad, raising an element of suspicion in Norm's mind. But his immediate responsibility was to lead New Zealand Maori against Scotland, and then to prepare for Wellington's NPC campaign.

In the NPC lead-up games, coach Dave Rennie decided to experiment with a new style of play based on that of the ACT Brumbies. Encouraged by Mourie, Rennie's strategy was based on ensuring a continuous line across the park for both offensive and defensive purposes. The forwards would be split in two, with each responsible for their own half of the paddock — the theory being that they would hit all the rucks and mauls in their half without overcommitting the team's resources and leaving gaps in the defensive line. Norm was resistant from the start.

'To be fair, it was Goss's idea, and although he was the assistant to Dave, it was obvious that he had the clout and that he wanted both Wellington and the Hurricanes to copy the Brumbies' style. I hated it. I hated it when it was put to us, I hated it when it was explained to us and I hated playing it. It was completely foreign to me, and all you ended up with was a game of rugby league. In fact, it was worse than rugby league, because at least they've got two less players per side and the 10-metre rule [the gap dividing attacking and defending teams at the tackle].

'The thing that irritated me most was that we didn't have a Hurricanes or a Lions style. Goss had borrowed the Crusaders' defensive strategy and then some of the Brumbies' offensive pattern. He was a follower. We needed our own pattern, given the player resources and the strengths and weaknesses of our team. Our strength was our outside backs so we had to create the space and the opportunities for them. You can't do that with thirty players strung across a rugby field.

'There's nothing wrong with the Crusaders' defence pattern — essentially you split your forwards, size up how many players they've got at the ruck and spread. If they've got six, you've got three with a guard dog on the fringes and a back door man in case. Then you take two steps forward and out so that you've got the momentum and you're closing down their gaps. It takes a lot of practice and a lot of drill to make that system work. Our problem was that we were trying to run before we could even crawl.'

Norm's antipathy to the Lions' tactical approach was shared by most of his team-mates. Although they enjoyed an opening win against Canterbury and a narrow away victory over Otago, they were also aware that the teams' All Blacks were absent on international duty. Instead of having the tight forwards blow over the tackle situation and pressure the opposing team at the breakdown, Norm and his fellow 'fatties' were obliged to station themselves in the backline and act as defenders or attackers depending on the situation.

The dissension within the team was not publicly known, and the crowds that attended the Hurricanes' next three home games, against Northland, Taranaki and Auckland, assumed that the tight forwards were 'seagulling' — trying to steal the glory from the back division instead of grafting away in the tight. A shock loss to Northland was followed by a fortuitous victory against Taranaki. It was a spiteful game, with the country boys well aware that Super 12 contracts were up for grabs, and the Lions' players equally determined to retain theirs.

'There's a good rivalry between Taranaki and Wellington but the move to professionalism definitely added an edge to these games. They really tore into it, with old-fashioned rucking, all the forwards hitting the ruck together and blowing over us. If they'd kept fifteen players on the paddock we would've been in trouble.'

Fortunately an act of madness from Taranaki halfback Brendan Haami crippled his side's effort. He grabbed Jason Spice, his opposite number, dragged him clear of a ruck, and stomped on him in full view of the touch judge, the referee and 15,000 baying spectators. Red card — and not even a quarter of the match played. But even with flanker Neil Crowley reverting to the halfback role and the Taranaki pack reduced to seven men, the Lions were still embarrassed at rucks and mauls by the more direct and aggressive approach of their opposition. Fortunately for them, Taranaki's ill-discipline continued. A yellow card and then another red finally gave the Wellington team the space they needed. The final 41-13 scoreline definitely flattered the hosts.

In the next game against Auckland, the strategic horrors returned. Derisive cat-calls followed Norm as the game finished and he walked off the park. The weekly *Rugby News* singled him out as a prime culprit in what it called 'the capital's clutter problems'. 'The site [sic] of props, hookers and locks appearing in the backline, slowing the distribution of ball while the speedsters on the flanks languish has Wellingtonians tearing their hair out ... Particularly guilty are Norm Hewitt, Mike Edwards and Dion Waller. None can call themselves speed merchants, but time and time again they end up in the chain. While they were fanning out, that left holes in the Wellington ruck, and several times Auckland simply did a pick-and-go up through the middle.'

The next week's loss to a poor North Harbour combination proved the last straw. The team played as they looked and looked as they felt — hesitant, disorganised and dispirited. With a three-three win-loss record, the season was virtually over.

'I was angry,' Norm recalls. 'I seethed that whole weekend because it was so bloody obvious that we were playing the wrong pattern. On the Monday morning I met most of the players at the Bodyworks gym for our usual work-out and they felt pretty much the same. We were being bagged in the local press, a lot of Super 12 contracts were flying out the window and we were getting totally turned off. When you stop enjoying your rugby, then you're in real trouble.'

Norm abandoned his usual diplomacy and let rip at his team members for their collective lack of guts. Were they men or not? Were they playing for themselves or the team? Were they thinking of the next game or their next Super 12 contract? But his real anger was directed at Rennie and Mourie. Why couldn't the forwards do what forwards do best, and the backs do what backs do best? Why was everything so pointlessly complicated?

'Goss came up afterwards and reckoned I'd gone over the top. But I think they had started thinking along the same lines. They weren't blind, and there was nowhere else for them to go. It was back to the traditional pattern or kiss the season goodbye. I don't know what would've happened if they hadn't agreed to the change [in tactics]. I was bloody close to mutiny.'

BOUNCING BACK

The revised team pattern had an immediate benefit. In their next game, against lowly Counties-Manukau at Pukekohe, the forwards attacked the breakdown, Jason Spice and David Holwell fed the backline, O'Halloran and Ieremia created the breaks, and Umaga, Lomu and Cullen finished them off. It was far from a complete performance, but both Norm and the rest of the team felt comfortable about their work. Forwards were being forwards, backs were being backs and God rested in His Heaven.

The next away game, against a doughty Southland, tested the team's resolve. On another typically bleak Invercargill afternoon, the Lions squeaked a narrow win and were thankful for the four competition points that had put them back in the race for the semi-finals.

'But you could feel the pressure building in the team. The guys who had played in the Tri-Nations were getting their puff back, and even though we'd lost Filo [Tiatia] with a broken leg, the two young loosies Jerry Collins and Rodney So'oialo had really come on and with Kupu [Vanisi] gave us the best loose forward combination in the whole NPC. I could feel it starting to come together, especially in the set-pieces like the scrum and the lineout.'

Norm's confidence was not misplaced. Wellington dismembered a powerful Waikato at the stadium on a brilliantly fine winter's afternoon, scoring six tries and thrilling the home crowd with the skill and speed of their play. New stars had been born, with So'oialo and Collins excelling in the loose, and Brad Fleming seizing his chance as a replacement and scorching 80 metres for the match-winning break. The final score of 48-23, and a place in the NPC semis, reinvigorated the whole province.

Yeah right, countered the cynics — Tarzan one day, Jane the next. Besides, they were drawn to play Auckland — the capital's hoodoo team. They hadn't defeated the Auks for eight years. In addition, the northerners had just despatched Otago by 50 points — the kind of demolition job that conjured up visions of their all-conquering predecessors. Nah, forget it. Not a chance. When Norm fearlessly predicted that Wellington would not only defeat Auckland but go on to win the NPC championship, rugby reporters gave him the kind of smile they might reserve for a simpleton.

'I knew we would beat them. I just knew it. Everything was coming together — the boys were fizzing. You had to be inside the team to experience that. We'd lost Filo and then Alama in the Waikato game and everyone was saying we couldn't win without those two. But I knew different. We'd recruited [South African prop] Morne van der Merwe and he was hitting form, Kevin Yates was playing his best rugby ever, Dion and Inoke were ultra-solid at lock . . . mate, we had the best forward pack that Wellington has ever had since I started playing first-class rugby. And I didn't rate Auckland's forwards. We'd held them the year before and we were stronger now. They lacked ticker, in my book. I knew they'd crack.'

It is now history that the rugby scribes and the cynics were wrong and Norm Hewitt was right. The Wellington victory was created by the tight five, who applied fearsome pressure at scrum time, disrupted the usually reliable Auckland lineout and neutralised the mercurial Carlos Spencer and his backline by ensuring that they received both ball and tackler at roughly the same moment.

Auckland coach Wayne Pivac later admitted that his team were outmuscled, outpassioned and outplayed. Even when the Wellingtonians were twice reduced to fourteen players, after yet more indiscretions, they still possessed the vision and the energy to score tries. The final scoreline was exactly the same as the week before — 48-23, five tries to one against the best defensive team in the NPC. Despite possessing no fewer than nine past or present All Blacks in their starting XV, Auckland had been abjectly humiliated.

Reporting on the game, *Rugby News* paid tribute to the much-maligned Lions' forwards, singling out 19-year-old Jerry Collins for his athleticism and sheer physical presence. 'And then there was Hewitt. He seemed to be in the centre of everything and clearly seemed to relish going forward for a change.'

'The press reports were ironic all right,' Norm remembers. 'Halfway through the season and I'm getting bagged by the media. And then after we start winning, they're suddenly all over me. But I wasn't playing any better. All that had changed was the game plan. And that allowed us tighties to do the business and we proved that we could.'

But the sterner test would be the NPC final, to be hosted by mighty Canterbury at Jade Stadium. Super 12 winners, Ranfurly Shield holders, and now boasting the All Black captain Todd Blackadder and virtually the entire All Black forward pack. They had defeated a brave and resourceful Taranaki in the other semi-final and seemed to have no weaknesses — with a back division that included the brilliant halves Andrew Mehrtens and Justin Marshall, and a speedy back three in Ben Blair, Caleb Ralph and Fijian international Marika Vunibaka. The NPC title would simply complete the treble.

To make matters worse, Canterbury were forewarned of the Lions' challenge. As the Crusaders they had been defeated by the Hurricanes, and as Canterbury they had dropped their opening NPC game to the Wellington team, their only loss of the season. There was the small matter of revenge. That it could be extracted in an NPC final, with 30,000 one-eyed Cantabrians cheering them on, would only make the retribution that much sweeter.

'There were also All Black touring spots up for grabs,' recalls Norm. 'The next day the selectors were to name the squad for France and also the New Zealand "A" team to the UK. So no-one could say they lacked motivation. This was as big as New Zealand provincial rugby ever gets.'

CHAPTER TWENTY

Hero

The build-up to the NPC final was not unlike that before a test match — the ever-tightening tension within the team, the coaches nervously fine-tuning their tactics, the constant demands of the media. The whole country seemed focused on the Saturday night game — first, debating whether the perennial losers might upset the Super 12 champions, then, having discounted that possibility, debating the margin of the final score. Most agreed that this would be the season's crowning triumph for the red-and-blacks — the final piece to a remarkable treble that included the Super 12 and the Ranfurly Shield. After an unsuccessful Shield challenge, Otago captain Kevin Middleton had labelled the Cantabrians 'unbreakable . . . they always come back at you'. Almost every NPC first division coach made the same call. At home, and with the treble at stake, Canterbury were unbeatable.

Whatever the supposed odds, Norm remained confident that his team had Canterbury's measure. Wellington will win, he told every reporter who asked. The tight five had proven themselves and were peaking, the loosies were young, skilled and enthusiastic, the backline had ironed out its earlier wrinkles. The stars — Umaga, Cullen and Lomu — were back to their best form and jumping out of their skins, and the whole team wanted to farewell their Samoan mate, Alama Ieremia, in the best way possible. The big centre had signed with a Japanese factory team and the NPC final would be his last game on New Zealand soil.

For Norm the game also rated as a much more personal challenge. He would be leading his much-maligned eight into battle against, essentially, the All Black forward pack. The Canterbury front row of Greg Somerville, Mark Hammett and Greg Feek was regarded as not just one of the best in the country but one of the best in the southern hemisphere. There was also the prospect that he might impress the All Black selectors sufficiently to make either the All Blacks or the New Zealand 'A' squad due to tour France and Italy the next month. Sure, it was unlikely that he would displace either Oliver or Hammett from the top squad, but New Zealand 'A' had to be a good chance.

Yet his concentration was not solely on the coming game. He was hosting 11-year-old Nathan Hamlin and his family, who were up from Invercargill especially for the final. Norm had met the youngster in Dunedin Hospital six years earlier when he was touring the children's ward as part of his All Black duties in the build-up to a Carisbrook test. The young boy was suffering from leukemia, but his eyes lit up when he saw his visitor.

'Something between us just clicked. I saw this tiny kid sitting in bed, tubes and machines all around him, and I thought to myself, "Mate, you don't know how lucky you are." So I just sat on his bed and started chatting. He was a bright little kid, and at the end of it all I said, "Keep in touch." And he did. So when I went down to play for Southland we met up again, he introduced me to his family, and we've all been mates ever since.

'He's such a little battler that I find him inspirational. I really wanted him to be there in Christchurch for the final. I wanted the whole thing to be special for him — something he would never forget.'

Despite the gesture there were those who sneered at the image of the small boy, in an oversized Wellington Lions jersey, leading the team out onto the ground for the season's ultimate match. Hewitt was using the kid, ran the accusations, blatantly massaging his public image. Such sniping wounds him to this day.

The cynics were unaware that Norm had personally arranged sponsorship for the Hamlin family to attend the NPC games leading up to the final — a gesture at odds with his mercenary reputation. But then there had many such gestures over the past couple of years —donating his time to the 'Books in Homes' project or the 'Ronald McDonald House' charity. Even, in the wake of the Queenstown debacle, accepting a role as a part-time family counseller for at-risk teens. Many found it hard to reconcile their impression of Hewitt the business opportunist with Hewitt the charity worker. So they decided not to bother. He was still out for himself. There had to be a selfish stratagem in there somewhere.

Nathan apart, however, all altruism was put on hold in the week of the final. Wellington had last won the NPC in the mid-80s — before the semi-finals and final format, before professional rugby, before Norm had even played a first-class game. Year after year, the capital boys had initially flattered only to later deceive — their immediate past a litany of failed coaches and frustrated supporters. It would require something extra special to overcome such a losing mindset, especially against the team the All Black selectors had built their current team around.

'All that history crap meant nothing to me or the players. Actually, I reckoned we had the psychological advantage — Canterbury hadn't beaten us in two years at either Super 12 or NPC level. So although we couldn't sneak in under the radar like we had with Auckland, we still had the mockers on them. We weren't scared of them like other teams were. Belief is a big part of rugby. If you have the littlest doubt, you're gone.'

As the Lions ran out onto Jade Stadium, on a clear and cold Saturday night, a chorus of boos and jeers rose to greet them. But rather than cower the team, the hostility acted as a spur. They refused to be intimidated by the crowd, the media or the opposition. At the first clash of the packs, Norm decided that he should lead by example, a flying forearm the surest indication that he had rediscovered his old aggression. The hate was back.

Indeed, in these early exchanges Norm was a one-man demolition squad, clearing out players with genuine ferocity. If a red and black jersey strayed within distance, damage was done. This was war, and the Marquis of Queensbury and the IRB rulebook were irrelevant niceties. It was a style of rugby that Canterbury knew and understood — the same brutal physicality that they had imposed on other teams, and a key to their remarkable success. It was based on an aggressive defence that made attackers flinch, pressured ball carriers and their support runners into mistakes, and aimed to hurt and force errors. The defenders might then convert the turned-over ball into attack, the speed of Canterbury's outside backs — Fijian Marika Vunibaka, Caleb Ralph and the gifted young Ben Blair — a vital factor in their success.

'When you play Canterbury you always know what you're going to get a hard physical game. Unlike, say, the Brumbies, Canterbury base a good part of their attack on hurting you. It's part of their culture. So I decided that we should get in first.'

He did not battle alone. Waller, Collins and So'oialo put a series of big hits on Canterbury runners around the ruck and maul area, while Norm directed their defence like some on-field sergeant. Then, in one fluid movement, the Lions' backs launched an attack, O'Halloran propped, spied the gap and grubber kicked to the corner, behind the now flailing Vunibaka. A big brown shadow zoomed past the Fijian, gathered the ball and dotted down — Jonah Lomu. David Holwell converted from the sideline. Seven-nil. The red flags fell limp, the embankment crowd went silent.

And not just because of the score. The Wellington forwards had gained an early and surprising ascendancy, which was putting pressure on the star halves Marshall and Mehrtens. Meanwhile pockets of Wellington supporters were yelling themselves hoarse. The boys were on fire.

However, referee Paul Honiss was proving troublesome. Twice Christian Cullen scythed through flimsy Canterbury defence; twice the goal-line beckoned. And twice Honiss blew his whistle to indicate transgressions that no-one else, not even the parochial crowd, had noticed.

'He called one for obstruction and the other for a knock-on. Both were bullshit — bad mistakes at this level — but we couldn't let it affect us. We had them in the backs and when Christian eventually put Nokes [Afeaki] over, everyone knew that our stars had come out to play. It was something like 20 points to nine at half-time. Solid enough, but it would have been 30 but for Honiss.'

As they filed off for the break Norm felt a touch of unease. Given their first half domination, eleven points wasn't much of a margin. They had the advantage out wide, no question, and the crowd had been taken out of play, but the margin was not enough. Canterbury had been curiously off the pace — hesitant in the forwards, stumbling in the backs. Surely, they wouldn't put two such halves together.

In the dressing room the message from Rennie and Mourie was simple. Ball retention, field position, tackle. They were forty minutes away from glory. Don't let Canterbury back into the game.

Minutes into the second half and the instructions looked to have been in vain. Todd Blackadder rallied his forwards, they became more precise and patient at the breakdown, and Mehrtens was kicking for both territory and field position. The results were immediate — two easy penalties to Ben Blair. Yet still Wellington's defence held, Dion Waller a colossus. And it was strong defence that produced the next try — the ball spilled in a tackle, spun wide, Cullen taking the pass at pace, Umaga freed and thundering down the middle of the field, with O'Halloran on hand to complete the try. Holwell converted. 27-15.

Four minutes later came the *coup de grâce*. Or so it seemed. Mehrtens, under pressure, passed wide and behind his support. O'Halloran snaffled the ball, freed Lomu, and suddenly the big man was in space. Twice

Vunibaka came at him, twice he swatted the big Fijian away as he rampaged towards the try-line. Back on the halfway mark Norm raised his hands in triumph. Surely that was the killer. With Holwell adding the extras, the gap was now nineteen points.

But no. As Middleton had noted, Canterbury did not know when to give up. It was a feature of their play — the refusal to surrender, the stirring fight-back that delivered victory in the last minutes, even the last seconds, of a game. In contrast, Wellington's concentration began to waver.

'We thought we had them and our intensity dropped away. It was like air escaping from a balloon. Sometimes it's dangerous to be too far ahead because mentally you let go. Often that doesn't matter because the other team are stuffed anyway. But we were becoming too loose, and we needed to tighten up on "D".'

At a maul, with Wellington back on attack, Justin Marshall leaned over from the Canterbury side and tried to slow down the release. As all good tight forwards should, Norm decided Marshall needed to be cleared away. His action was legitimate, the execution less so. Norm's forearm struck the solid bone of the halfback's forehead. Pain shot up the hooker's arm and he visibly recoiled from the contact. At the next stop in play Norm jogged to the sideline and motioned to Wellington physio Glenn Muirhead.

'I've broken my arm. Tape it up.'

'Don't be so fucking ridiculous.'

'Do as I fucking say. Tape it up.'

Muirhead obeyed.

As Norm ran back on, a wad of tape covering his entire right forearm, he had a quick word to locks Waller and Afeaki — don't call any lineouts to the back — he couldn't throw that far. Dion would have to be the money man at number two for the rest of the game.

'There was no way I was coming off. Morne van der Merwe had injured a leg and Tyson [Edwards] had come on to replace him. I reckoned that if Shane [Carter] came on for me then we'd depower our scrum. We couldn't afford to let Canterbury start dominating the scrum because they were starting to get a roll on as it was.'

After a sustained build-up, Wellington's defence was stretched beyond breaking point and Mehrtens scooted in for a soft try near the posts. The home side had regained momentum. Again and again they attacked, wave after wave of red and black jerseys throwing themselves at the tiring Lions. Finally captain Blackadder crashed over. With nine minutes to go, only five points separated the teams. And in the Lions camp things had just gone from serious to critical — Yates had joined van der Merwe on the sideline with a dislocated shoulder. There was nothing for it — Norm would have to go to prop, Shane Carter to hooker.

'They [the coaches] wanted me to go to tighthead, but there was no way . . . I'd have to use the broken arm to bind on the opposite prop. So I went into loosehead and instead could protect my arm a bit by putting it around Shane's shoulder. But it was really starting to hurt. And we were running out of puff and Canterbury knew it. So did the crowd — they were going off big-time — and we just kept hanging on, plugging the gaps, trying to slow the ball down, tackling anything with a red and black jersey.'

Still Wellington held out. But it seemed inevitable that they must finally yield. And now that his forwards were giving him the space, Mehrtens was coming into his own, giving the midfield of Daryl Gibson and Mark Mayerhoffler the space to probe and find gaps for themselves and their speedy outsides.

Referee Honiss was also a factor. Correctly, he warned Norm that the Wellington players were illegally slowing the ball at the breakdown. Penalty followed penalty. But Norm didn't care. Canterbury needed a try — a penalty wouldn't do. Finally, Honiss's patience snapped, and Dion Waller was sent to the sin bin for slapping down a Canterbury pass metres from the line.

'If Dion hadn't done that, they would have scored. Yeah, they probably did deserve a penalty try, but I put that decision against the two tries we were robbed of in the first half. I was getting frustrated too. All I could think of was that no bastard was going to steal this game from me. This was our game. This was our title. They were not going to score.'

Finally, the last frenzied Canterbury attack was put to ground, the last tackle made, the last error forced. Honiss blew his whistle. Immediately a wave of relief swept over Norm. The pain in his arm was forgotten, the exhaustion pushed away as his team-mates whooped, embraced, pointed and clapped at their supporters, then embraced some more. Victory was theirs. For the first time in fourteen years, Wellington were the top provincial team in the country.

'It was an amazing moment. I'd never felt such exhilaration before — not only because we'd won but because we'd done it the hard way by winning both the semi and the final away from home. Six weeks ago we'd been dog tucker — now we were the champs. Shit, it felt good.'

The adrenalin dulled the pain in his arm as he mounted the presentation dais and raised the Air New Zealand trophy above his head. This was as good as it gets, he told himself. Whatever comes after this . . . this is as good as rugby gets. Two years ago he had been sitting in a

Queenstown gutter watching blood pump out of his arm and not caring if he lived or died. Now here he was celebrating victory. On top. And yet it felt as unreal as Queenstown — as if he were in a dream and begging not to be woken.

'There was a party back at the team hotel that night but it was pretty flat. There were fish-heads everywhere and the players were knackered. I felt a bit weird actually. Like I couldn't really take it in. All the players had come down by then — I think the fish-heads enjoyed it more than us. I had a couple of Cokes, smoked a cigar, then went off to bed.'

SACKED

The next morning a weary Wellington team caught the bus to Christchurch airport and flew back to the capital. On arrival they were greeted by a sea of well-wishers that swamped the terminal and spilled beyond. As Norm emerged from the corridor, the trophy raised high in his left hand, he was greeted by an enormous roar. As the players made their way through the throng each was cheered as if he was a hero returning from war.

For Norm the crowd's enthusiasm was a mixed blessing. His right hand was seized and pumped by any number of excited supporters, his right shoulder slapped in appreciation. He began to recoil from the crowd, trying to protect his arm from further damage. But as he got into the shower at home, in preparation for a team-only party at a local bar, the pain overwhelmed him.

Somehow he struggled to the function, managed a couple of soft drinks, then surrendered to the inevitable. Manager Tony Bedford drove him to the hospital and Norm's on-field diagnosis was confirmed — a clean break of the radius. Within an hour his right arm and elbow were encased in plaster.

The next day the *Dominion* banner and front page lead paid homage to the Lions' captain. The banner read simply: 'And he played with a broken arm', with a picture of Norm underneath. The *Evening Post* joined the celebrations with a massive four-page spread on the NPC final, and over the next two nights ran maps of the route of the victory parade plus tips on the best vantage points from which to cheer the conquering heroes. It seemed the whole city had gone mad. 'Captain Hurricane' — now sporting a plaster cast — was praised anew for his leadership and spirit. It was a classic story of guts and glory, and the capital's media wallowed in it.

'The whole team was blown away by the reception. It was like everyone in Wellington was buzzing — like they'd all taken happy pills. Everywhere we went you could see the joy on people's faces — the kids, their parents, the old people in particular. As long as I'll live, I'll never feel like that again. The parade and the civic reception was awesome. It was almost too much — we just couldn't take it all in.'

Less enthused was ACC minister Ruth Dyson. The minister pronounced herself appalled that Hewitt had played the final quarter with a broken arm; far from being an act of courage, she said, his decision was an act of mindless stupidity. What kind of example was this supposed role model setting for young kids?

The politician's strident censure was picked up and amplified by the national media. But instead of having a chastening effect, Dyson's outburst only added to Norm's public lustre. In sporting circles, the ACC minister was ridiculed for misunderstanding the sacrifice required at the elite level of sport. Was it any wonder the All Blacks lacked mongrel, growled the talkback hosts, if the country was led by politically correct types like Dyson? Sports minister Trevor Mallard quickly distanced himself from his colleague's comments, appalled at her misjudgment of the public mood. The critics were less charitable. Dyson was a Cantabrian — if it had been Todd Blackadder or Norm Maxwell, many wondered if she would have been quite so quick to condemn.

Norm had a more immediate worry. He had received an email from former All Black team-mate Jamie Joseph, and its content shocked him.

'Normie,' it read. 'Heard from a source back home that the Wgtn union, or more so the coaches etc, are going to jerk you for next year. It came from a pretty reliable source as they are looking in Otago for a hooker to replace you, and have rang [sic] different agents around the country on the availability of there [sic] hookers on a move to Wellington.'

The email struck a raw nerve, confirming an impression Norm had gained over the NPC season about Mourie's evasiveness. He hadn't been able to get a straight answer to the composition of next year's Super 12 team or even his place in it, let alone the captaincy. The email seemed to provide the answer.

Yet how surreal — here he was being lauded for both his leadership and the quality of his play, with *Rugby News* describing his performance at Jade Stadium as 'the team's inspiration'. And here was Mourie giving him the cold shoulder and Jamie warning that he was about to be shafted.

Indeed, Mourie had made up his mind.

'There were two factors for me [in sacking Norm as captain]. There was a question of form, and I'd felt during the 2000 season that he might not get picked for the [Hurricanes] squad. From the Waikato game on, his play had picked up and that's why he was selected. But there were peripheral issues that affected my decision about the captaincy. It seemed that he had conflicts of interest. He was acting for players in the marketplace and involved in placing some [Wellington] players out of town [to overseas clubs]. And he had other business interests as well . . . In the end, I decided to select both [Southland hooker] Davin Heaps and Norm and let them battle it out for the number one slot. As for captain, I thought Gordy [Slater] was the better choice.'

The decision, and especially the reasoning, floored the hooker.

'I couldn't believe it. And I was bloody angry because I didn't have a chance to argue about all the extracurricular stuff. Sure, I involved the boys in a lot of charity work and was arranging [commercial] deals for them but, as far as I was concerned, that was part of my job. You look after your players off the paddock as well as on it. And if the guys came to me and said, "Norm, I need your advice about this contract," then I wasn't going to tell them to piss off or let them be screwed. I was there for the players — they were my priority. Not the union and not the bloody fish-heads.'

Norm was also annoyed that Davin Heaps was deemed to merit a place in the Hurricanes squad over local talent, let alone the coach's verdict that he would be a worthy challenger.

'Davin was having a lot of health problems and had struggled to nail down a starting spot with Southland [during the NPC]. So when Goss told me that it was a scrap between the two of us for the Super 12, I couldn't believe it. It was bullshit. I represented a threat to Goss and the way he wanted to run things. The decision to challenge the Brumbies' style of play midway through the season was a part of it, I reckon. I still think that was the real reason I was dumped.'

Mourie denies the accusation. 'I have real respect for Norm as a player and a person. But I had to think of who was going to be the best hooker and where the team needed to be in a couple of years' time. I think, overall, that dropping Norm [from the captaincy] was good for him. He could have been bitter and he certainly thought it took away some of his mana. But he battled back. He had a good Super 12 and is probably still the best scrummaging hooker in the country.'

Nevertheless, the loss of the captaincy widened the division between the two men. Norm no longer trusted his coach. This was John Hart all over again. And that he'd heard of his imminent dropping by email from a mate in Japan suggested that Mourie had told others long before he'd bothered to consult the player. The fact that he rated Davin Heaps the better hooker and Gordon Slater the better captain was hardly a vote of confidence in his abilities.

Bewildered by the decision, Norm sought advice from others. Both friends and players tendered the same message — stick it up Mourie, prove him wrong. Besides, they said, there was little he could do — the power lay with the coach and selectors. There was no other option bar spit the dummy. It proved unpalatable advice.

'I knew they were right. But I hated it. It was a huge blow to my pride, and it was hard to take because I didn't think I'd deserved it. Although looking back, maybe Goss was right. It was a bloody good lesson, although maybe not the one he intended. It reminded me that a player is just a player — a piece of meat. We're here at the whim of others.'

There was no question that he felt stabbed in the back, aggrieved at both the decision and its timing. But Mourie had chosen his successor well. Gordy was a mate and, given his inexperience, Norm felt obliged to offer advice and assistance to the big Taranaki prop.

'Eventually I got over it,' he says, shrugging his shoulders. 'I didn't say anything to the media when they asked me, bar a bullshit press statement about pledging my loyalty to the team. Which was crap, but the sort of things the fish-heads were looking for. It wasn't how I felt and I was fair bursting to have a go. But I knew it wouldn't do me any good in the long run. Besides, I was still playing footy and I was still getting paid for it. That's not a bad consolation.'

GOSS

Over the off-season Norm trained hard, determined that the Southland draftee would not get an easy go of it. He knew Davin Heaps from his days down in Southland and liked the guy. It wasn't Heaps' fault, he reasoned. Then when Heaps' health problems resurfaced any lingering resentment was replaced by sympathy. By the first practice games it was obvious that Norm would retain his place in the Hurricanes' starting XV for the 2001 season. It was equally obvious that Mourie would persist with the Brumbies-style pattern of play, and that Bryan Williams was no closer to getting on the same wavelength as the Hurricanes backline than he had been the previous year.

'Goss was heavily into the computer stuff by now and he'd started handing out diagrams and executive summaries for each of the games. It was all a bit technical for some of the boys — and I must admit I wasn't all that impressed either. You had to fill in a sort of pie-chart after each game as to how you thought you'd played. Then Goss would have a go and fill in some squares and hand it back to you. I mean, why? Why couldn't he just say, "Norm, work on your lineouts" or "We need you hitting up the ball more"? It was like going back to school with all these pieces of paper floating around.'

The new style represented perhaps the clearest evidence that Norm Hewitt did not fit the new brand of physical chess that now dominated the southern hemisphere, a style of rugby that requires players to make programmed as well as intelligent choices. Norm had been brought up on a diet of intimidation and intuition — on the need to dominate one's opponent. And that was still the case in the front row and at the set-plays.

'I knew where Goss and BJ were coming from, but I'm not sure that kind of coaching works with a team like the Hurricanes. We have certain strengths that a Brumbies type of game detracts from. Because of all the stars out wide, both the Lions and the Hurricanes need ball winners and grunters up front — people who can get to the breakdown and dominate that area. I thought we'd proved that by winning the NPC. But Goss kept on with this idea of splitting up the field, not committing too many players to the breakdown, working the angles in close.'

There was also the matter of the team's education and academic intelligence. And their culture.

'Us Polynesian boys don't write things down. We were never that good at school. We learn by doing things, by being shown. Goss is a smart guy and I bet he's got a varsity degree or two tucked away somewhere. So sometimes what he says, and the way he says it, goes over the players' heads.

'In Australia, rugby is a private school game. They're generally bright white boys who play at that level. League is the working class game over there. So they've developed a game that isn't too physical but is very structured. And good on them. That suits their culture. But I don't think it suits ours. We need our own style of play, our own rugby culture. At the moment we're borrowing defence patterns from league, our tactics from the Brumbies and Australia. We've lost our rugby identity, I reckon. And the Hurricanes is a bloody good example of that. We were being given a game-plan that wasn't us. Man, I was glad I wasn't captain. Because I knew 2001 was going to be a right balls-up.'

CHAPTER TWENTY ONE

The Last Haka

Norm winced as he reached over and flicked on the bedside lamp. The clock informed him that daybreak on this early August morning was still hours away. He sat up carefully, trying not to knock his throbbing arm. He had taken three digesics before going to bed, but their effect had worn off and now the pain was severe enough to wake him. Just like the night before. And the night before that.

The specialist's advice was that he may need a bone graft to repair the damage. He had hoped the arm would come right — that over the Christmas period his recuperative powers would do their usual trick and he would report fit and healthy for the Super 12. But the break had not healed properly, and it had been further battered during the competition. Even the arm guard that he wore during each game — a piece of PVC piping overlaid with a padded wetskin — provided scant protection. He'd even arranged for the injection of a local anaesthetic, directly into the fracture, to get him through recent games but that was no help whatsoever at three in the morning.

He had become one of the 'jab-jab' boys, the collection of players who only made it on to the field with the assistance of a needle. Invariably these were the older players who were coming to the ends of their careers, their bodies' need to rest and heal overridden by the demands of the team and their own obstinacy. Top class rugby required players to confront and conquer the pain barrier. Playing with injuries was just part of that requirement — and when the pain became too intense, there was always the needle.

Norm had one small consolation that August morning. Just two days earlier he had captained Wellington to their first NPC win of the new season, against a tough Taranaki forward pack that had been all fired up for the local derby, playing on their home ground at New Plymouth and well aware that Super 12 contracts were up for grabs. Wellington had won well, Christian Cullen's return from injury inspiring an otherwise stolid Lions backline.

It was certainly better than being booed off the park, as had happened the previous weekend when they'd played Bay of Plenty. The team had resembled a cast of extras from a zombie movie — disjointed, lifeless, brain-dead. They had not been helped by a succession of crooked lineout throws from their captain. When Norm was replaced by Shane Carter the jeers had followed him all the way to the reserves bench.

That was rugby, he thought. You're only as good as your last match. And fans are a fickle bunch. They'd already forgotten the previous year's championship, and they were in a sour mood after the Wallabies' retention of the Bledisloe Cup at Carisbrook the day before. Now their champion team was being defeated by the lowly Bay, and it was more than they could take. Norm felt some sympathy for them. In all his time with Wellington he doubted the team had ever played a worse game.

But other matters were also weighing on his mind. His old Hurricanes front-row mate, Kevin Yates, who was contracted to Sale for the coming premiership, had phoned from Manchester. Sale were short of a scrummaging hooker for the 2001/2002 season, and the chunky Maori hooker had been suggested as ideal for the heavier English ground conditions and the northern hemisphere focus on set-pieces and forward confrontation.

Within days their interest had been formalised, with Sale's management offering a basic contract worth £84,000 (NZ$260,000) for seven months, starting from 1 November. In addition they were offering another £300 (NZ$1000) for every match Norm played in, an extra £200 (NZ$700) for every win, and a share of any bonuses should the team qualify for the European club competitions. There would also be a one-off payment of £3500 towards accommodation, £3000 towards a car, and all the usual medical and insurance cover. It was a more than tempting offer, and when he'd discussed it with his mates they'd all told him the same thing — he'd be mad not to go. Against the NZRFU contract offer of $130,000 for the 2002 season, an offer subject to his selection in both the Hurricanes and the Lions, the Sale offer was outstanding.

Yeah, but it wasn't that simple. It would mean he'd have to quit the

Wellington Lions now, leave the team when their front five was particularly vulnerable, get the operation on his arm and then rest ahead of the November deadline. He was also sitting on 292 first-class rugby games, more than any other current New Zealand player, and he desperately wanted to finish his career by cracking the magic 300 mark. If he played every remaining match in the NPC round-robin that would be the 300. Of all New Zealand's rugby players, only Colin Meads, Andy Haden and Sean Fitzpatrick would have played more. Not bad company — not bad at all.

There was also the new home that he had purchased at Pauatahanui — a peaceful retreat set on 6 hectares of land just outside Wellington. He and Arlene had only moved in a couple of weeks earlier, and he was loving it. No near neighbours, the smell of the land, the sweep of the surrounding hills. It had felt like home as soon as he'd seen it. But it would still be there when he came back. If he went to Sale then he and Arlene could tour Europe, enjoy the experience of a new culture and a fresh rugby environment. It would be a perfect cap to a long career, and provide him with enough money to launch any number of business initiatives after he retired.

For the first time in his life, though, money was not a factor. Until now he had been acquisitive, the 'shop' mentality that he had acquired at Te Aute governing a good part of his outlook. Rugby had become a business as well as a sport. But now there was a new contentedness within his personality, a generosity that hadn't been there before. The Cloud 9 children's trust and other charities were consuming a good deal of his time, Arlene had established an aerobics school, and their relationship was strong and secure. He was happy. Yeah, he was content. This was where he wanted to be.

'I'm a bloody mug,' he muttered as he headed for the bathroom cabinet and the painkillers.

THE HORROR-CANES

They were the Super 12 team voted by the pundits as most likely to challenge the Crusaders and Brumbies for the 2001 title. And no wonder. Not only had Wellington won the NPC the previous season but Taranaki, the Hurricanes' other main constituent province, had also reached the NPC semi-finals. Graft Taranaki grunt onto Wellington finesse and here was a team that would really shake the big boys.

Despite the loss of Alama Ieremia to Japan, the Hurricanes had no shortage of talent. Of the backline, Cullen, Umaga, Lomu and O'Halloran

Left: *Happy hookers. The indestructible Sean Fitzpatrick survives a dip in the shark infested waters of Durban, South Africa.*
Right: *One of the very best. Norm shakes hands with Waratahs and Wallaby No 2 Phil Kearns after the 1999 Hurricanes win 13-7 at Napier.*

Left: *All Black captain Anton Oliver. Norm's international career was caught between the immovable object that was Fitzpatrick and the irresistible force that was Oliver.*
Right: *The best hooker that Norm encountered in his long career. Irish and British Lions tyro Keith Wood — the complete No.2.*

Dion Waller earns a yellow card and the grateful thanks of his team-mates for illegally preventing a Canterbury try in the final minutes of the NPC final.

Left: *Glory. The Wellington NPC bask in the wake of their 34-29 victory over Canterbury at Jade Stadium to win the 2000 NPC title.*
Right: *Norm and special fan Nathan Hamlin share the sweet taste of success.*

'Goss' Mourie and BG Williams — the ill-fated Hurricanes coaching duo of 2000/01. Great All Blacks do not necessarily make great coaches.

Left: *Even the freakish Stephen Larkham could find no way through the Hurricanes defence during the Brumbies 19-34 drubbing.*

Right: *The night the stadium rocked. Tana Umaga helps Christian Cullen celebrate a try against 2001 Super 12 champions, the ACT Brumbies.*

Norm promoting the 'Books in Homes' scheme. He sees his future in the education and welfare fields.

Beauty and the beast. Norm and former world aerobics champ Arlene Thomas have been partners since 1999.

had toured France and Italy with the All Blacks at the end of the previous year, while Holwell and Spice had been selected for the New Zealand 'A' squad. Winger Brad Fleming would also have been a certainty for the latter had he not been injured. The forward line-up was only slightly less impressive, with Filo Tiatia and Gordon Slater in the same All Black party to France while Jerry Collins, Kupu Vanisi and Dion Waller had all made the New Zealand 'A' team. The rest of the forward pack wasn't bad either, with Kevin Yates and Norm teaming up with captain Slater in the front row, the fiery redhead and New Zealand Colts captain Paul Tito at lock, and blindside Rodney So'oialo and utility Inoke Afeaki completing a genuinely competitive unit.

'I think it was the best Hurricanes side — in terms of pure talent — that there's ever been,' Norm says. 'But it was the classic story. We were a team of champions but not a champion team. We didn't have it from day one.'

Part of the problem was the appointment of Gordon Slater as captain. He was inexperienced, didn't have sufficient rapport with the Wellington players, and lacked on-field tactical nous. The light touch favoured by the coaches required a powerful on-field presence, and Slater was not cut out for the role. From the sidelines it became obvious that Norm, Dion Waller and other senior forwards were contributing more talk and direction than Slater, and the players would sometimes be at cross-purposes as to what the next play should be.

In addition, some of the star players were carrying injuries, and they seemed jaded after the previous year's gruelling season. The All Blacks who had toured France had had just six weeks off before training for the Super 12 began, and Christian Cullen in particular seemed curiously sluggish, his post-tour stint with the Barbarians exacerbating a leg injury. In the first few Super 12 games Cullen was just another journeyman, a pale shadow of his former self.

'The ones who had played in the All Blacks were a bit off the pace to start with. Most of them had played for eleven months out of the year before, and we were back into practice games on hard grounds before their bodies had properly recovered. Mentally they weren't there either, but then neither was I.'

Still smarting from the loss of the captaincy, Norm came to loathe the coaching staff's heavy reliance on video analysis and motivational tools. His dissatisfaction became focused on the team's psychologist, Dave Hadfield.

'I don't get the need for these sorts of people. All they do is mess with players' minds. Rugby is a simple game. And a good coach or captain should know his players well enough to know what motivates each of them. You don't need a shrink. That's a cop-out in my book. An excuse for a coach, captain or manager not to be doing their job. I hated it. And I never saw one player play better as a consequence. Always the opposite.'

Mourie also used tools like wagon wheels and printed game plans. The wagon wheel listed a variety of skills required by each player during a game, and then required both player and coach to analyse the player's performance against those objectives. While it wasn't Norm's preferred technique — indeed, he doubted its effectiveness in view of the largely Polynesian character of the Hurricanes — he at least could understand where Goss was coming from. The game plans themselves were particularly useful in getting each player to understand their role in the coming match.

'My only concern is that I think most rugby players are show-and-tell people. We're not into written memos and that sort of drama. As a coaching aid they're OK, but they can't replace the one-on-one hands-on stuff. That's why I thought Laurie Mains set the bench-mark. I'm sure he uses video analysis, but he's into the detail stuff on the training paddock as well. He shows you what you're doing wrong and how to make it better.'

Whatever the cause, the Hurricanes started the Super 12 poorly and got steadily worse. After five games they had just one win to their credit — a poor effort against the lowly Northern Bulls. Their lack of on-field intelligence seemed best exemplified by a last-minute decision against the Cats at Bloemfontein. Trailing 15-18, and with a penalty straight in front of the Cats' goal-posts, Slater instead opted for the tap kick. The play was easily defended, and the Cats escaped with the win and four competition points. In a competition as tight as the Super 12 every bonus point was crucial, and not only had the Hurricanes sacrificed one themselves by not taking the draw, they had gifted the Cats additional points.

Mourie defends the decision. 'Gordy was unfairly criticised over that. It was our [the coaches] decision to go for it. It didn't come off — that's the way it goes sometimes.'

Norm is less philosophical. 'In the Super 12 every bonus point is critical. That's been the lesson over the last five years — where you end up on the table is often determined by just a point. We came tenth in the end — if we'd taken the kick we would have ended up eighth. But that wasn't my reasoning at the time. The team needed a morale boost. Drawing with the Cats on their home patch would have been a damned sight better than losing. And we gifted them two points [as a result of not taking the draw]. Too bloody generous in my book.'

Back at the team hotel, a still bemused Norm was drawn aside by manager Tony Bedford.

'He said something like: "You didn't hear this from me but I've had a phone call from [Wellington rugby official] Brett Jackson and the word is that you're part of the dissension in the team. [Jackson] had heard through media sources that you are to blame for the losses and a factor in the rift between Goss and BeeGee."

'I just looked at him and shook my head. It was bullshit. I wasn't the captain anymore, but I was still getting all the criticism. It was true that the coaches weren't seeing eye to eye — they had argued [about tactics] in front of us players and you don't like to see that. That lets you know that something is really wrong.'

Norm's mood was not improved by the surroundings, or the warning the team received not to venture outside their hotel at night.

'Bloemfontein is a hole of a place. We were warned by the South African police and the SARFU liaison that we shouldn't take taxis because there was a good chance you'd end up dead.

'We've just lost to the Cats through a dumb decision, I'm copping the crap for the team's losses, and we're stuck in this shit town with nowhere to go. Man, that was definitely my low point of the Super 12.'

It didn't look as if it would get any better. The team had to fly back from South Africa, deal with a generally critical Kiwi press then take on the Super 12 champions, the Crusaders, back down at Jade Stadium. Although their mood lightened perceptibly on the flight back. Any public expectations were gone and the Hurricanes had nothing to lose. Nobody gave them the ghost of a chance, despite the NPC heroics a few months earlier.

'I never need any motivation when I play Canterbury or the Crusaders because the crowd down there are so bad. They're on a par with the worst Afrikaners crowd. The kids swear at you with their parents looking on — the number of times I was told to "fuck off home" or called a drunk while I was waiting to throw the ball in was amazing. The racist abuse could get pretty bad too. If the "Jerry Springer Show" is ever looking for any foul-mouthed screamers they should trawl the terraces down at Jade Stadium.'

That night the locals had more reason than usual to curse the capital boys as they dealt to the Crusaders 41-29. Yet again the Hurricanes pack confounded the critics, making their opposites look slow and wooden.

'We didn't play all that well. But the Crusaders were poor. They kept stuffing up at the break-down, fumbling the ball under pressure, and our lineout went really well. Dion Waller sure showed up Blackadder and Maxwell that night. Their best player was the Brisbane Broncos guy [league convert] Brad Thorn. He came on as a replacement and played really well. I went to tackle him at one stage and he just bumped me off, sat me on my arse and took off again. I looked a right idiot. But I thought to myself that if the Crusaders pack were meant to be the base for the All Blacks this year we were going to be in real trouble.'

BASHING THE BRUMBIES

The team's next match was against the ACT Brumbies — a team that had annihilated the Crusaders in the opening round and were leading the Super 12 at the midway point of the competition. To qualify for the semi-finals, the Hurricanes would need to defeat the artful Aussies and then keep winning. But beating the Brumbies was a totally different proposition to beating the out-of-sorts Crusaders. The gifted halves combination of George Gregan and Steve Larkham were in top form, George Smith and Owen Finegan were ruling the loose, and coach Eddie Jones had honed the team into a rugby machine. From numbers one through to fifteen there wasn't a weakness.

Or so ran the conventional wisdom. The previous season the Crusaders had discovered the chink in the Brumbies' attack — that it was overly reliant on phase ball and could be frustrated by an attacking defence around the fringes of rucks and mauls. The key playmakers were Gregan and Larkham, particularly the latter. The theory ran: neutralise Larkham and the machine would start to miss. But outside Larkham lurked the squat Rod Kafer — a clever ball player who could take the pressure off his first-five if required and free up runners coming into the line from depth. Against such a disciplined and ordered team, Norm found that Mourie's video analysis and tactical planning had its place.

'The game against the Brumbies made me respect Goss a lot more because it was like he was playing chess with Eddie Jones. I mean it was the master and the pupil, but Goss sussed Jones that night. We got the game plan, Goss took us through it during the lead-up week, and we all knew our jobs. It was a bit ironic because the Brumbies play to such a pattern that once you tumble them they don't appear to have a Plan "B". Although I don't think they're that dumb. Jones had them playing one pattern in the round-robin and another one in the semis and final. He wasn't going to make the same mistake he'd made the year before. He kept something back in reserve.'

Mourie also fired up his team with an unexpected threat at practice on the preceding Tuesday night. This was a key game — lose and the season was as good as over. And if they did lose he would have no hesitation in playing the reserves and other squad members the next week.

As the teams ran out onto the stadium with a sell-out crowd of 34,000 cheering them on, Norm was conscious that as many had come to watch the Brumbies as to support the Hurricanes. Within seconds of the start Larkham ghosted down the blindside, almost conjuring a try for winger Bartholomeusz. In the stand, people looked at each other and raised their eyebrows. Shee-it. These guys were good all right.

So what unfolded over the next seventy-odd minutes was no less than a miracle. The Hurricanes attacked the runners off the Brumbies' breakdowns as if each was personally responsible for every setback they had ever suffered. They picked up the runners taking the inside passes and smashed them to the ground. They nagged and worried at Gregan like a troop of hyenas. Eventually the Brumbies began to make mistakes, and first Cullen and then Lomu managed to finish off midfield breakdowns and counter-attacking busts. When David Holwell converted both and then slotted a couple of easy penalties the halftime score read 20-nil.

The second half began much the same as the first, with the Brumbies relentless in attack but knocked down time and time again by the Hurricanes forwards, young Jerry Collins a brown destroyer. When Holwell went over and then converted his try it was 27-nil. Twenty-seven points to zip. The crowd roared its approval, at the same time half expecting to be woken from this dream or for someone to be sin-binned and the Brumbies storm back. Instead it was the big Brumbies breakaway Owen Finegan who was sent to the sin bin — his frustration causing him to lash out in front of a vigilant referee. Eventually the Hurricanes relented and the game ended with a final score of 34-19, but the message had been well and truly sent. The Hurricanes were back — both of last year's finalists swatted away like annoying insects.

Then the dreaded bye round. It is one of the accepted truths of the Super 12 that teams take the bye badly, that the relaxation from the weekly grind frustrates a team's momentum.

'It all depends on where the bye comes. The best time is midway through — like it was for us. If you get it too early it's a waste of time, and if it's too late the week-in week-out grind has already done its damage. I really needed the rest and so did most of the team. All the same, the Super 12 organisers should space it so that all the teams get their byes in, say, rounds six, seven and eight. At the moment, it's a dog's breakfast.'

Norm used the time to sleep, rest and let his minor injuries heal. His arm was getting worse but it would need more than a week's rest to solve that problem. And he mused on the events of the last few weeks. Maybe he'd been wrong, he thought. Maybe the team was gelling as it should — maybe it was getting used to Goss and BeeGee, or they were getting used to the team.

'They say winning is a habit and it is. The problems don't so much go away as are masked. I mean, that's human nature. If you're winning, you feel happier. And if you're losing you get a bit down and maybe you start looking to share some blame. When we beat the Waratahs in the next game, it looked like we might make the semis. Three wins on the trot and an easy road home.'

An easy road home — maybe that was the problem. Maybe the team felt that with the Chiefs at the stadium and then the underperforming Blues away, the Hurricanes were already in the final four. To this day, Norm remains mystified about what happened next.

'The next game the stadium's packed. The Chiefs are playing well but not well enough to think they can roll us at home. Steiny [Paul Steinmetz] scores in the corner. Dave Holwell converts and it's seven-nil before anyone's even got a sweat up. Then Jonah takes off and almost scores and it's starting to look easy. Boy, did we ever get that wrong. The Chiefs began to play out of their skins and we had no answer.'

In the blink of an eye the Hurricanes team became fifteen individuals playing as if they were all meeting each other for the first time. In contrast, the Chiefs' forward pack hunted as one, and the backs created space — while all the Hurricanes' stars decided to have their worst defensive game of the season. The final result was a 51-27 thrashing that left the crowd stunned. They had come to party, but they left as if they had each lost the winning Lotto ticket.

Graeme Mourie blamed the loss on his team 'still having stereotypes of the Chiefs', despite the fact that their new coach John Mitchell had instilled a winning pride into the hapless franchise. But even worse was to follow. On a sodden Eden Park, and still with an outside chance of reaching the top four, the Hurricanes were soundly defeated by the Blues — the worst New Zealand team in the competition.

'We were abysmal,' says Mourie. 'We didn't play to the team pattern, there were basic errors of technique — it was the worst performance in my two years of coaching them. The forwards went OK but the backs tried to do too much as individuals and didn't follow instructions.

'Our team can be a bit like an old Rolls Royce — you've got to push it to start and it's expensive to run, but once it gets going it's very impressive. Unlike Canterbury and the Crusaders, who are more like a Toyota — they can't go above 120 kph and they only come in the one colour, but they're reliable. They start every time.'

The loss not only scuppered the Hurricanes' season, it dropped them to tenth on the table. It had been an appalling Super 12 for the New Zealand franchises — for the first time in the competition's history none would feature in the final four, and three of the four bottom teams hailed from New Zealand. But that was no consolation for the Hurricanes — yet again, they had underperformed.

In his end-of-competition review *Evening Post* rugby writer David Ogilvie laid a good part of the responsibility on the team's jaded All Black stars and an out-of-sorts management team. Mourie was criticised for the team taking 'too long to get organised and going properly. Maybe he was also a little too detailed in his work for some of the players.' The clash between Williams and his back-line charges was also emphasised. '[Maybe] he wanted too much structure for them. But then maybe he was right.' Gordon Slater's captaincy did not escape comment either: 'Battled adequately all competition,' wrote Ogilvie, 'but seemed uncomfortable with the captaincy.'

In the end only a handful of players drew Ogilvie's praise — he named Dion Waller his player of the season, but also had positive comments for Jonah Lomu, Rodney So'oialo, Jerry Collins, Paul Tito and Norm Hewitt. 'The odd lineout throw came back to haunt him but generally an excellent season and seemed to adjust to the non-captaincy well enough. Important as a scrummager.' That five of the season's top performers were forwards was not lost on anyone. Far from being a weakness, the Hurricanes' pack had actually been a consistent strength. It was the star backline that had proven the weakest link.

THE WALLABIES

The Chiefs game had not just been a disaster in terms of the Hurricanes' Super 12 chances, but it also firmly nixed Norm's ambition to captain New Zealand Maori for one last time. Waikato's Deon Muir had been in outstanding form as both the Chiefs' captain and as their No. 8, and his performance at the stadium convinced Matt Te Pou and Jim Love that he was ready to assume on-field responsibility for the Maori team as well.

While it may have been another blow to Norm's mana, this time he accepted the captaincy decision with a measure of equanimity. Te Pou had been upfront from the moment the issue was raised, and had provided Norm with explicit reasons for his choice. In addition, Muir was the captain of a performing Super 12 team and had led Waikato with distinction at NPC level. It was a sharp contrast to the Slater choice and the evasiveness that accompanied it.

'All players want is honesty. Tell us early and tell us why. I respected Matt for his decision and had no problem working with Deon. Then when Matt offered me a leadership role within the team — a sort of vice-captain role in charge of the tighties — man, I was motivated. Off the scale.'

And little wonder. New Zealand Maori had been invited to play the world champion Wallabies at the Sydney Football Stadium as a warm-up game prior to the British and Irish Lions' tour. There would be further matches against a Wasps selection at Rotorua and the touring Argentine team, but nothing ranked with the Wallabies international.

'Every Maori player, whether they were an All Black or not, wanted to be in that team. To play the Aussies over there was going to be huge. And it was a real honour too. They could have played warm-up tests against, say, the Samoans or the French or the Argentinians, but they chose us. They wanted a tough game and they deliberately chose us. That meant a lot to the players and to Maoridom. Mana is a big part of our culture — the invite gave us that mana. So we weren't going to let them or ourselves down. We were going to take it to them from day one.'

To increase the status of the Maori team, and to provide some of their players with an early taste of the coming Tri-Nations, the All Black selectors released their Maori players to the team. The addition of Taine Randell, Norm Maxwell and Troy Flavell added class and size to the Maori pack. It also provided an opportunity to test Randell as an openside flanker at the top level, Flavell on the blindside and big Mark Cooksley as a locking partner for Maxwell.

'We assembled in Auckland and within minutes we were a team. It was amazing. The karakia, the waiata, our whole culture bound us as tight as a team can get. We were so close, like brothers, and so determined. We knew that a lot more was on the line than just a rugby match. I doubt if a Maori team has ever played a bigger game. The whole rugby world was going to be watching and we were the warriors for our people. I've played for the All Blacks, led the haka in test matches, captained my province and Super 12 teams, but it was nothing to how I felt before that game. It was the ultimate rugby experience.'

Certainly the team the Maori put on Sydney Football Stadium that night would rank as one of the best ever assembled — a side that could confidently expect to beat most international teams and even trouble the mighty All Blacks.

'Eleven of us had played for the All Blacks so we all had big match experience. I mean look at that team — Carlos Spencer at fullback, Randle and Reihana on the wings, Ralph and Gibson in the centres, the Chiefs pair of Glen Jackson and Rhys Duggan at first-five and halfback ... and the forward pack of Deon, Taine, Troy, the "Big Rig", Normie Maxwell, with Greg Feek, Deacon Manu and me in the front row. Kees Meeuws was originally to play at prop but he got injured, so young Deacon stepped up and he was bloody good. He'll be an All Black one day.'

Against them was ranked a Wallaby team that included all its stars — Matthew Burke, Daniel Herbert, the magical pairing of Larkham and Gregan, Toutai Kefu, dreadlocked openside George Smith, the living legend John Eales, and a useful front row that included dynamic young Brumbies hooker Jeremy Paul.

'Our tactics were simple. We wanted to dominate them up front and attack their midfield. They were experimenting with Elton Flatley at second-five but we identified him as the weak link — or at least the gap between Flatley and Larkham as an area we could attack. In the forwards we wanted to upset their lineout because we had three tall jumpers in Cooksley, Maxwell and Flavell, as well as attack their front-row at scrumtime. It was old-fashioned stuff — be physical and pressure them all over the field. Smash them at the breakdown and don't let them get into their pattern. The Springboks used exactly the same tactics later in the Tri-Nations.'

But there was a risk to such a strategy. The wafer-thin line between vigorous and over-vigorous play would be set by the match referee and his assistants. And Norm was shocked when a leading New Zealand referee privately informed the team that the choice of match officials would cost them dear.

'We were warned that we wouldn't get a fair go with South African match officials involved. Basically this New Zealand ref said that not all the old attitudes had died with apartheid. To be honest, a number of Island and Maori players are still a bit suspicious about some of the white South African refs. So when we hear something like that we take it a bit more seriously than you might expect.'

But as the team ran out onto the SFS to await the Wallabies, Norm put such concerns to one side. The Maori support was spectacular — it seemed as if every Maori in Australia had made the pilgrimage, with black and white flags, banners and scarves draped over every part of the ground. Their raucous reception easily eclipsed that for the home team.

'It was awesome. We were revved up already, but seeing all that support

— hearing your name shouted out from the stands — man, that was something else. It was huge. Spine-tingling. Deon led the haka, the crowd were going off and the Wallabies looked a bit anxious, like this was not what they had expected. The trouble was, though, that maybe we were a bit over-excited, because Daniel Herbert scored early and it took that try to settle us down and remember our pattern.'

But the Australians were not having it all their own way. The Maori forwards gained an early ascendancy and gave Duggan the time to free his backs and Gibson, in particular, to start probing the midfield. By midway through the first half New Zealand Maori were clearly in charge, with the Australian backs increasingly hesitant in the face of some fierce defence. Each time Larkham or Flatley received the ball they found Taine Randell or Daryl Gibson arriving a millisecond later.

And then the winning and losing of the game — the ball among the Australian backs, a kick under pressure, regathered by the Maori and a thrilling counterattack launched down the middle of the field with Flavell raising his fist in triumph before he scores under the bar. But way back down the field touch-judge Mark Lawrence has his flag pointed out onto the field. Referee Tappe Henning gets the word through his microphone and jogs back to his countryman. A late charge by Caleb Ralph. Henning motions to the captains — the try is disallowed, Ralph sent to the sin bin, a penalty to Australia back where the offence took place.

Months later Norm was still seething over the decision. 'It was bullshit. Bullshit! Caleb was committed to the tackle. I would see similar incidents in every Super 12 game and the worst you might get is a warning. Look what [Sharks first-five] Butch James got away with all the Super 12. I was filthy about it and I sure remembered what had been said before the game.'

Yet a more dispassionate view would suggest that both penalty and subsequent actions were justified. That Ralph had the time to pull himself away from contact but, perhaps mindful of the Maori imperative to physically intimidate, did not do so. A line had been crossed. Whether or not he deserved the yellow card is a matter of debate. But once the offence was drawn to Henning's attention then the disallowance of the try and the subsequent penalty were inevitable.

The Wallabies duly took advantage, aboriginal winger Andrew Walker exhibiting the rarest of skills to somehow squeeze between four tacklers and take Australia out to a 14-3 lead. It was a dagger to the heart of the Maori team's ambitions.

Or at least it should have been. But this was a Maori side that refused to yield. Cooksley was a dominant presence in the lineouts, Taine Randell had made George Smith anonymous, and the Maori front-row was getting on top. Five minutes before half-time they had battled back to 13-14, with Carlos Spencer scoring the first of his two tries after some great preliminary work by the forwards — only to concede a soft try to prop Nick Stiles and turn 13-21 down at the break.

The second half started much the same as the first, with the Maori having an edge in the tight but the lack of combination in the backs producing turnover ball and blunting a series of promising attacks. When Larkham slipped between a gap and scored it looked as if the game was over. But still the Maori refused to yield, and after another try to Spencer and two penalties only two points separated the teams. The crowd were yelling themselves hoarse. An incredible upset was on the cards — an untried New Zealand Maori combination was putting the heat on the world champions and Australia were not responding.

'With about ten minutes to go we knew the game was there for the taking. But we were having no luck — a lot of the 50/50 calls were going against us and we'd get a bit of momentum going and then make a silly mistake. If we'd had just one warm-up game I reckon we would have beaten the Wallabies. It was a bit of rustiness, but mostly the lack of combination. And we were playing a team that had been together for three or four years.'

The Wallabies held on, their admirable defence extinguishing raid after raid. Each time it looked as if the Maori must score there would be one last defender who would do something special — wrap the ball-carrier in the tackle, get a hand in the way of the final pass, anticipate the overlap and snuff out the first receiver. With an Andrew Walker penalty and a final try to replacement winger Graeme Bond the score blew out to 41-29, a flattering result for the hosts.

'We were shattered because we knew we had them. But we were also very proud. To have taken the Wallabies that close and to have played that well without much preparation — we'd proven ourselves. And that's what the game was about. About mana. About Maori rugby proving itself against the best.'

But physically, Norm was exhausted. After touring the ground with the Maori team and thanking their supporters, he slumped in the dressing room and found it difficult to stand. The pace of the match, along with the combination of mental concentration and physical strength, had drained him of all reserves.

'It took me days to recover. Arlene had come over for the match and we stayed on in Sydney for a while, but each day it was a real effort just getting out of bed and doing normal things like walking straight. It taught me a huge lesson. Since I'd played my last test back in '98 the international game had got even more physical and faster. And I realised then, for the first time I reckon, that I couldn't play that top level of international rugby again. I mean that Wallabies–Maori game would have been the equal of, say, a Six Nations test and probably superior in intensity to an All Blacks v Argentina test. But as for stepping up to Tri-Nations and playing four such tests in six or seven weeks — I knew then my body could never have done it. And that was a big call for me. I'd kidded myself that I could.'

But if this was his last big international then what a way to go out. The atmosphere in the Maori camp had been exceptional, the reception in Sydney outstanding, and the game one that would be remembered in rugby circles for years to come — the day the Maori boys came to town and almost beat the world champions on their own home patch.

A week later the Maori team comfortably accounted for the visiting Argentinians at Rotorua, but it was a low-key affair — an anti-climax after their efforts in Sydney. And in many ways it was symbolic of the host union's arrogance, forcing their Argentinian visitors to play four games in ten days and even refusing to allow their test players to fraternise after the international in Christchurch.

'I talked to a couple of the Argies after the game and they were dirty about their treatment. Fair enough too. It was shabby stuff. We knew where they were coming from because Maori rugby gets treated like that every year.

'The Australian union treated us better than the New Zealand Rugby Union treats Maori rugby. For a start, they'd offered us the game, and they had a sense of occasion and respect that is missing from our union. When Jeremy Paul and I swapped jerseys at the end of the game it was something special. I really like the way the Australians make their jerseys unique. This one had "Wallabies v NZ Maori, Sydney 2001" stitched over the left breast. And here we were — a Maori Australian and a Maori New Zealander respecting each other after battle. I'll treasure that jersey until the day I die because it's symbolic of my Maoriness and the fact that we can, as a people, get to the top no matter where we are.'

Epilogue

It's the knee again. The newspapers say he'll be out for a couple of weeks but Norm knows it will be longer than that. He may be out forever. His last rugby act to be at the bottom of a collapsed scrum against Southland on a spring afternoon at the Wellington Stadium. His medial ligaments are damaged and although the specialist is optimistic he can't give the hooker a definite time-frame. It may require an operation — it may not.

It is yet another dilemma for the veteran gladiator. So, is his career over or not? Should he retire or wait for some never-never recovery? And even if the knee does come right, will the Super12 selectors still consider him worthy of a contract? The NZRFU have offered him $130,000 for the 2002 season but that's only if he makes the team. And while he's confident that he's among the top ten hookers in the country, it's not his call. His fate rests in the hands of others and he loathes that uncertainty.

Although his greatest fear is not of being dropped but of what lies beyond. Of what happens once the rugby stops. This is the only life he has known, the only job he's had in the past eight years. Indeed he's only been trained for one thing in life and that is to play rugby. A part of him feels that his life is nearly over. And he's just turned 33 years of age.

'It's a weird feeling. Everything I've done, everything I've been, everything I've ever dreamed is connected with rugby. When I was a kid, that's all I wanted — to be a top rugby player. I'm being pushed out of my comfort zone and, yeah, it's unsettling.'

They are natural qualms for a top sportsperson approaching the end of his career. He has lived a strange, self-absorbed existence that has delivered

285

reward, celebrity and the respect of his peers. But with the collapse of a scrum, and maybe the flick of a selector's pen, it is all about to end. Norm Hewitt will be converted into Joe Average. The 'phone will stop ringing, the contract monies dry up, and the camaraderie of his playing mates will fade away. He appreciates this inevitability but it doesn't make it any easier.

He need not be so apprehensive. Despite having no formal qualifications, his life and organisational skills are highly valued by others. His twin mentors, Ray Thompson of TV production company Cloud 9 and Trevor Grice of the Life Education Trust, want him to work in their chosen fields of expertise. Similarly there is the prospect of a contract with Te Puni Kokiri — keen to engage his undoubted ability to relate to at-risk youth and inspire them.

But it is a measure of Norm that he views the future with trepidation. His whole life has required an order, a discipline, a measure of control over his immediate environment. One is tempted to trace such needs back to his childhood and most especially his adolescence. Rugby provided him security. By retiring from the game he will be stepping into the unknown.

'I'll get there. Rationally, I know what needs to be done and I want to continue my work with kids and teenagers and get involved in business. But it's given me a decent jolt, I can tell you that.'

He has made one decision. There'll be no hanging on. Once he's retired, then that's it. He doesn't want to be a dreaded has-been — an ex-player drawn back to the fringes of the game because nothing else makes any sense.

'I've seen a lot of All Blacks stay on in the rugby environment because they can't do anything else. They try real life for a bit and then shoot straight back. Or they never leave — they end up working for the NZRFU or rugby type organisations. If that's all I have to offer then they may as well shoot me now.'

Yet rugby is a game that Norm will always love. It has been his consuming passion over all the adult years of his life. In turn, it has rewarded him for his devotion. Without rugby he would have evolved into nothing more than a criminal statistic. Which is why he inherently appreciates what the sport has given him — financial security, strong friendships, a diverse range of business contacts and the chance to fulfil boyhood dreams.

It is a game that has changed much since he played his first first-class match at Nelson Park, Hastings in 1988. Professionalism has transformed everything — from the physical shape, strength and fitness of the players through to the way in which the players themselves view the sport.

'It's a job now,' says Norm. 'And a real career choice for young Maori and Island boys in particular. There's no question that rugby has become a brown game. That's because of the emphasis upon size and strength and that goes right down to schoolboy rugby.'

The changing ethnicity of the modern game is an issue that Norm believes rugby administrators and coaches still don't properly understand.

'Most of New Zealand's top coaches and officials are white and most of the top players are brown. It's not the colour so much as the cultural gap. It's not rugby becoming more Polynesian that's the problem — it's that this movement has practical effects. You have to respect the different way in which players might have been brought up, or think and are motivated, if you're going to mould them into a top team.'

The other major difference over the past thirteen years is that rugby has become less spontaneous, less intuitive, less reliant on individual skill.

'We play programmed rugby now. It's a combination of gridiron and chess and it can be very frustrating to play and boring to watch. We're patterning ourselves on the Brumbies and the Wallabies . . . it's all rehearsed moves with the aim of getting the smallest advantage. It's clever but robotic. Combine that with the league and Crusaders-style defence and most tries are scored from turnovers. Not from set plays or backline moves.

'Kiwis aren't robots. But we're becoming like that — followers, not innovators. Our strength in recent years has been our flair and if we breed that out of players — if they become too scared to make mistakes and not have a go then we'll lose something special out of New Zealand rugby.

'Also the field is too small. I know that sounds strange but rugby was originally designed for thirty players who weren't all that fit and who were divided into forwards and backs. Now there are the same thirty guys but they are fast, fit and strong and they're lined out across the field with the aim of getting continuity — in other words, phase after phase of play until there's a half-gap somewhere.'

Norm looks to rugby league for the solution. He advocates a 13-a-side game by dropping the flankers and imposing a five yard offside rule for any player not involved in the breakdown. That way space will be created on the field and backlines given more room in which to craft innovative plays.

'If rugby keeps going the way it is, then we'll drive the crowds away. It's got to become a more open, more spontaneous, more entertaining game.'

However, Norm is not convinced that rugby administrators actually perceive there to be a problem.

'They're still getting their heads around professionalism which means they keep copying the corporate model. The NZRFU bureaucracy is top-heavy and becoming increasingly remote from the fans and even us players. The commercial way isn't always the best way. This is a game not a business.'

But those are decisions for others. Norm has his own future to make. Whatever those choices, his relationships with Arlene and his family are central. No matter his early difficulties with his father, recent years have seen a steady rapprochement. The bond of family binds all the Hewitts and was never better illustrated than in the immediate wake of the Queenstown incident.

Similarly his relationship with Arlene has progressed to the point where they now live together and share similar thoughts about their future.

'Sometimes I have to pinch myself to believe that Arlene is with me. I'm not sure I deserve her. She's been so tolerant as I've had to work through all my personal stuff and been so focussed on rugby. I have a lot of making up to do. I'm looking forward to that.'

And what about his drinking?

'Since Queenstown, I've had a couple of glasses of wine and that's been it. I don't drink now. The [Lions] boys rib me that I'm a boring bastard these days- "where's Boris?" they say. "Bring back Boris". But I don't need to drink any more. It's not who I am. I know that it will always be there and it will always be a temptation. I mean, what happens if I strike rough times ahead — if something happens to Arlene or my Mum and Dad? That's what they say about alcoholics — it's never over. But with the spiritual support and the backing of those closest to me, I should be right.'

Indeed, he should be. He understands himself now — has an understanding of his weaknesses as well as his strengths. And with that knowledge has come insight and a measure of wisdom.

Still, it will be a reluctant departure from rugby. No longer will he captain companies of men, hear the roar of the crowd, battle fierce opponents and refuse surrender. No more fans baying for blood and victory at the stadium — the camaraderie and status of the champion gladiator will be gone. Instead there will be different challenges and a future unseen and unscripted.

He rubs his shaven head and smiles. 'Let me at it,' he says.